Paul B. Kidd is a Sydney-based author, crime historian, Radio 2UE talkback broadcaster, freelance *60 Minutes* researching producer and photo/journalist who specialises in Australian true crime, big game fishing, adventure and humour.

Paul's articles, interviews and photographs have appeared in most Australian major outdoors and men's publications and in numerous magazines and websites worldwide.

Paul B. Kidd is Australia's recognised authority on the history of Australian serial killers and criminals who have been sentenced to life imprisonment with their papers marked *Never To Be Released*.

The author of twenty books, mainly on Australian true crime, he lives in Sydney's eastern suburbs.

OTHER AUSTRALIAN TRUE CRIME TITLES BY PAUL B. KIDD

Never To Be Released: Australia's Most Vicious Murderers

Never To Be Released Volume Two

Never To Be Released Volume Three

Never To Be Released Volume Four

Australia's Serial Killers: The Definitive History of Serial Multicide in Australia

The Knick Knack Man: Inside the Mind of Australia's Most Deranged Serial Killer

Shallow Graves: The Concealments of Killers

Til Death Us Do Part: Australian Marriages That Ended in Murder

Australia's Serial Killers: The Definitive History of Serial Multicide in Australia: Revised Edition

The Australian Crime File

The Australian Crime File 2

Celluloid Serial Killers: The History of Serial Killers in the Movies

The Mutilator and Australia's Other Signature Serial Killers

THE AUSTRALIAN CRIME FILE 3

More Stories from Australia's Best True Crime Collection

Paul B. Kidd

The Five Mile Press

*For Susie. Thanks for the help and advice.
It's a long way from Mary Poppins.*

The Five Mile Press Pty Ltd
1 Centre Road, Scoresby
Victoria 3179 Australia
www.fivemile.com.au

Copyright © Paul B. Kidd, 2012
All rights reserved

First published 2012

Printed in Australia at Griffin Press.
Only wood grown from sustainable regrowth forests is used
in the manufacture of paper found in this book.

Cover image © Shutterstock
Typesetting by Shaun Jury

National Library of Australia Cataloguing-in-Publication entry
   Author: Kidd, Paul B. (Paul Benjamin), 1945-
   Title: Notorious true crime stories / Paul B. Kidd.
   ISBN: 9781743005545 (pbk.)
   Series: Kidd, Paul B. (Paul Benjamin), 1945-
                        Australian crime file; 3.
   Subjects: Crime—Australia—Case studies.
                        Criminal investigation—Australia.
   Dewey Number: 364.994

CONTENTS

	Introduction	ix
1	Where is Jodie Larcombe?	1
2	The Arthur Coningham Conspiracy	7
3	David Hicks: Terrorist or Tourist?	11
4	Is Derek Percy the Wanda Beach Killer?	17
5	Charles 'Lucky' Luciano: The Founder of the Modern Mafia	21
6	The Murders of Bruce Burrell	27
7	The Sef Gonzales Family Murders	33
8	Justice Jeffrey Shaw and His Missing Blood Samples	37
9	The Mysterious Disappearance of Samantha Knight	41
10	The Many Lives of Fred Many	45
11	The John Christie Murders of Notting Hill	49
12	The Wales-King Murders	53
13	The Murder of MP John Newman: Australia's First Political Murder	57

14	HIH: The Cash Cow for Corporate Crooks	61
15	The Love-struck Jailer: How Heather Parker Helped Peter Gibb Escape	67
16	The Saint Valentine's Day Massacre: When the Gangsters Ruled Chicago	71
17	The Persecution of Harry 'the Hat' Blackburn	75
18	The Real-life Cannibals	79
19	The Final Indignity for Darryl Raymond Beamish	87
20	The Real-life *Psycho*: Ed Gein	91
21	Mr Froggy and His Ill-gotten Millions: The Ponzi Frauds of Karl Suleman	95
22	Who Poisoned Bobby Lulham?	101
23	The Injustice of Colin Campbell Ross: A Century Too Late	105
24	The William Moxley Murders	109
25	The BTK Serial Killer	113
26	The Canberra Cop Killer: The Murder of Colin Winchester	121
27	Who Killed Adrian Kay?	131
28	The 'Mistakes' of Justice Marcus Einfeld	135
29	Little Has Changed in 100 Years: The Mount Rennie Rape Case	141
30	Murder Inc.: The Mafia's Own Private Death Squad	145

31	The Two Lives of Al Grassby	149
32	The Perils of Pauline Hanson	155
33	The Shootout at Dangar Place: When Detective Roger Rogerson Met Warren Lanfranchi	161
34	Not a Good Time to be Named Jodie: The Crimes of Jodie Harris	165
35	Double Jeopardy Justice: At Last a Murderer is Tried Twice	171
36	Born to Steal: The Facts Behind the Australian Shoplifting Industry	175
37	Final Justice for Mersina Halvagis: Serial Killer Peter Dupas Gets His Just Desserts	183
38	Where is Peter Falconio?	187
39	Three Strikes and Gone for Good: Justice at Last for John Leslie Coombes	191
40	The Yorkshire Ripper	195
41	Death on Bondi Beach: The Bizarre Death of Roni Levi	199
42	Sydney's First 'Chicago-style' Gangland Hit: The Public Demise of Pretty Boy Walker	205
43	Peter Foster: Australia's Dumbest Conman	209
44	Son of Sam	215
45	Is Arthur Brown Australia's Worst Child Killer?	219

46	Dr Death: The Crimes of Dr Jayant Patel	223
47	Bali Justice for Schapelle Corby	229
48	London's Notorious Kray Twins	233
49	The Jury's Still Out on Sir Joh	237
50	Protecting Paedophiles From the Pulpit: The Naivety of Peter Hollingworth	241
51	The Adventures of Captain Moonlite	247
52	Dead Wrong: When the Law Makes a Fatal Mistake	253
53	Who Framed the Mickelbergs? The Story Behind Western Australia's Biggest Gold Heist	263
54	The Devil Made Me Do It: The Violent World of Darren Osborne	267
55	The Japanese Tourist Murder Mystery: The Crimes of Robert Raymond Day	271
56	America's Worst Serial Killer Ever: Pogo the Killer Clown	275
57	The Case of the Persistent Poisoner	279
58	Should The Bulli Rapist Be Free To Walk Among Us?	283
	Index	287

INTRODUCTION

When I compiled the first *Australian Crime File* way back in 2005, I thought that perhaps there would be a *Crime File* 2, but at the time I never dreamed we would do a third. However, the first two have been so successful that another book is not really so surprising. Let's face it, crime stops for no man! And given that the books are based on the Crime File segments that I write and present with George Moore on our radio program each weekend on radio 2UE in Sydney, you could say that I am compiling a new chapter every week as I go.

When I'm compiling these stories for the radio, I include the maximum amount of information in the minimum amount of space. Each crime file on the radio takes about 12 minutes to read out to the listeners and in that short time I must tell them every bit of information about the case. I pack details into the stories – times, days, dates, years, motives, modus operandi, capture/non-capture, and sentences of the offenders. You are getting the best of everything in these informative chapters.

I have also endeavoured not to be opinionated and tried to be as non-judgemental as possible and just report the facts. But in some cases I simply can't help myself. My intense dislike for the serial and child killers, the pack rapists and heartless conmen is always simmering beneath the surface and on occasion it shows in the writing. You must remember also that I have written this for a huge radio audience which comprises people of all ages. There really are stories for everyone in this collection.

After spending a lifetime writing and broadcasting so many stories about every major crime, as well as most of the not-so-major crimes, in Australia's history, I am proud so say that now I have now achieved the status of Crime Historian and

ix

The Australian Crime File 3

that now appears as my by-line on my regular appearances on *Today*, *Sunrise* and *60 Minutes* shown across Australia and in print media articles.

And I am very pleased to bring you the latest collection of Crime Files from our radio program. There is crime for everyone. Not just murder and rape but also lots of crimes about the ordinary and very respected members of our community, the least likely people that you would imagine would fall foul of the law and then have to face the judgement of their peers.

On behalf of George and myself I'd like to thank all the listeners for making our show the number one weekend show in Sydney.

Paul B. Kidd, Sydney, 2012

1 | WHERE IS JODIE LARCOMBE?

Finding someone guilty of murder without a body is very difficult . . . but it does happen. Take the conviction of Lindy Chamberlain for the 1980 abduction and murder of her baby daughter, Azaria, at Uluru. Lindy Chamberlain was eventually exonerated, released and pardoned after years in jail when, by fluke, her baby Azaria's matinee jacket was found near dingo lairs in 1986. Until then it was believed that the missing baby wasn't wearing any such jacket and that her mother had been lying, saying that her child had been taken from their tent by a dingo.

But there was no fluke in the case of Bruce Burrell for the abduction murders of Mrs Kerry Whelan and Dorothy Davis, whose bodies were never found. Burrell was caught through diligent police work from a team of detectives who knew he was as guilty as sin and would never give up until he was caught.

Another person convicted of murder without a body is Bradley Murdoch, for the outback murder of Peter Falconio, whose body has never been found. Murdoch made the mistake of leaving his blood DNA at the murder scene, on his second intended victim, and in her car.

You can read more about both the Bruce Burrell and Peter Falconio stories later in this book.

The following story is a lesser-known case of a murder without a body, which also resulted in a conviction due to relentless police diligence and detective work.

On or around 22 December 1987, the day she was released from Pentridge Prison, 21-year-old prostitute and heroin addict Jodie Maree Larcombe went missing. Three months later, in March 1988, in an unrelated incident, police were called to an isolated property in Pooncarie in the south-west of New South Wales to investigate the sexual assault and abduction of a woman named Sophie Carni, who had escaped her assailant and informed a neighbouring farmer of her ordeal.

There, local police arrested 51-year-old Daryl Francis Suckling, a property caretaker, and charged him with sexual assault and false imprisonment. Police checked Suckling out to find that he had been in and out of jail all of his life, with 138 convictions for a huge variety of offences including burglary, stealing cars and fraud dating back to when he was 11 years old. Suckling had twice escaped from jail and in 1978, at the age of 42, the skinny, inoffensive-looking little man had been convicted of carnal knowledge with a girl aged between 10 and 16. In 1984, he had miraculously managed to get very serious charges of abduction and rape dropped.

Sophie Carni told police that her assailant had abducted her at knifepoint in Melbourne, taken her to the property in New South Wales, drugged and raped her and forced her to pose for explicit photos. In her statement she said that her assailant had told her that he had killed another woman and her body was buried nearby. But he didn't say exactly where. Police conducted numerous thorough searches of the farm and surrounding areas but no body was ever found.

But while they found no human remains in their search, police did find jewellery, clothing and a set of dentures that belonged to

Where is Jodie Larcombe?

a Jodie Larcombe, who had gone missing three months earlier. But it was the discovery of explicit photos of Jodie Larcombe, who appeared to be drugged or drunk and whose body appeared to be battered and bruised, that lead police to believe that she was the woman Suckling had boasted to Sophie Carni of killing and burying.

On 3 April 1989, police charged Daryl Suckling with the murder of Jodie Larcombe, along with the charges relating to Sophie Carni. On 3 June 1989, Sophie Carni died of a drug overdose, making her evidence at Suckling's trial inadmissible, and the judge ordered that Suckling be acquitted. But Suckling still had the charges of abducting and murdering Jodie Larcombe to answer to and his trial date was set down for 25 February 1991.

Soon after, police prosecutors and Jodie Larcombe's family were shocked to receive a letter from the NSW Director of Public Prosecutions, Reg Blanch, informing them that the trial of Daryl Suckling on the charge of murdering Jodie Larcombe would not go ahead. The letter from Mr Blanch said in part:

> *I advise you that after careful consideration of this matter, I have directed that there be no further prosecution. I have received advice from two Queen's Counsel that the evidence available at this time is such that if the evidence which is admissible were presented to a jury a verdict of acquittal would be inevitable.*
>
> *I agree with the assessment. Such an acquittal would make it impossible to prosecute the matter again. By directing now that there be no further proceedings it is open to prosecute the matter again if any relevant evidence should come forward.*

Mr Blanch and the NSW Department of Public Prosecutions came under heavy fire for the decision and in February 1992, Mr Blanch provided the following facts of the case:
- No one had seen or heard of Jodie Larcombe since she was released from Pentridge Prison on 22 December 1987.

- She lived and worked as a street prostitute in St Kilda.
- On 26 December 1987, Daryl Suckling withdrew $40 from an automatic teller machine in that suburb.
- It was the same amount that Jodie Larcombe charged for sex.

In March 1988, police found in Suckling's possession at his remote Wyrama Station home, 170 kilometres from Wentworth, Miss Larcombe's false teeth, silver chain and watch. Police also found explicit photos of Miss Larcombe in Suckling's car. A dress believed to belong to the missing woman was recovered from Suckling, as was a notebook with an entry 'Jodie 27.12'. Suckling was charged and subsequently committed for trial on murder charges by Magistrate Derek Hand.

The DPP then dropped the charges.

Mr Blanch was not alone in agreeing to drop the charges. High-profile Sydney solicitor Chris Murphy said, 'Mr Blanch would have destroyed the credibility of his office by taking the easy alternative of sending this man to trial. It would have been a lynch-mob mentality to put Suckling up for trial looking for a conviction on emotional grounds.'

But the police who had worked tirelessly piecing the evidence together against Suckling did not agree that the case should be dropped. They believed that they had enough on Suckling to convict him. In late 1991, Jodie Larcombe's parents collected thousands of signatures on a petition calling for the prosecution of the man who was once charged with the murder of their daughter. 'We will fight this in every way and hope someone will sit up and take notice,' Mr Larcombe said.

Nothing came of it. But the investigating police and Jodie's family and loved ones never gave up hope that Daryl Suckling would one day be brought to justice.

On 2 September 1996, nine years after Jodie went missing, presumed murdered, her family's prayers were answered when Daryl Francis Suckling, now 60, faced the jury after being tried for her abduction, rape and murder. Suckling had fallen into the oldest trap of them all. He couldn't keep his mouth shut.

Where is Jodie Larcombe?

While in prison for another offence, Suckling had made the fatal mistake of boasting to a cellmate about killing Jodie Larcombe. The cellmate went to the police and when the two men teamed up on release from prison, police fitted the informant with a listening device that recorded Suckling telling the terrible details of how he had murdered and dismembered Jodie with an axe and disposed of her body parts. This time the DPP elected to prosecute.

The jury found Suckling guilty of the murder of Jodie Larcombe, 21, on or about 27 December 1987 at an unknown place in New South Wales. Justice Bruce James said that it was a crime in the worst category and sentenced Suckling to life in prison without the possibility of parole.

Jodie Larcombe's body has never been found. Police have good reason to believe that she may not have been Suckling's only victim.

The Jodie Larcombe case is the subject of a brilliant book titled *Killing Jodie* by Sydney journalist Janet Fife-Yeomans.

2 | THE ARTHUR CONINGHAM CONSPIRACY

If you think complicated divorces that eventually wind up in the courtroom are restricted to the litigious times we live in right now, then think again. At the beginning of last century Australia was treated to a court case that had the lot . . . and then some. The characters included a Test cricketer, his beautiful English wife, adultery, blackmail and even an Irish Catholic priest. They'd even have trouble topping that these days.

It became known worldwide as the Coningham Conspiracy and is one of the most famous divorce cases in our legal history. As the sordid details were published daily in the press the case divided the readers – some choosing to side with the handsome international cricketer and others taking the side of the kindly priest.

The Coningham Conspiracy began at the end of 1900, when famous cricketer Arthur Coningham claimed that his beautiful English-born wife had repeatedly committed adultery with the handsome Irish-born priest Reverend Dr Denis Francis O'Haran, and began divorce proceedings.

Reverend O'Haran was well respected in the community as the administrator of Sydney's St Mary's Cathedral and was private secretary to Cardinal Moran. For their part, The Coninghams seemed to be the perfect young couple. Arthur Coningham was a Test cricketer who had represented Australia when they toured England seven years earlier. Coningham, a chemist when he wasn't playing cricket, had married the much-pursued Alice Dowling in March 1893 at the Bondi Church of England the day before he sailed for England with the Australian team. By 1899 the happy young couple had three children.

So Sydneysiders were shocked when local hero Arthur Coningham filed for divorce in late 1900. They were even more mortified when it was rumoured that Coningham was to name the Reverend O'Haran as the co-respondent and claim £5000 damages. It was said that Mr Coningham also wanted custody of his two eldest children, claiming he didn't want the youngest as he alleged that his wife had told him the child wasn't his, and that the real father was in fact the Reverend O'Haran.

But before Arthur Coningham actually lodged the official petition for divorce in court outlining the alleged circumstances and subsequent demands, he sent a letter to the Reverend O'Haran's boss, Cardinal Moran. In it he hinted that an outrageous scandal that would cause endless damage to the Church could be avoided if he, Cardinal Moran, agreed to a settlement out of court – all of the sordid allegations would go away.

Outraged, and seeing the thinly disguised blackmail attempt for exactly what it was, Cardinal Moran went immediately to the police. After careful examination of the letter, the police told His Excellency that due to the clever wording of the threats there was little they could do to prove it was blackmail. The divorce trial would go ahead. The petition with all of its juicy details was lodged and the public waited in sordid anticipation for early December, when proceedings would begin in front of Mr Justice Simpson.

The Arthur Coningham Conspiracy

Arthur Coningham's case was based entirely on his wife's signed admission that she had been having an affair with the Reverend O'Haran. Even more shocking was the allegation that the infidelities took place inside St Mary's Cathedral. The public gallery gasped at the horror of it all. It was also alleged that Alice Coningham's third child was named Vincent Francis after the Reverend Denis Francis O'Haran, the child's alleged father.

When called to the witness stand to give evidence, Mrs Coningham not only admitted to having the torrid affair with the reverend, but also gave times and places where the lovemaking had taken place. Much to the disappointment of the court reporters, she stopped just short of giving the exact intimate details, though it appeared she would have if the court had asked her to. She was a very credible witness.

Under cross-examination by the Reverend O'Haran's counsel, Jack Want, who was the Perry Mason of the time, Alice Coningham convincingly denied that she was party to a conspiracy with her husband in an attempt to blackmail the Church at the expense of the reputation of an innocent man of the cloth.

Then it was the Reverend O'Haran's turn in the witness box. He vehemently denied all of the charges of sin and adultery levelled against him. He was saddened to think that anyone could accuse him of doing such things in his church. Arthur Coningham elected to cross-examine the reverend himself in an attempt to trap him into an admission but try as he may, the Reverend O'Haran held his ground and admitted to nothing, saying over and over that there was nothing to admit to and that the charges against him were absolutely untrue and ungodly to boot.

With the evidence of two totally credible witnesses before them, the jury retired to consider its verdict. With Sydney evenly divided on the outcome, it was even money which way it would go. After 12 hours the jury had to admit that they were divided equally down the middle and couldn't possibly arrive at a result. Much to the delight of Sydney's gossipmongers, Mr Justice Simpson took the only course of action that the law allowed, dismissing the jury and calling for a second trial.

But this time the Reverend O'Haran decided that if he couldn't prove his own innocence in the eyes of God then he would go about it another way – he would prove the Coninghams' guilt. For the forthcoming second trial the reverend employed the services of solicitor WP Crick, who was also the NSW Postmaster General and had a reputation as an investigator that was second to none in the country. Mr Crick had an equally devious sidekick named Dan Green, and together the pair looked deep into the activities of Alice and Arthur Coningham.

Dan Green quickly discovered that not only were the Coninghams on very friendly terms, given the circumstances, but they were clandestinely meeting and sleeping together at a farm just out of Sydney. Green also discovered letters the pair had written to each other, which told in detail of their plot to concoct evidence against the reverend and exploit the church.

At the second trial, which began in March 1901, Arthur Coningham was bombarded time and again with the new evidence and at one stage he became so desperate that he pulled a revolver and pointed it at the reverend, declaring that he should shoot him on the spot for ruining his marriage to the woman he loved. He was quickly disarmed and the one-sided trial was allowed to continue to its inevitable result. The jury returned a unanimous verdict in favour of the Reverend O'Haran.

Disgraced and in danger of being charged with conspiring to commit blackmail, the Coninghams wisely left Sydney and moved to New Zealand. Soon after, Mr Coningham was caught in the act of adultery and his wife divorced him. The Reverend Dr O'Haran's reputation remained intact and he worked out the rest of his life at his beloved St Mary's Cathedral.

3 | DAVID HICKS: TERRORIST OR TOURIST?

Born into what is generally described as an average family in Adelaide in August 1975, there was little in David Hicks' early years to suggest he would become one of Australia's most infamous people. But along the way, Hicks' thirst for the sort of adventures you don't normally find in tourist brochures found him locked up in solitary confinement by the US in the notorious Guantanamo Bay in Cuba – the world's most secure prison – accused of being an al Qaeda terrorist. He was held without a trial for almost three years, without a charge being laid. It just proves that you never know what life has in store for you.

Hicks' controversial story is a polarising one in Australian society. According to the Adelaide journeyman turned Muslim convert himself, he just happened to be in the wrong place at the wrong time. Others believe he was a terrorist and therefore deserved everything he got.

Despite his uneventful early years, life threw Hicks the proverbial curve ball when he was 10 years old. His parents separated and – like so many troubled children in similar situations – he turned to alcohol, drugs and petty crime through his teenage years. With no real direction in his life, Hicks started to wander. He held a variety of jobs through the years, including a stint droving cattle in the Northern Territory. As unlikely as the setting may seem, that was the first place he started studying the Koran.

Back in Adelaide, Hicks fell in love with a woman named Jodie Sparrow. They had two children together, but the romance didn't last. They split in 1996. David Hicks cast his eye at the wider world; that same year, 21-year-old Hicks moved to Japan to train horses. This was during the build up to violent conflict in Kosovo. Every day, Hicks read the newspapers and, dismayed by the way Slobodan Milosevic oppressed the Kosovan people, he vowed to help.

Hicks travelled to Albania early in 1999 and joined the Kosovo Liberation Army, determined to fight against the invading Serbian forces. Even though the conflict only lasted a few months and he never got near the frontline, it was a pivotal experience in Hicks' life. It appealed to his sense of adventure, while letting him feel he was working towards a greater good. It was the turning point in his life that led him to Guantanamo Bay.

When Hicks returned to his country of birth later that year, he applied to join the Australian Army, but his low level of education saw him rejected. He instead converted to Islam. Hicks started to visit the various mosques around Adelaide, where he prayed and studied his new chosen religion, but it never seemed enough for him. He still craved adventure.

Hicks got in touch with some Muslim missionaries in Pakistan. With nothing more than a promise of accommodation, a 24-year-old's burning desire to forge his own path, and a backpack, he made his way to Pakistan, ostensibly to learn Arabic and gain a deeper understanding of the Koran. Before long he linked up with the Lashkar-e-Tayyiba terrorist group and trained for three months at one of their desert camps. But this was just a stepping stone on Hicks' path as a terrorist.

David Hicks

He hadn't been in Pakistan long before he got to know a Saudi national with connections to one of the training camps in Afghanistan that had been set up by the US and Saudi Arabia in the 1980s, to drill Muslims to rise up against Russia's occupation of Afghanistan. The man asked Hicks if he'd like to train there. His answer shouldn't be much of a surprise by now.

It was at the camp in Afghanistan that Hicks first laid eyes on the man that would change the course of the 21st century, the man who used passenger-filled planes as bombs against the US, the man who has come to personify evil to the Western world, the man the US spent a decade and countless billions of dollars hunting down and killing for his actions – Osama bin Laden. Hicks saw the al Qaeda leader eight times in total during his time at the camp. He even spoke to him once.

Hicks was back in Pakistan on 11 September 2001 when commercial jets crashed into the World Trade Center, the Pentagon and a field in Arlington, Virginia. He claims he was there on his way back to Sydney. Instead, after watching the carnage, he decided to head back to Afghanistan.

He later told the Australian Federal Police that he had made the decision to retrieve his belongings – his clothes, money, birth certificate and passport. Like many other discrepancies in his story, there is no explanation for why he had left them there if his plan was to return home.

Instead, the US Department of Defense contends that he returned to Afghanistan to rejoin his al Qaeda associates to fight against the US, British, Canadian, Australian, Afghan and other coalition forces.

When he arrived in Kandahar, Hicks was given an AK-47 automatic rifle, ammunition and grenades. He allegedly chose to join al Qaeda fighters defending the Kandahar airport, where he was allegedly assigned to guard a Taliban tank when the US started their bombing campaign.

Hicks eventually decided it was time to get out of Afghanistan, but he was captured by a Northern Alliance warlord in early December 2001. The warlord gave him up to the US Special Forces for $1000.

By this stage in the War on Terror, the US was going hard. President George W Bush had sworn to overcome terrorism. As a result, it had been decided that al Qaeda and Taliban suspects would no longer be classified as 'prisoners of war'. The reasoning was that the Taliban was not recognised as the official government of Afghanistan. They were instead classed as 'illegal combatants', and thus were not covered by international humanitarian laws such as the Geneva Convention. That meant they had no access to a US trial, but would instead have to face a Military Commission. Basically, they would be denied their basic human rights as guaranteed by the US constitution.

A month after the warlord collected $1000 for him, Hicks found himself shackled to the floor of a 2 metre by 3 metre cell at Guantanamo Bay, the notorious US military base in Cuba. The only other humans he saw for 16 months were his guards. It was almost a year before he saw natural light. As for a lawyer, Hicks had to wait two years before he could get any legal advice. He wasn't even charged until 2004.

According to Hicks, he spent 23 hours of every day in solitary confinement, and was subjected to regular interrogations. He also says he was forced to run in shackles, deprived of sleep, beaten while handcuffed and blindfolded, bashed while under sedation, and assaulted anally while wearing a bag over his head. He also had to endure watching other prisoners being savaged by attack dogs. A total of 775 detainees have been taken through Guantanamo Bay since 7 October 2001.

When the legal wheels finally started to turn, Hicks was charged with attempted murder, conspiracy and aiding the enemy. But the US Supreme Court declared the Military Commission to be unconstitutional in June 2006 and the charges against Hicks were dropped.

In March 2007, he pleaded guilty to a new charge of providing material support to a terrorist organisation. He was sentenced to seven years in prison, with six years and three months suspended as long as he didn't speak to the media. Another provision was that he agree that he was never illegally mistreated in Guantanamo Bay.

Once the negotiations between the US and Australia were complete, Hicks was flown home to serve the remainder of his sentence at Adelaide's Yatala Prison, which must have felt like Buckingham Palace compared with where he had been for almost the past six years.

David Hicks was released from jail on 29 December 2007. His only concern today is whether or not he can claim the royalties on his bestselling book of his adventures. After all, it's against the law in Australia to profit from a book about your crimes.

But David Hicks would have us believe that he didn't commit any crimes. It was all a terrible mistake. He was just in the wrong place at the wrong time in history.

4 | IS DEREK PERCY THE WANDA BEACH KILLER?

Police have believed for years that the convicted child killer, the certified insane Derek Percy, may be responsible for the unsolved murders of as many as another five juveniles on top of the murder for which he was convicted. They include the 1965 New South Wales Wanda Beach murders of two teenage girls and the murders of three other children in Canberra, Sydney and Melbourne in the 1960s.

Born into a loving family in 1948, Percy and his two brothers and parents travelled throughout rural Victoria for his father's work with the Victorian Electricity Commission, before settling in Mount Beauty near Bright. A shy boy with an IQ of 122 who never had a girlfriend, Percy was an excellent student and rose to become school prefect. Then, in 1964, women's undergarments began to regularly go missing from the local clotheslines. There was a 'snowdropper', or underwear thief, in town.

At around the same time, Percy's grades plummeted and he began acting strangely. When he was discovered in a ladies' petticoat at a secluded waterhole by a couple of his fellow students, the rumours flew that Percy was the snowdropper. When his father was promoted to a job with the Snowy Mountains Scheme and the family moved to Khancoban in New South Wales, the snowdropping moved with them. It also seemed that a peeping Tom had moved into the tiny town with a population of 500 on the edge of the Snowy Mountains.

When a neighbour told Ernie Percy that his son had sexually assaulted his six-year-old daughter, Percy persuaded the neighbour not to call the police. Mr Percy later told police that around about this time he caught his son in women's clothing, and he and his wife discovered their son's diaries of sexually depraved writings about children and the atrocities he would like to inflict upon them. Police discovered later that many of Percy's teenage writings were blueprints for the crimes he would later be suspected of committing.

Under the watchful eye of his brothers and father, Percy finished school and at 19 joined the navy, graduating at the top of his class as a naval rating. When on leave Percy did as he had done all of his life and joined his family on caravanning holidays that took them all over Australia. Some of the beaches they visited to watch yachting regattas would be of significance in the investigations ahead.

On 11 January 1965, when Derek Percy was 16, teenagers Marianne Schmidt and Mary Sharrock were found murdered in the sand dunes of Wanda Beach at Cronulla in Sydney's south. They had been hideously mutilated and sexually assaulted. There were similarities between theirs and a later Percy murder that could link the crimes. It is believed that the Percy family were holidaying at a nearby regatta at the time, and Percy's grandparents lived within walking distance of where the girls caught the train to their deaths. There were numerous other 'coincidences' connecting Percy to the Wanda murders.

On 27 September 1966, six-year-old Allen Geoffrey Redston went missing in the Canberra suburb of Curtain. The following day his hogtied body was found in a creek with a plastic bag over his head, exactly the same thing that an unidentified

Is Derek Percy the Wanda Beach Killer?

fair-haired teenager had been 'jokingly' doing to children in a Canberra park during the previous week. Percy had holidayed with his family in Canberra in September 1966.

The identikit drawing for the crime was the image of Percy and witnesses described his distinctive bike to police, but the mysterious teenager was nowhere to be found.

On 9 March 1968, while Derek Percy was based at Sydney's Garden Island, three-year-old Simon Brook went missing from the front yard of his home in Glebe. A witness said that he had seen a little boy hand in hand with a young blond-haired man at nearby Jubilee Park. The identikit looked remarkably like Percy. Simon's body was found near his home and alongside it were two distinctive razor blades used by the navy. It was later discovered that Percy had written in his diary of abducting and killing a three-year-old 'baby' and detailing information that only the police and killer would have known.

On 10 August 1968, seven-year-old Linda Stilwell became separated from her brother near Melbourne's Little Luna Park. She was last seen with a young man wearing a distinctive navy blue spray jacket and answering to Percy's description. Percy had transferred to the HMAS *Sydney*, based in Melbourne in July 1968, and was on 18 days' leave, which began five days before Linda disappeared. Her body has never been found.

In July 1969, 12-year-old Shane Spiller was lucky to escape with his life when he threatened Percy with a tomahawk and ran away. Not so lucky was Shane's 12-year-old friend Yvonne Tuohy, who couldn't break free when Percy tried to abduct them both from Ski Beach, at Warneet in Victoria. Soon after, Yvonne's raped, tortured and murdered body was found nearby. Some of Yvonne's mutilations were the same as those on the Wanda Beach victims. Her lucky friend described Percy and his car, which had a distinctive navy sticker in the back windscreen. Police arrested Percy as he was washing Yvonne's blood from his clothing at the nearby HMAS *Cerberus* naval base.

After Percy was arrested for Yvonne Tuohy's murder and a photo of him wearing the same distinctive spray jacket appeared in the paper, a witness said that he was unmistakably the young

The Australian Crime File 3

man who had been sitting in the park when Linda Stilwell went missing. At his trial for the murder of Yvonne Tuohy, Percy was found unfit to plead on the grounds of insanity and, given an indeterminate sentence, he is still locked up. Percy has been questioned many times about the other murders but isn't talking, in the belief that one day he may be released.

Given that he is considered to be arguably the most dangerous man in Australia, that's highly unlikely.

5 | CHARLES 'LUCKY' LUCIANO: THE FOUNDER OF THE MODERN MAFIA

Many people throughout the world questioned *Time Magazine*'s judgement when it named the infamous New York gangster of the 1930s, Charles 'Charlie Lucky' Luciano, as one of the world's 100 Most Important People of the 20th Century, alongside such luminaries as Mahatma Gandhi, Franklin D Roosevelt, Pope John Paul II, Nelson Mandela, Bill Gates, Walt Disney and Henry Ford.

In the wake of heavy criticism of Luciano's inclusion in such an illustrious list, *Time* magazine explained that while Luciano may not have been of good character, 'he modernized the Mafia, shaping it into a smoothly run national crime syndicate focused on the bottom line'. New York mayor Rudy Giuliani was outraged: 'The idea that Luciano civilized the Mafia is absurd. He [Luciano] murdered in order to get the position that he had, and then he authorized hundreds and hundreds of murders.' However, in defending his controversial choice, *Time* business editor Bill Saporito called Luciano 'kind of an evil genius' who had a 'deep impact on the underground economy'.

But no matter what, there is no doubt whatever that Luciano single-handedly turned the common ramshackle Mafia, with hundreds of various unorganised factions throughout America, into the biggest and best-run – albeit illegal – organisation in the USA. Here is how he did it. You make up your own mind.

The foundations of the Mafia in America as we know it today were the original Black Hand gangs of criminal Sicilian immigrants who, around the turn of the century, made capital cities such as New York their home and illegally exploited their decent fellow Italians for money. These gangs of violent thugs stood over ordinary citizens with threats of violence and death if they didn't pay them protection money. It worked, and soon the gangs throughout every capital city in America branched out into drug trafficking, gambling, bootlegging, union racketeering, organised theft, hijacking and numbers rackets.

By the late 1920s, the New York underworld was controlled by two opposing Black Hand gangs run by Giuseppe 'Joe the Boss' Masseria and Salvatore Maranzano. Both had hundreds of 'soldiers' under their control, who were prepared to commit murder should the directive come from the boss. Joe the Boss headed the largest crime family in New York but Maranzano wasn't far behind, and had ideals of taking over and becoming the Boss of all Bosses in New York.

Although Joe the Boss had a hundred or so more soldiers than his opposition, Maranzano ordered his thugs to kill any Masseria gang member on sight or, better still, kill Joe the Boss himself. But the Boss kept himself heavily guarded at all times. And so, in 1928, began what became known as the Castellammarese War, so named after a district in western Sicily from where the Black Hand was said to originate.

Joe the Boss' Underboss was an ambitious young gangster named Charles 'Lucky' Luciano. 'Lucky' was so named because he had once been taken on a 'ride' by opposition gangsters – from which no one had ever returned before – and miraculously survived. Luciano's escape from certain death had left him with a scar running the length of his face as a memento.

As the gangland killings mounted up to 50 and more over the next couple of years, Luciano saw an opening for a smart young businessman. If he could get rid of both Joe the Boss *and* Maranzano and call a peaceful truce, he could take control. One day in April 1931, Luciano suggested to his superior, Joe the Boss, that they have lunch together at the Nuova Villa Tamora restaurant at Coney Island, which was run by a friend of Luciano's.

With their bodyguards waiting outside in the car, the pair finished a feast of pasta and seafood and after all of the other patrons had left, Luciano suggested to Joe the Boss that they play a game of klob, a popular two-handed card game of the time, drink wine and discuss business. They had played only a single hand when Luciano excused himself to go to the toilet. No sooner had Luciano left the table than four of Luciano's lieutenants, Vito Genovese, Joe Adonis, Albert Anastasia and Benjamin 'Bugsy' Siegel, rushed into the restaurant and filled Joe the Boss full of lead. As he lay on the ground, in his bloodsplattered right hand the late Boss held the ace of spades. The owner of the restaurant, who was the only witness to the killing, was mysteriously murdered several weeks later.

He wasn't sure who killed Joe the Boss – though he had his suspicions – but Maranzano appointed himself as the Boss of all the Bosses, with Luciano his Underboss. It was a big mistake. With the war now allegedly over and the two gangs combined to form one army of about 500 soldiers, Maranzano wasn't content to leave it at that. He ordered his men to keep killing those who had offended him during the war, and the murders went on. Luciano decided it was time to make his final move.

Six months after the murder of Joe the Boss, four supposed federal tax agents raided Maranzano's posh offices on Park Avenue on the pretext of inspecting his books. As he was forever being investigated, Maranzano wasn't suspicious and let them in. The men set upon Maranzano and shot him many times, but he would not give in. In the end they had to stab him to death.

To everyone Luciano was now *Capo De Tuti Capi* or 'Boss of all the Bosses'; the underworld was at peace and the killings finally stopped.

Charlie Lucky Luciano named the combined organisation the Unione Siciliane after a secret criminal society believed to have first developed in the mid-19th century in Sicily. Members of all of the crime families were collectively called 'Mafioso', Mafia or 'members of the Mafia'. The humble Luciano refused the title of *Capo De Tuti Capi* and chose simply to call the national crime organisation over which he was the supreme ruler 'the outfit'.

Now the newspapers and gossip columnists called him 'the Boss' when they wrote about him, although they had no idea what he was the boss of. And while his friends, associates and underlings still called him Lucky, Charlie or Charlie Lucky, everyone thought of him as the Boss. He modestly insisted that he wasn't the boss of anything other than his own outfit, and was of no more importance than any of the other family leaders in the Unione Siciliane. But despite his protestations, to everyone he was the Boss and whatever he wanted was done without question. And Lucky Luciano was a good Boss.

Luciano instigated the five New York crime families – Bonanno, Gambino, Colombo, Genovese and Lucchese – which had their own territories, and he set up a commission or 'board of directors', of which he was the head. Only Italians could sit at the new Commission, which mainly comprised the heads of the families. Luciano sat above all of the leaders of the five families.

All of America's smaller crime families had to fall into line and kick back a percentage of their earnings to the Commission under threat of death from Murder Incorporated, Luciano's personal band of assassins. As the Jewish brains behind Luciano's organising skills, Myer Lansky, once reportedly said: 'We're bigger than US Steel.' And he was right. In the early 1930s and all through the Great Depression, nationally the Mafia was turning over hundreds of millions of illegal dollars annually, and Lucky Luciano was getting a direct percentage from all of New York's activities and distributing it among his lieutenants.

Charles 'Lucky' Luciano

The charismatic Luciano set up home in a penthouse at the Waldorf Towers and wore elegant suits, silk shirts, handmade shoes, cashmere topcoats and fedora hats. He was the walking fashion statement of the day. Charlie Lucky always had a beautiful showgirl or a nightclub singer on his arm and actor George Raft and comedian Jimmy Durante were among his friends.

But the good life for the supreme leader of America's biggest and most profitable organisation ended abruptly when special prosecutor Thomas E Dewey – who was totally oblivious to the fact that organised crime even existed – charged Luciano with multiple trumped-up counts of compulsory prostitution. Convicted on 62 counts in June 1936, Luciano got 30 to 50 years in Dannemora Prison. But for all his crimes, Charlie Lucky was definitely not a pimp. To this day, where gangsters gather, it is still said of their beloved leader that it was a 'bum rap'.

Such was Luciano's power that he ran the Mafia like a Swiss watch from prison. In return for his freedom, Luciano struck a deal with the US government that he would keep the allied docks free of Nazi sympathiser bomb attacks on supply ships, and that his friends in Sicily would aid the allied war effort. In 1946 he was deported to Italy, from where he ran the American Mafia until he eventually retired in the 1950s on a substantial pension, delivered to him from the USA in cash each month. Lucky Luciano dropped dead of a heart attack at Naples airport in 1962. He was aged 64.

So secretive was Charles 'Lucky' Luciano's organisation, which was making billions of dollars each year, that it wasn't until a lowly Mafia soldier named Joe Valachi broke the code of Omerta that anyone knew it existed. For a breakdown of a murder rap, Valachi revealed all of the secrets of the Cosa Nostra (as Valachi called it) to a 1963 Senate Subcommittee. Until then America hadn't the slightest idea of what had been going on right under the noses of law enforcement agencies for decades. They knew there were gangsters and crime, but had no idea that it was organised like a huge corporation. It was so secretive, in fact, that the head of the FBI, J Edgar Hoover, refused to acknowledge that it ever existed.

And therein lies a tale. Rumour has it that Hoover really had known of the Unione Siciliane's existence for many years but had been convinced that it wouldn't be a good idea to acknowledge its existence, otherwise photos of Hoover and his assistant, Clyde Tolson, in compromising sexual positions, which had come into the possession of Mafia accountant Myer Lansky, would be released to the newspapers.

Hoover and Tolson's relationship was suspect as it was. They went on every vacation together, ate breakfast, lunch and dinner together, went to work together, lived together, never had families, never had girlfriends, and when they died they were buried together; the pictures would confirm their sexual relationship.

It seems that even the most important crime fighter in the history of the United States, like everything else in America, was under the control of the Mafia.

6 | THE MURDERS OF BRUCE BURRELL

In September 2007, at his trial for a second murder, the jury got it right with the conviction of Bruce Allan Burrell. For the first time in our history, Burrell had now been found guilty of not one, but two murders, where the bodies of his victims have still not been found to this day.

Burrell had been a suspect for 10 years in both the women's disappearances. Outside of the fact that his victims were both wealthy women, they may well have lived on different planets. The only thing they had in common in life was that they both knew Bruce Burrell. But in death it is highly likely that they could be very much closer, their bodies perhaps buried in the same grave or secreted together forever in any of the many bottomless mineshafts on Burrell's southern New South Wales highlands farm.

The beginning of the end for Burrell began on 6 May 1997, when 39-year-old Mrs Kerry Whelan, the mother of three and wife of Bernard Whelan, a successful Sydney businessman and

CEO of Crown Forklifts, went to a hairdressing appointment in Parramatta and vanished. A surveillance video from where Mrs Whelan had left her car revealed a distinctive two-tone Mitsubishi Pajero with a bullbar leaving the scene a few seconds after she left the car park.

Soon after, a ransom note arrived at Mr Whelan's work, demanding $1 million in US dollars or his wife would die. The ransom note instructed that when the money was ready, sometime in the next seven days, an advertisement was to be placed in Sydney's *Daily Telegraph*. The ad was to read: 'Anyone who witnessed a white Volkswagen Beetle parked beside the eastern gates of the Sydney Olympic site at 10.30pm on Tuesday 8.4.97 please call . . . then put your home telephone number at the end of the advertisement.'

The Whelan family nanny came forward and told police of an unusual circumstance that had occurred just a month earlier when a former sales employee of Mr Whelan, a Bruce Burrell, had arrived unannounced at the Whelans' rural home during the day and had secretive discussions with Mrs Whelan over a cup of tea. What Mrs Whelan would be doing associating with Burrell was a mystery. Burrell was a 44-year-old balding, portly braggart who was always broke, swigging on a can of VB and smoking a cigarette.

When Burrell had left, Mrs Whelan said to the nanny, 'Can you do me a favour? You never saw him here. Don't tell anybody. Give me a couple of weeks and I'll tell you why. Don't worry. I'm not having an affair.' It has since been proved as close to conclusively as possible by police and author Candace Sutton that this was definitely the case and that Kerry Whelan had never been unfaithful to her husband, least of all with a lowlife like Bruce Burrell, who had been sacked by her husband years earlier because he couldn't be trusted.

Police raided Burrell's farm on the southern highlands and found a Mitsubishi Pajero identical in every way to the one in the surveillance video, a typewriter that could have typed the ransom note, two handwritten cryptic lists that could have been the outline of a kidnap plan, empty bottles that contained traces

The Murders of Bruce Burrell

of chloroform and a map book in which the car park where Mrs Whelan parked her car was highlighted.

Hundreds of police converged on Burrell's farm looking for Mrs Whelan, but apart from some stolen cars and rifles they found nothing. On further investigation they discovered that Burrell was unemployed and desperately broke and couldn't keep up the mortgage payments on his farm.

It wasn't until police began investigating Mrs Whelan's disappearance that they considered Burrell a suspect in a similar case that had happened two years earlier. Between 1pm and 1.30pm on 30 May 1995, 74-year-old grandmother Dorothy Davis left her house in Sydney's exclusive Lurline Bay and told a builder she was on her way to visit a cancer-stricken friend down the street. She has not been seen since.

The sick friend was Bruce Burrell's wife, who was a nearby neighbour and had been a friend of Mrs Davis for many years. Police believe that when Mrs Davis arrived at the flat, her sick friend was not there. Instead, Bruce Burrell was waiting alone to murder her.

That same afternoon Burrell made a 'sudden and unexpected trip' to his farm near Goulburn and returned the same night, before making the same five-hour round trip again the following day. It would later be concluded that Burrell had murdered Mrs Davis in his apartment and on the first trip he left Mrs Davis' body at the farm; the second trip was to conceal it. But why did Burrell murder the elderly lady? What was his motive?

It seemed that in 1994 Bruce Burrell secretly approached Mrs Davis, a very wealthy widow who had been left a lot of money by her late husband, and borrowed $100,000, which he said was to purchase a unit in the street. He repaid Mrs Davis $10,000 and when she kept asking for the balance, Burrell confided in a friend that 'she had gone as far as saying that she would take legal action to get the money back'. Burrell had allegedly gone to comfort her to get her to back off from her threats. Soon after, Mrs Davis disappeared. Burrell had never come under suspicion. Until Mrs Whelan's disappearance.

But despite the mountain of circumstantial evidence against Burrell, police desperately needed him to make a mistake in order to charge him with the murder of Kerry Whelan. It happened early on 23 May 1997. As police turned his home upside down with the media camped outside his property, Burrell drove to Goulburn, where, seemingly under the belief that calls from public phone boxes weren't traceable, he made a call from the phone box outside the Empire Hotel.

At 9.21am – the exact same time as Burrell was in the phone box – a call was received at Crown Equipment. A man spoke to a receptionist and asked her to write this message down and give it to Mr Whelan. He said: 'Mrs Whelan is okay. Mr Whelan must call off the police and media today. Tell him, the man with the white Volkswagen,' and hung up.

Only the kidnapper, the police and the Whelan family knew about the white Volkswagen reference. Phone traces showed the call came from a phone box outside the Empire Hotel at exactly 9.21am. Burrell told police he had made a call from that phone box but said it was to his lawyers. That was soon disproved. They had their man, but the absence of a victim was going to make proving the case almost impossible.

In the meantime, Burrell was charged with six counts of stealing cars found on his property, including the Pajero. On 22 October in the Parramatta District Court he pleaded guilty and was sent to prison for two and a half years. Police now had him where they could keep an eye on him and have the run of his property.

On 31 March 1999, Bruce Burrell was charged with the abduction and murder of Kerry Whelan, but the charges were later withdrawn through lack of evidence. In 2002 a coronial inquest found a 'known' person was responsible for the kidnapping and murder of Kerry Whelan and referred the case to the Director of Public Prosecutions.

In August 2005 Burrell went on trial in the NSW Supreme Court for kidnap and murder, but after nearly two weeks of deliberation the jury could not reach a unanimous verdict. On March 2006 Burrell was re-tried and on 6 June 2006, after nine days of deliberations, he was found guilty in a unanimous verdict and sentenced to life in prison without the possibility of parole.

Charged with the abduction and murder of Mrs Dorothy Davis, under the laws of subjudice, mention of Burrell's previous conviction for an almost identical crime was not permitted at the trial or in the press during the trial. But it seems it wasn't necessary. All the evidence pointed to a clear case of murder of an old lady in the pursuit of personal greed. In September 2007, Burrell was also found guilty of the abduction and murder of Mrs Dorothy Davis and received a further 28 years.

We can only wonder if the details of the Kerry Whelan murder, which was one of Australia's most sensational and publicised trials, had any sway on the jury's decision in finding Bruce Burrell guilty of murdering and concealing the body of Dorothy Davis.

But then again, who really cares? Do you? The chances of the same set of circumstances ever happening to an innocent man would surely run into the trillions.

7 | THE SEF GONZALES FAMILY MURDERS

Soon after police arrived early on the morning of 11 July 2001, to investigate a triple murder at the home of the Gonzales family in Sydney's suburban North Ryde, they became suspicious of the sole surviving family member, 21-year-old student Sef Gonzales.

The Gonzales family – Sef, his father Teddy, his mother Mary Loiva, and his 18-year-old sister Clodine – had immigrated to Australia from the Philippines 10 years earlier, and had prospered through their family-run immigration law firm. Now the baby-faced Sef Gonzales was huddled up in the garage sobbing uncontrollably, but no tears flowed down his face.

After a while he seemed more concerned that detectives would find a pornographic video in his bedroom than he was about his family, the members of whom lay throughout the house, savagely beaten with a baseball bat and stabbed to death sometime between 3pm and 6pm the previous afternoon.

Sef Gonzales said that when he arrived home at 11.45pm that night he'd found 'one or two' men in the house and he chased them down the street on foot. He'd returned to find the house covered in blood and his family murdered. He'd cradled his father in his arms and then tried desperately to stem the flow of blood gushing from a gaping wound in his sister's side, which was impossible given that she had been dead for hours. But Gonzales had very little blood on his hands or clothes. And he couldn't explain why an anti-Asian slur 'FUCK OFF ASIANS. KKK' was sprayed on the lounge-room wall in blue paint, except to say that perhaps it had something to do with a road rage incident that had happened the night before when three men had racially abused his family over a traffic incident and followed them home before driving off.

At the funeral, police and family members watched in disbelief as a calm and sad-faced Gonzales stood behind the three caskets and sang a solo rendition of the Mariah Carey/Boys II Men duet 'One Sweet Day' as if he were auditioning for *Australian Idol*. After the funeral, Gonzales appealed for help to find the killer and said in a public statement, 'It is difficult to explain the love and ties in my family . . . but if you were to picture the four corners of the world, in my world we were the four. The three corners of my world are now gone.'

From then on, relatives began distancing themselves from Sef Gonzales in the belief that all was not as it seemed, and that they were not safe as long as he was on the loose. With his family in the ground Sef Gonzales became the sole beneficiary of his father's estate, which was estimated at $1.5 million, and he was free to do with it as he pleased as soon as he could get his hands on it. Within three days of the murders, Gonzales was with his father's accountant finding out exactly how much the inheritance was. To speed up probate, Gonzales created false death certificates on his computer. Gonzales told friends that he was coming into big money, and test-drove a Porsche and a Lexus. He sold some of his mother's jewellery and his parents' cars, rented a luxury apartment and was seen in all of the local nightclubs dancing and drinking and having a wonderful time.

The Sef Gonzales Family Murders

In the meantime, detectives were working around the clock to bring the Gonzales family's killer to justice. There was no other suspect than Sef. Searches of emails that Gonzales thought were deleted from his computer revealed that in February that year he set in motion a plan to purchase seeds of highly poisonous plants over the internet, apparently to mix with his family's food. To cover his tracks, he sent a typed letter to a major food company saying that three of their most popular products had been poisoned and were on unnamed supermarket shelves. He also wrote similar letters to the Federal Police and the Australian Quarantine and Inspection Service. Traces of these letters were later found on his computer and his fingerprint was on one of the envelopes.

In early July, just over a week before the murders, Sef's mother fell violently ill and was rushed to hospital with suspected food poisoning. Gonzales also allegedly suffered a mild dose of food poisoning, telling friends that it may have been from a restaurant where the family had dined the night before. After his mother recovered, Gonzales apparently put the poisoning plan on hold and threw the incriminating seeds in the backyard where, three years later, a poisonous plant was found growing. When asked to explain the purchase of the poison seeds, Gonzales told police that he had planned on killing himself after finding out he had cancer and then losing the girlfriend he adored at the same time.

In December 2001 police leaked to Gonzales through a friend that they didn't believe his alibi of being away from the family house at the time of the murders, as two separate people had seen his car there at the time. While police listened in on a tapped phone, Gonzales set about establishing a new alibi that he was at a brothel at the time of the murders. Trouble was that the prostitute he was supposedly with was on holidays at the time. Then he paid a taxi driver $50 to sign a dictated statement saying that he had driven Gonzales to Chatswood on the day in question. Gonzales also handed police a forged email that a wealthy Filipino businessman had allegedly sent to him, claiming responsibility for his family's deaths and saying that police should search his father's business records for the truth.

But Gonzales had no answer for the traces of blue paint – identical to that in which the racist message had been written on the wall – that were found on the sleeve of the jumper he had been wearing on the night of the murders. In the end it was found that Sef Gonzales lived a Walter Mitty existence and nothing he told his friends or police was even remotely close to the truth. He didn't have cancer, he wasn't a taekwondo black belt, he wasn't offered a recording contract for his rendition of 'One Sweet Day', which he'd sung at the funeral, he wasn't such a stud that prostitutes didn't charge him, he didn't own a television production company and he was not training for the Olympics. In reality he was a law student in fear of failing university due to abysmal grades and disgracing his family. By murdering them all, he thought he'd found a way to solve all of his problems and live the lavish lifestyle he craved at the same time.

Still protesting his innocence at his trial in May 2004, it took a jury just four hours to find Sef Gonzales guilty on all counts; he was sentenced to three terms of life imprisonment without the possibility of parole.

In December 2004, North Ryde real estate agent LJ Hooker was fined more than $20,000 after being ordered to refund an $80,000 deposit to an unsuspecting buyer after selling the Gonzales house as a 'deceased estate', yet failing to tell the purchasers of the real terrible circumstances.

8 | JUSTICE JEFFREY SHAW AND HIS MISSING BLOOD SAMPLES

There's a common perception that the Justices of the courts, those who decide who is right and wrong in this country, are above reproach – in both their legal and moral character. They would never, we are led to believe, succumb to the temptations and evils that get us, the regular people of Australia, into the sort of trouble that can land us on the wrong side of them, waiting to hear their verdict.

But while we really only know them by name or the occasional picture in a newspaper, Supreme Court Justices really are normal human beings with the same health and social frailties as the rest of us. And believe it or not, some of them have even been known to have an alcoholic drink from time to time. And yes, even a little too much at times – which is certainly no crime. Unless, of course, you do something you shouldn't while inebriated.

A car, too much alcohol and a few hundred metres was all it took for NSW Supreme Court Justice Jeffrey William Shaw's life to turn upside down on the night of 13 October 2004. Shaw had attended a NSW Law Society function, then kicked on with a meal in the city with a colleague before catching a cab home. But not all the way home – and that's where the trouble started.

No one is really sure why Justice Shaw – well over the legal limit to drive after his night out – decided to get the taxi to drop him off at his grey Alfa Romeo parked near his local oval at around 11.30pm, instead of going the short distance further to his house on Louisa Road, the only street on an arm of land that stretches into Sydney Harbour in exclusive Birchgrove, near Balmain in Sydney's inner west.

But the Justice must have believed he was fine to operate a vehicle, especially if he drove slowly. He wasn't, though. His Eminence managed to slam into a parked Toyota Corolla while navigating down the quiet road, the impact of the crash so loud it echoed out along the quiet street. Tired residents came out in their dressing gowns to see what the commotion was. They dragged the semiconscious Shaw from his car, blood flowing from a gash in his head, the smells of a smoking clutch and booze thick in the air. Shaw denied that he had been drinking, but the neighbours took his keys away from him anyway. It was clear that something was up. He begged them not to call his wife or the police, and protested strongly when one of his neighbours insisted on taking him to hospital to have his head wound treated.

Shaw arrived at the Royal Prince Alfred Hospital in Camperdown at around 12.30am. Police attended the crash site and had both of the vehicles involved towed away.

Complying with hospital procedure dictated by the authorities, nurses took two blood samples from Shaw at 2.15am. They were stored in identical vials and sealed to prevent tampering. One of the samples was for the police in case a drink-driving charge had to be laid. The other was for Shaw to keep. It is believed that the blood alcohol reading of the samples was .225 – a massive four times the legal limit for anyone in charge of a vehicle.

Once the Justice was left alone, he dressed himself and walked out of the hospital. He got a cab out the front at 2.30am. Security

Justice Jeffrey Shaw and His Missing Blood Samples

cameras next snapped Shaw using his security pass to gain access to his office at the Supreme Court building back in the city at 3am. In his hands were what appeared to be the two vials holding his blood samples.

The Justice was back at the hospital a little over an hour later. Doctors gave him a final examination before discharging him. It was around 9am when his wife drove him back to their Birchgrove home.

It took 19 days for police to issue a press release, stating that both of Justice Shaw's blood samples had gone missing after the accident. The next day – 20 November – Shaw's wife was shocked to find officers of the law at her door looking for the samples. She turned them away.

Next, the authorities declared that an inquiry would be held to determine exactly what had happened to the missing blood samples. Shaw knew his bluff had been called. He decided it was best to turn them in to the police investigating his case. Of course, no one could say exactly how they had ended up in his possession. No one was about to say that a Justice of the Australian courts had stolen police evidence. Had it just been a big mistake, either by Shaw or the hospital, perhaps?

There was even debate about what had happened with the blood samples during the weeks they had been missing. Some questioned whether or not the blood in them was even Shaw's.

One of the doctors on duty that night said that he had believed he'd secured the sample taken for the police in the special police safe box, but now he wasn't positive that he had after all. A nurse insisted that the vial containing Shaw's personal sample had been left on a shelf above his bed.

The police suggested that Shaw himself had taken the samples from a trolley, but he was quick to deny the accusation, despite the fact that he had also said he didn't actually remember much from the night. The best the Justice could come up with was that someone at the hospital must have simply given them to him.

Because of all the confusion about what had really happened on the night – and what had happened with the blood samples afterwards – the high-range drink-driving charge against Shaw was dropped in March 2005. Instead, he was found guilty of negligent driving and driving under the influence. These lesser charges earned him a $3000 fine and a one-year suspension of his driver's licence.

Justice Shaw resigned from public service in November 2006. The next month, a Police Integrity Report regarding the matter was presented in Parliament. It damningly found that Shaw had indeed swiped the blood samples from a hospital trolley. It also stated that he had – against medical advice – left the hospital of his own accord and taken the vials in question to his office at the Supreme Court building. A week later, the report stated, he gave the vials to a fellow barrister for what was called 'storage'.

The claim that Shaw had come to possess the vials by means that 'did not involve misconduct' was disavowed by the report, which also recommended that Shaw be charged with perverting the course of justice. If found guilty, he could expect to spend as much as 14 years in jail.

It wasn't until August 2007 that the Director of Public Prosecutions Nicholas Cowdery told the Police Integrity Commission that former Justice Jeff Shaw would escape a charge of giving false evidence – aka lying. Neither would he be charged with attempting to pervert the cause of justice. Cowdery said that the charges would not be pursued because he didn't believe Shaw could be proven guilty beyond any reasonable doubt, because of his defence – that someone at the hospital must have given him the samples but he couldn't properly recall what had happened on the night in question.

Strangely, men all around the country try to pull that one every Sunday morning. The wives of Australia don't often let them get away with it.

After a distinguished career in politics and as a jurist, Justice Jeff Shaw passed away in May 2010. He was just 60. It seems a terrible shame that one human mistake that is common to all of us could blemish such a career.

But judges aren't supposed to make mistakes.

9 | THE MYSTERIOUS DISAPPEARANCE OF SAMANTHA KNIGHT

It was one of Sydney's most enduring mysteries that saw the face of Samantha Knight in her urchin's cap become deep-etched in the memories of those of us who lived through that terrible time. And then, as is so often the case when children come to harm, Samantha's killer was there all the time, just a heartbeat away, a trusted friend of the family. But it took many years to catch the beast and during that time he assaulted countless other kiddies on his way to his cell in protective custody, away from the other prisoners who would gladly tear him to shreds if they could get their hands on him.

At 4.30pm on the Tuesday afternoon of 19 August 1986, nine-year-old Samantha Knight left her Bondi flat, where she lived with her mother Tess and their black cat Midnight, to go to the shops in nearby Bondi Road to buy some lollies and a pencil. Samantha made her purchases and soon after was positively identified by a neighbour walking alone along Bondi Road. Three other witnesses said that they may have seen Samantha walking – perhaps hand-in-hand, but not for certain – with a man that afternoon, but it couldn't be confirmed. Then the pretty little girl in the cap simply vanished.

Samantha's disappearance triggered one of the biggest investigations in Sydney's history, an investigation which saw her face on posters all throughout Sydney's suburbs and as far away as Newcastle. They asked the question: 'Have you seen this girl?' But no one had. There were countless alleged sightings, the majority from well-meaning citizens and the rest from cruel hoaxers, but none offered the slightest positive clue as to what may have become of Samantha Knight.

Despite relentless campaigning by Samantha's family to keep the case in the public awareness, a $50,000 reward offered by the NSW Government for any information and the press running stories at the slightest opportunity to keep the case alive, it wasn't until 14 years later that relentless investigators revealed that at last they had a definite suspect.

On 11 February 2000, convicted Sydney paedophile Michael Anthony Guider, 49, was convicted of sex offences against two five-year-old children between 1982 and 1985. Guider was four years into a 10-year sentence for 60 counts of drugging and molesting 11 children aged two to 16 and possessing thousands of pornographic pictures of children, which he had taken.

Although found guilty, Guider wasn't given any additional jail time on top of his existing sentence. 'There is little point in my imposing an additional term – he's already looking at six more years which in my opinion is long enough to deal with any problems that he has,' Judge O'Reilly told the court.

Apparently, shortly after Michael Guider was initially sent to Lithgow jail for 10 years in 1996, he was questioned by detectives about Samantha Knight's disappearance. He was questioned about the matter again in 1999. And he was questioned again before, and after, his 2000 conviction. It seemed that Michael Guider had once been a family friend who had acted as babysitter on several occasions to Samantha Knight and some of her friends.

The Mysterious Disappearance of Samantha Knight

A year later, on 21 February 2001, Michael Guider stood before the court at his committal hearing charged with the murder of Samantha Knight, more than 14 years earlier. Those who had known him previously gasped as he was brought into the court. Dressed in prison greens, his bespectacled face was almost completely covered in a prison-grown bushy grey beard, and long unkempt hair hung down over his face and shoulders. Guider was unrecognisable. He had grown the ultimate disguise.

Documents presented to the court stated that Guider, a former North Shore landscaper and gardener, had admitted to witnesses that he had drugged Samantha to take naked pictures of her, but he had given her too many sleeping pills and she had accidentally died. Documents also said that Guider had admitted to molesting and taking pornographic pictures of many children over the previous 20 years. Two of the victims were Samantha's girlfriends.

The documents said that Guider had initially endeared himself to Samantha when she was five and lived at Manly, and had two girlfriends of similar age. Guider was a friend of their families. When Samantha moved to Bondi at the age of seven, she stayed friends with the girls and would regularly visit their homes, sometimes for sleepovers. During the following years Michael Guider occasionally babysat for Samantha and her two girlfriends, drugging them with sleeping pills in soft drink and taking obscene pictures of them while they slept.

Medical records verified that Guider regularly bought the prescription drug Normison, a sleeping pill that could undoubtedly cause toxic overdose, especially in a nine-year-old child, if too many were taken. Michael Guider had purchased Normison in the month leading up to Samantha's disappearance.

Samantha's mother Tess and father Peter O'Meagher, who had separated before their daughter went missing, sat intently through the proceedings. They listened as, one by one, three prisoners who had been in jail with Michael Guider told of his confessions to them.

One told the court that Guider had told him he had given Samantha too much Normison, and that if police had looked under bushes in nearby Cooper Park they would have found her. Another said that Guider had told him that he was the man the three witnesses thought they saw Samantha with, and that he had taken her to a cave in North Sydney. There he drugged her and photographed her and went away for a brief time. When he came back she was dead. He buried her in a park then dug her body up later and put it in the garbage, and it was taken away, never to be found.

Michael Guider was committed for trial where he pleaded guilty to the manslaughter, not murder, of Samantha Knight after arriving at a deal with the Crown, with the approval of Samantha's family. It carried a maximum of 25 years in jail. Guider received 17 years with a minimum of 12, to be served concurrently with the term he was already serving. This means that all he really got for killing Samantha Knight was eight years. That's if he's a good boy. But then again, there aren't any little girls in jail, are there?

It turned out that one of the three prisoners who gave evidence against Michael Guider was his own brother Tim, who was serving a 10-year sentence for matters relating to an armed robbery. Given that it was alleged that it was Tim's information against his brother that brought about the conviction in the first place, Tim was given a pardon and released from jail.

Here's a scary thought. Michael Guider will be eligible for parole in 2014. He will be 63. At the very worst they can only keep him in jail until 2019, when he is 68. No one knows what he looks like without a beard, long hair and glasses. Just a nice, cuddly old man with some Normison. That's unless someone puts him in the mainstream section of the prison by mistake. We can only wish.

10 | THE MANY LIVES OF FRED MANY

Frederick Glen Many was a career criminal who specialised in armed robbery and rape and had it not been for the fact that he was deaf in one ear, his crimes would most certainly have included murder. Many spent so much time in jail during his life that he knew the system backwards and devised methods to exploit it and get time off his sentence. His favourite was informing on his fellow prisoners. Another time, in prison folklore, he allegedly saved a prison officer from being bashed.

Fred Many was born into a decent, hardworking rural family, none of whom had ever been in trouble with the police. After Many began his career as a thief he was in and out of institutions at first, and then jail, for every crime in the book, including drug offences, common assault, robbery with assault, rape, car theft and armed robbery.

On 11 July 1986, Many was released from prison while he still had seven years to serve of a 22-and-a-half-year jail term for a combination of serious crimes. It seemed that Many had saved the life of a prison superintendent who was being viciously attacked by another prisoner, Raymond Hornby. Many had dragged Hornby off the incapacitated officer and if it wasn't for his intervention – something that is heavily frowned upon by inmates who believe that whatever happens, let it happen – there seemed little doubt that the officer would have been killed.

Fearing for Many's life in jail given that he had intervened – and also due to his unselfish act of bravery – his sentence was dramatically reduced and he was allowed to go home on parole seven years early. After Many was released, Hornby admitted to police that the attack was in fact a set-up between himself and Many, to make Many look good so that he would get early parole. We can only wonder at what would make a man do that, and get more years on his sentence, to get another man off early. We shall never know. And as it sadly turned out, letting Fred Many back out on the streets wasn't a good idea.

Upon release, Many moved to the NSW Central Coast with his younger partner. Seven weeks later, on 2 September 1986, he offered a 15-year-old schoolgirl, who was walking home from the beach, a lift to the nearest bus stop. Against her better judgement the girl accepted and sat in the passenger's seat. She had no way of knowing that Many had earlier offered two other girls lifts but they had refused.

Against her will, Many took the young girl to a deserted bush area where he sexually assaulted and tried to strangle her. Lying on the ground with her head buried in the sand after Many had bashed and repeatedly assaulted her, the teenager pretended to be dead, daring only to breathe faintly and not ruffle the sand near her nostrils. Many accepted that he had killed her and, convinced that there was no living witness, left her for dead. If Fred Many hadn't been deaf in one ear he surely would have heard the faint breathing coming from his victim and finished her off. But the young lady lived to identify her attacker, who was back behind bars within three days.

Charged with rape and attempted murder, Many set about finding the crims in jail about whom the authorities would like to know things. Having found his targets, he endeared himself to them in order to find out useful information that the National Crime Authority (NCA) and the New South Wales police would be interested in, in exchange for favours and a reduction in his sentence, which by now had been set at 20 years.

And if Fred Many couldn't find anything in which the authorities would be interested, he would simply make it up. Over his years in jail Many had learnt that it was easier to get by if he told people what they wanted to hear, truth or otherwise, rather than not telling them anything at all. With this principle in mind, Many began passing on information about several of his fellow prisoners to the NCA, one of whom they were especially interested in.

While it couldn't be said that Fred Many was rocket-scientist material, it could at the very least be said that he was game. The main bloke that Many elected to 'allegedly' inform on was none other than Tom Domican, or 'Tough Tom' as he was known, the toughest guy in the joint, who was both respected and feared by villains and law enforcement agencies alike.

Domican was on remand in custody on the charge of shooting at hitman Christopher Dale Flannery and his wife and children with a machine gun in a drive-by shooting at Flannery's home. Although Flannery survived, since the incident occurred he had mysteriously gone missing, presumed dead.

Fred Many told the NCA that he was Tough Tom's best mate and that Domican was confiding all sorts of juicy tidbits in him. Anyone who knew Tom Domican would tell you that he would sooner pull out his own toenails with a blowtorch and a pair of pliers than part with his secrets, let alone confide in the likes of a halfwit such as Many, who was the type of weak individual that Domican despised.

But when Fred Many told the NCA that Domican had told him not only about his attempt to assassinate Chris Flannery, but also about two other murder plots, and that Domican had actually solicited Many's help on one, investigators almost choked with glee. Many gave evidence in court against his 'best mate' Tom Domican. The evidence was unreliable and full of holes and Domican was exonerated; despite this fact, Fred Many still had his sentence reduced by eight and a half years.

This was also despite a solicitor stating that Many had told her he had often lied in court. It left those who chose to believe Many's lies and knock the time off his sentence looking very stupid.

Many served most of the nine years of his 20-year sentence looking over his shoulder for fear of reprisals. It was only his rat cunning that kept him alive. Amid uproar that such a beast should be released, let alone 11 years early, he was set free on the eve of the 1995 New South Wales election that voted in Bob Carr's opposition Labor Party, which had campaigned heavily against Many's release.

No sooner was Many out of jail than his former partner told police of two armed robberies he had committed during his seven weeks of freedom before he raped and almost murdered the schoolgirl nine years earlier.

Charged with the robberies and on bail, Many prolonged his trial by appealing that he wouldn't get a fair trial due to his notoriety. But before it ever got to court, in September 1997, Many died while watching TV in his western suburbs home. The story goes that Fred Many died of a sudden heart attack when he awoke in front of the TV and thought he saw Tough Tom Domican through the window knocking at the front door, wanting to have a word with him.

11 | THE JOHN CHRISTIE MURDERS OF NOTTING HILL

As seen in the movie of the same name, Notting Hill is a very fashionable part of London. But there was a time when it was a grimy slum that one of England's most vile beasts made his private killing field.

John Reginald Halliday Christie and his wife Ethel took up residence in the small, rundown ground-floor apartment of a terrace house at 10 Rillington Place in Notting Hill in 1938. A timid clerk with a bald head and thick glasses, Christie had grown up with a violent father and four domineering sisters. From an early age Christie developed a love-hate relationship with females – no doubt brought about by his bullying sisters. To make matters worse, when some of his first amorous encounters with females ended in failure, he earned the nickname 'Can't-make-it Christie'. He was plagued by impotence for the rest of his life.

After World War I broke out, Christie left school at 15 and joined the army as a signalman. After leaving the service,

Christie became a clerk and married Ethel Waddington in 1920. Christie's long-time practice of seeing prostitutes carried on into his marriage. He became a postman and was sent to prison for three months for stealing postal orders. On his release he moved to London, leaving Ethel at home at Sheffield.

When Christie was 29, he was sent back to jail for nine months for stealing. From jail Christie contacted Ethel and asked her to come back and the couple were reunited in London in 1933, after a decade apart. In 1939, with World War II brewing and now living in Notting Hill, Christie joined the War Reserve Police. Not bothering to check his record, police issued Christie with a uniform in the rank of Special Constable with the Harrow Road Police Station.

In a position of authority for a change, for the first time in his life Christie was happy. He stayed in the position for four years, and was so intent on maintaining law and order he was nicknamed 'the Himmler of Rillington Place'. Little did people know he used his position to illicitly follow women and spy on them undressing.

In 1949, newlyweds 19-year-old Beryl and 24-year-old Timothy Evans and their baby daughter Geraldine moved into the flat above. The lorry driver Evans was a short man with a quick temper and a fondness for alcohol, with an IQ of around 70, who could barely read or write. What little money Evans brought in barely covered their living costs. They fought, often physically, and the baby was neglected.

To make matters worse, Beryl found herself pregnant again. She tried various methods to terminate the pregnancy, and spoke to several people – including the Christies – about her desire to get an abortion. Soon after, according to Christie, Tim Evans told them that Beryl had moved back to Bristol. A day after that, he told the Christies that he was selling up and joining his wife. But when he left town it was by train to his aunt's house in Merthyr Vale in South Wales. He returned six days later, informing Christie that Beryl had left him, then he went back to Merthyr Vale where he informed the local police that his wife had been murdered.

The John Christie Murders of Notting Hill

The police contacted their colleagues in Notting Hill, who went around to 10 Rillington Place, where they eventually found Beryl Evans and her baby Geraldine both strangled to death in the washhouse. Evans was arrested and went on to confess that he had murdered Beryl because she kept getting the family into debt. He said they had fought and that he had hit her before strangling her with a piece of rope. Two days after that, he quit his job and killed his baby girl, strangling her with a tie and placing her body with her mother's in the washhouse.

The confession was so contradictory to the facts that popular belief was that the police had led the not-so-bright Evans through his statement and that he was also threatened with physical violence if he didn't admit to the murders. Evans then changed his tune and said that his wife Beryl died during an abortion attempt by Christie, who also murdered their baby afterwards. But no one believed him.

Evans faced court at the Old Bailey on 11 January 1950, charged with the murder of his daughter. The soft-spoken, unassuming Christie was the main witness for the prosecution, telling the court how Tim Evans beat his family and was more than capable of murder. Also against Evans were four separate confessions he had made, and after a trial that saw the defence try to pin the blame on Christie, Evans was found guilty and was hanged on 9 March 1950.

Nothing further was heard from 10 Rillington Place until three years later; Ethel Christie disappeared and John Christie told neighbours she had gone to Sheffield, where he would soon join her. Around this time, he began laying a strong-smelling disinfectant about the house and garden and sold his furniture and Ethel's wedding ring. With no job, Christie forged his wife's signature and took all the funds from her bank account. He then had his dog put down, gave his cat to the neighbours and left.

When new tenants moved into the Christie house they discovered Ethel's putrefying body under the floorboards, along with the bodies of three women in a large wall cavity behind recently applied wallpaper. Police also discovered the remains of two other females who had been buried in the backyard for six years.

Broke and with nowhere to stay, Christie was soon picked up and taken to Putney police station, where he openly spoke about the six murdered women found at his house. It seemed as though due to his impotence he preferred his sexual partners to be dead so they couldn't make fun of his inadequacies. This also explained why he kept the corpses in and around his house long after their deaths.

While in Brixton Prison awaiting trial, Christie confessed to killing the baby Geraldine but not her mother Beryl. Charged with murdering his wife, Christie pleaded insanity. The jury took just 80 minutes to find him both sane and guilty and he was hanged on 15 July 1953.

In the following years there were numerous public inquiries to clear Timmy Evans' name. A 1965 government inquiry stated that Timothy Evans had killed his wife, but that Christie had murdered Geraldine Evans. As a result, Evans was granted a posthumous pardon for the murder of his little girl and reburied in consecrated ground. Also in 1965, and largely due to the fact that an innocent man had been hanged, the death penalty was abolished in Britain.

In 2003, the British Home Office awarded Timothy Evans' family compensation for the miscarriage of justice. The independent assessor for the Home Office, Lord Brennan QC, said that 'the conviction and execution of Timothy Evans for the murder of his child was wrongful and a miscarriage of justice', and added that 'there is no evidence to implicate Timothy Evans in the murder of his wife. She was most probably murdered by Christie'.

In 1971, the spine-chilling movie *10 Rillington Place*, featuring Richard Attenborough and John Hurt, was filmed at the address where it all happened. In 1972, 10 Rillington Place, which had become more popular than 10 Downing Street as a tourist destination, was bulldozed and replaced with a housing development renamed Bartle Road, Notting Hill.

12 | THE WALES-KING MURDERS

The brutal bashing murders of Margaret Wales-King and her husband Paul in April 2002 were dubbed by the Melbourne press as 'The Society Murders', yet nothing could be further from the truth. Admittedly, Paul and Margaret Wales-King had all of the trappings of high society, but besides their wealth and comfortable townhouse in the leafy establishment suburb of Armadale, they were just ordinary people beyond reproach who were much more interested in their children and family life with their 11 grandchildren than any glittering fundraising cocktail party where they could be photographed for the social pages in the Sunday papers. Well off, yes. But A-list society? Never.

At the time of his murder, 70-year-old retired investor Paul King was an invalid due to two strokes and was 68-year-old Margaret Lord's second husband. She had previously been married to airline pilot Brian Wales, with whom she had five children. When she married Paul King, who was of independent means, the now Margaret Wales-King was substantially wealthy in her own right in that she was estimated to be worth in the vicinity of $5 million, which consisted of her home, car, jewellery and antiques, cash, substantial shareholdings and superannuation. Mrs Wales-King had made out her will, with her husband and five children each getting a sixth of her estate upon her death. But one of the children wasn't prepared to wait that long.

It was no secret within the family that the youngest son, Matthew, 34, and his mother had been rowing for years over Matthew's reckless financial affairs and her refusal to keep giving him more money to seemingly throw away. But all seemed to be peaceful on the evening of 5 April when Brian and Margaret Wales-King arrived at Matthew and his Chilean-born wife Maritza's home for dinner. Nor was there anything odd about the simple meal of vegetable soup and then a homemade risotto. Nothing unusual, that is, except for the handful of potent painkillers and blood pressure pills that had been blended and mixed through the main course.

When Matthew's mother and stepfather became drowsy at around 9.45pm, Maritza stayed inside the house while Matthew ushered them through the front door to their car, suggesting they best go home, just five minutes away, where they could find medication for their ailments. Then, as they left the Glen Iris townhouse by the front door and headed towards the driveway, Matthew took to them with a 1-metre piece of four-by-two pine he had hidden in the garden, bludgeoning them both severely about the head. First he hit his mother over the back of the head and then he set upon his invalid stepfather until he lay in a bleeding heap at his feet. Then he finished his mother off. There was little doubt that it was premeditated, cold-blooded murder.

Having murdered his parents, Matthew now had the dilemma of what to do with their bodies. As it turned out, his planning to do away with them hadn't gone past the murder stage. With his wife, who had in no way taken part in the killings, watching on in horror from the kitchen window, Matthew Wales-King dragged the lifeless bodies of her in-laws across the front lawn and concealed them beneath their two-year-old son Dominik's deflated kiddie's wading pool.

The Wales-King Murders

So, what to do now with his mother's silver Mercedes, which was parked in the driveway? In a hastily planned scheme to throw any suspicion away from him, Matthew drove his mother's car to the inner-city bayside suburb of Middle Park, where he parked it in the street, locked it and caught a cab home. Along the way he threw the car keys into a drain.

Back home, Matthew Wales-King still had the problem of what to do with his parents' bodies. It was obviously something that he had not prepared for. First he used sheets to cover his victims' faces, obviously, as crime scene investigators would point out later, to hide their incriminating stares as he went about the business of preparing them for burial. He then placed the deflated kiddie pool back over them and covered it with leaves to look like a pile of rubbish until he decided what his next step would be.

A few days later Matthew Wales-King set his bizarre plan in action. He rented a trailer and attached it to his own car. Then he loaded the bodies, which he had wrapped up in doonas, a mattock and new bags of mulch into the trailer and took off through Melbourne's eastern suburbs, to eventually arrive 20 kilometres past the mountain resort of Marysville, where he drove off on a secluded sidetrack and into the forest. About 20 metres off the side of the track he dug a shallow grave no more than about a metre deep and lay his mother's body face down, then laid his stepfather on top of her. He then filled in what was left of the hole.

He then drove home to Melbourne, all the while convinced that what he had just done wouldn't convince anyone that it was anything other than a shallow grave. He would have to return and do it properly. A few days later he returned to the gravesite, where he covered it with rocks he had brought in the trailer, then added more soil and covered it with brand-new mulch, which only made it look more than ever like a new gravesite. On the way home he pulled into a car wash and put the car and the trailer through, giving them a really good scrub. Then he went home and with powerful disinfectant scrubbed everything in his home that could have come in contact with the dead bodies.

The Australian Crime File 3

If ever there was a bloke leaving elephant prints in the snow, it was Matthew King.

In the meantime, other family members had tried repeatedly to get in touch with their parents and eventually notified the police. A week later, when the silver Mercedes was found, it was all over the newspapers, and almost three weeks later, when the bodies were discovered by rangers who noticed car tracks and a mysterious mound in a protected area, it became one the biggest stories in Victorian criminal history.

Nine days after the bodies were discovered, Matthew Wales-King was inconsolable at his mother's funeral and offered prayers on behalf of the mourners. Two days later he was arrested and charged with double murder, after police had become suspicious on finding blood in his garage and had put him under full-scale investigation.

Confronted with the undeniable mountain of circumstantial evidence, Matthew broke down and confessed to killing his mother and stepfather, saying that initially he only meant to scare them into giving him some money but it had got out of hand. Given that his wife had full knowledge of what had taken place but hadn't told police for fear of going to jail, she was charged with attempting to pervert the course of justice.

Incredibly, for the premeditated bashing murders of his mother and stepfather Matthew Wales-King was sentenced to only 30 years' imprisonment. His wife Maritza received a two-year jail term, which was suspended.

13 | THE MURDER OF MP JOHN NEWMAN: AUSTRALIA'S FIRST POLITICAL MURDER

The murder conspiracy against John Paul Newman, State Labor MP for Cabramatta, in Sydney's south-west, was the district's worst-kept secret and almost comical in its stupidity. The first three planned attempts – which it seems as though most of Cabramatta knew about – never got past the planning stage. The first two *actual* attempts never happened because the murder scene was overpopulated and then the would-be assassins lost their nerve.

And when John Newman was actually murdered, his killers used their own cars to speed away from the shooting, left a succession of would-be hitmen who had been asked if they would do the job, and a club full of people who had either been asked to participate or at least knew that a murder was going to take place and who was the intended victim. But yet, despite the amount of work done by the task force, it took years to bring the culprits to justice, and even then the actual killers got away.

57

At 9.30pm on the Monday night of 5 September 1994, John Newman returned to his home in Woods Avenue, Cabramatta, from a branch meeting of the ALP and was gunned down by two assailants in his driveway in front of his partner Lucy Wang. Wang, severely traumatised, never got a very good look at her fiancé's killers. Although he never pulled the trigger, the man behind John Newman's murder was high-profile businessman and local Labor Councillor Phuong Ngo, who also owned the local Vietnamese newspaper and made no bones about the fact that he wanted John Newman's job in state politics.

The two men openly took each other to task about problems within the burgeoning Cabramatta Vietnamese community and about the crime rate, which was the highest in New South Wales and saw dealers openly approaching citizens in shopping centres and at the railway station, offering them deals of heroin. John Newman's car suddenly became the target of paint bombs while parked in his front driveway.

It didn't help matters when an anonymous flyer circulated throughout Cabramatta calling for an investigation into the unsubstantiated criminal activities of Phuong Ngo, his alleged dealings in drugs and association with leading crime bosses. Phuong Ngo decided to take matters into his own hands.

Basing himself at Cabramatta's Mekong Club, which he created to support the social welfare activities of the community and of which he was Honorary President, Phuong Ngo told one of the staff to make inquiries about getting a gun. The quest for the gun soon spread throughout the club as one associate asked another, and soon there were employees driving all over Sydney's southern suburbs with handfuls of money in search of a handgun. They came up with a sawn-off .22 rifle, a .32 Beretta, a Colt .45 and a Ruger.

With a Mekong Club poker machine attendant and another employee as his hitmen, Ngo sent them on their mission to kill John Newman. Plans at three venues – Mr Newman's office, the Fairfield Council Chambers and the Yagoona Greyhound Club – fell over at the last minute due to cold feet on the part of the hitmen. Their first real attempt outside a Cabramatta

The Murder of MP John Newman

Vietnamese restaurant failed when they missed their signal from Phuong Ngo that John Newman had finished his meal and was leaving. As it turned out it wouldn't have happened anyway, as the gunmen had decided that there were too many people about. A second attempt, outside John Newman's home, came to nothing when the hitmen got frightened and couldn't decide who was going to shoot first.

Phuong Ngo sacked his two would-be hitmen and recruited a bar attendant and the personnel manager from the Mekong Club to kill John Newman. On their reconnaissance of the proposed murder scene, the two new hitmen used their own cars, with Ngo following them in a car owned by the Mekong Club.

On the afternoon of Saturday 3 September, two days before the murder, a woman told police she recalled seeing a white car parked in nearby Bowden Street. It was identical to the one that was owned by the Mekong Club and driven by Phuong Ngo. That same night at the corner of Bowden and Huey streets, near John Newman's home, three sisters recalled seeing a green early-model Fairlane that looked conspicuously out of place. One of the girls also recalled seeing the same car parked there on and off over recent days. In nearby Judith Street, an Asian couple briefly saw a man answering to Phuong Ngo's description standing beside his car.

On the Monday night that the murder took place, Phuong Ngo and his two hitmen attempted to set up a fake alibi. This involved false minutes to a staff meeting that they had attended earlier stating that they all had left much later, thus supposedly accounting for their whereabouts at the time of the murder.

The conspicuous green Fairlane with the assassins inside parked near John Newman's home while Phuong Ngo waited with the Mekong Club's Camry parked nearby. John Newman arrived home just after 9.30pm with his fiancée, Lucy Wang, and got out of the car. The bar attendant approached John Newman, fired four times, hitting him twice, and then fled back to the Fairlane, which took off with the Camry driven by Phuong Ngo in hot pursuit. The cars stopped at a service station, where

The Australian Crime File 3

Phuong Ngo took the pistol for disposal and the others made their way back to the Mekong Club. Ngo dumped the pistol in the Georges River and joined the others later.

Despite a mountain of circumstantial evidence and hearsay that pointed to Phuong Ngo and his associates as John Newman's killers, and although they were questioned many times, there wasn't enough hard evidence to convict them. It wasn't until a 1998 coronial inquest into John Newman's murder that it was decided that there was enough solid evidence to charge Phuong Ngo and his associates with murder. But even then it wasn't going to be easy. The first trial was aborted and a second trial resulted in a hung jury.

Then the Crown hit the jackpot when Phuong Ngo's former personnel manager at the Mekong Club decided to tell the court all he knew in return for indemnity from prosecution. In June 2001, Phuong Ngo was finally found guilty of John Newman's murder and sent to jail for life with no possibility of parole. His two co-accused, who had actually carried out the murder but had also decided to roll over, were found not guilty and set free.

Phuong Ngo now resides in Goulburn Jail's Supermax prison, which is reserved exclusively for New South Wales' worst prisoners.

14 | HIH: THE CASH COW FOR CORPORATE CROOKS

When Australia's largest insurance company, HIH, went broke in 2001 for billions of dollars, there were tens of thousands of penniless customers who hoped that there was a special place in hell for the high flyers who had robbed them blind. And while they never got their money back, they achieved some personal satisfaction when crooked HIH directors Ray Williams, Brad Cooper and Rodney Adler found that special hell on Earth in prison, a long way from their lives of mansions, Rolls-Royces, Ferraris, first-class world travel and tipping food waitresses more than most people earn in a week.

When Williams fronted a royal commission into the collapse of HIH, ordered by then Prime Minister John Howard and presided over by Justice Neville John Owen in 2002, he maintained that he was a law-abiding citizen and pleaded ignorance. Williams maintained that his only crime had been that he hadn't fully understood the trouble his company was in. And when it came time to present the facts to shareholders – the shareholders that in March the year before had found out that all the money they had invested in good faith was now worth nothing – Williams didn't exactly tell the truth.

By April 2005, he had changed his tune – he was now complaining loudly and angrily to anyone who would listen that the minimum jail sentence of two years and nine months, with a maximum of four and a half years, that he had received as the result of his company imploding in spectacular fashion was far too harsh. The thousands of everyday Aussies who lost their homes and businesses didn't feel the slightest compassion for him. Far from it; they believed that the sentence was far too lean – he should have been given life.

As if in complete denial of the obvious, Williams was indignant after having to plead guilty in court to making misleading statements in an annual report, which overstated HIH's 1999 operating profit by $92.4 million to cover the company's huge, mismanaged losses. On top of that, he had also pleaded guilty to signing off on a letter in 2000 telling investors that Rodney Adler's newly acquired FAI Insurance had net assets of $200 million, when in fact it had just $35 million, making it worth considerably less than what the ailing HIH had paid for it. Williams was also found guilty of falsifying a prospectus to raise up to $155 million for HIH. When HIH went down the gurgler to the tune of $5.3 billion, it was far and away the biggest bankruptcy in Australia's history – and, as is always sadly the way, it took tens of thousands of innocent Australians out with it.

First to go were the small businesses – primarily ones in the building trade that relied on payments from HIH for construction jobs they were employed to do for insurance claims. Next on the financial chopping block were the thousands of everyday Aussies waiting for payouts from the insurance company for their regular claims. By 1 March 2001 the bubble had burst and HIH could no longer make any payments to anyone.

HIH had gone from being one of the country's leading insurance companies, with an alleged $7.8 billion in assets, to a barren financial husk. Provisional liquidator Anthony McGrath of accountancy firm McGrath & Riddell estimated that HIH had lost more than $800 million during the six months leading up to 31 December 2000, due to glaring mismanagement.

McGrath also quickly determined that the company had continued to trade even after they had become hopelessly insolvent, which, of course, was highly illegal. The company, it was said, eventually failed as a result of rapid expansion, unsupervised delegation of authority, underpricing, false reports, reckless management, incompetence, fraud and basic greed.

HIH was founded in 1968, as a small underwriting company, by Ray Williams and Michael Payne. It was originally named MW Payne Underwriting Agency Pty Ltd, and it went through a number of takeovers along the way – with Williams always staying on as CEO. It became CE Heath International Holdings in May 1996 and continued to acquire several companies under its wings both in Australia and overseas. One of those was local insurance company FAI Insurance, which it took on in 1998 and whose chief executive Rodney Adler became a director of HIH the following year, at which time the company also changed its name to HIH Insurance Ltd.

A year later the wild ride was reaching its messy end, with HIH going from a giant with net assets of $940 million to being down the tubes to the tune of $5.3 billion.

But how did no one in authority to monitor such matters notice what was going on at the time? If the Australian Prudential Regulation Authority (APRA) had been more alert to the situation, they may have been able to let shareholders know about the increasingly shaky situation, but the regulating body allowed HIH to keep on trading until early in 2001, even though it was looking like it would collapse by the end of 1999, finally becoming insolvent by September the following year. Those extra months allowed the crooked directors Williams, Adler and another especially greedy crook, Bradley David Cooper, plenty more time to keep their snouts in the trough and embezzle as much as they could from the failing company before it slipped into the ocean altogether.

Incredibly, the royal commission would later find that Williams, Adler and Cooper's corporate fraud played no part in the downfall of HIH. But just the same, that didn't stop the trio from going to jail. It turned out that their behind-the-scenes chicanery – offsetting HIH's assets with its debts and potential insurance claims against the company – had left them with net assets of $133 million.

In 2000, due to bodgie financial statements concocted by Williams, the accountancy firm McGrath & Riddell described HIH's solvency as 'marginal'. The report into the company stated that 'an extremely small movement of just 1.7 per cent in the value of assets, could move the balance sheet into net asset deficiency'. In the end, even the slightest setback to HIH would push the company into insolvency.

Of course, while his company fell apart, Ray Williams was still happily swanning around town in the latest Rolls-Royce, which he parked at his palatial mansion. He flashed the corporate credit card, even using HIH shareholders' money to support several notable Australian charities. To anyone who didn't know the trouble HIH was in, Williams appeared to be an unassuming Christian philanthropist. He was even awarded the Order of Australia and sat on numerous charity boards.

Four months into his prison sentence, Williams declared himself bankrupt. The circling creditors swooped – they obviously wanted to access whatever assets he had left, but they were too late. By that time, Williams had transferred all he had left into his wife's name.

For his part, Adler was fined $5.4 million and banned from sitting on a board of directors after being found guilty of inappropriately purchasing $10 million worth of HIH shares with HIH money through another of his companies. The move was highly illegal and a ploy to prop up HIH's share price, making his HIH shares worth considerably more. The court also determined that Adler, Williams and HIH Chief Financial Officer Dominic Fodera had breached corporate law statutes more than 200 times.

In February 2005, Rodney Adler was back in the Supreme Court and pleaded guilty to making false and misleading statements to encourage investors to buy HIH shares and misusing his position as a director of HIH to intentionally be dishonest, and failing to act in the best interests of the board. Adler was sent to prison for a minimum of two and a half years.

Like Adler, the chubby Ferrari-driving entrepreneur Brad Cooper – who had trouble squeezing into a Testarossa – had come across to HIH from FAI, which in turn was responsible for Cooper's debt-ridden company HSI (Home Security International). HSI wasn't just losing money – it was haemorrhaging it out an alarming rate. Ray Williams was worried that this would make HIH look bad, so, to protect his own name, he began pouring funds from his financially troubled company into his employee's cash-strapped company. It was a situation that was never going to end well.

Williams ended up injecting $85 million of HIH cash into HSI – of which more than $13 million in turn found its way into Cooper's greedy pockets, under the guise of fees and services rendered. Not bad money, if you can live with the guilty conscience. Cooper could, not a worry in the world.

With two waterfront mansions, a love of first-class travel and several luxury cars already to his name, it wasn't as if Cooper really needed to embezzle from HIH. But Cooper was just plain greedy. He saw a cash cow and went for it. He bribed HIH Chief Investment Officer Bill Howard with $124,000 to facilitate the payment of $4.9 million to him, while getting the bean counter to turn a blind eye to a $1.79 million debt Cooper owed HIH.

Cooper had no trouble pulling his scam. He just made up a bunch of fake invoices and Howard paid them. These dodgy invoices were for such dubious purposes as $1.2 million on non-existent seminars, more than $500,000 for random 'expenses' and almost $2 million billed for an 'introduction fee' involving a property deal with media mogul Kerry Packer that never saw the light of day.

When Cooper's crimes were discovered, he found himself in court in October 2005 on 13 charges of bribery and fraud. Proving there's no honour among thieves – especially the white-collar variety – Bill Howard gave him up. Cooper was sentenced to a minimum five years in jail, while Howard – in return for giving evidence against his former cohort – was given a three-year suspended sentence after being convicted on two counts of criminal misconduct.

And good riddance to them, all the investors and customers of HIH said. But it was little consolation to the thousands of decent Aussie workers and small businesses who are still suffering from their greed to this day.

The most recent news of Rodney Adler was that he was lecturing on honesty in business and how he had benefited from his mistakes. What a joke!

15 | THE LOVE-STRUCK JAILER: HOW HEATHER PARKER HELPED PETER GIBB ESCAPE

When Heather Parker and Peter Gibb were caught getting it off in a broom closet in the Melbourne Remand Centre in 1992, you couldn't be blamed for thinking that surely they could have found a better place. Trouble was, they couldn't. Gibb was on remand for armed robbery and looking down the barrel of a long sentence. Heather Parker was the jail warder assigned to look after him.

Although she was married with two children, 27-year-old Parker had fallen heavily for the swarthy, older career criminal Gibb, who was covered in jailhouse tatts and had been in serious trouble since he was a teenager. It was no secret around the remand centre that Parker had the hots for Gibb, as she was seen kissing him when she opened his cell in the mornings.

The broom closet incident caused an uproar in the remand centre; the other guards put the prisoners in lockdown and staged a stop-work meeting to demand that Parker be booted out. She was first transferred to Pentridge Prison and then to the security ward at St Vincent's Hospital. She finally wound up in a clerical position at the head office of the Corrections Department. Parker kept in constant contact with Gibb, who had by now received 12 years for the armed robbery charges.

With the aid of another prisoner, Archie Butterly, Gibb planned a bold escape. But he would need the outside assistance of Heather Parker. She couldn't volunteer quickly enough. She imported an automatic pistol and three stun guns from the US by mail order. Parker then recruited one of Gibb's friends on the outside to steal a station wagon and a four-wheel drive and some extra number plates. Then she equipped the stolen 4WD with gear that she and Gibb would need for a life on the run – food and petrol supplies, camping gear, mobile phones, police scanners and a camouflage net to hide them from nosy helicopters.

With all in readiness, Gibb and Butterly put their plan into action. At 6pm on Sunday 7 March 1993, they blew out a window on the second floor of the remand centre with a small piece of explosive that Parker had smuggled in. The men kicked out the bars and dropped into La Trobe Street by sliding down a knotted sheet. There they took off in a waiting Ford Falcon station wagon that had the keys in the ignition and a revolver hidden beneath the seat.

An alert warder, Donald Glasson, ran outside the remand centre just in time to hail down a passing taxi and keep police informed over the radio as to the escapees' progress. The Falcon wagon charged through red lights at great speed and didn't stop after smashing into another car, but eventually crashed into a ramp on the Westgate Freeway.

Although they were both badly injured, Gibb and Butterly stole a motorbike at gunpoint. When they crashed it and attempted to steal another, a police van pulled up and they were attacked by two police officers who broke Gibb's arm with a baton. In the brawl one of the officers was shot twice and his gun was stolen. In a hail of bullets Gibb and Butterly took off in the paddy wagon. A short distance away they abandoned the police van and were seen getting into a waiting Suzuki Vitara,

The Love-struck Jailer

which was registered to a Heather Dianne Parker. From there they vanished.

A huge police search across Melbourne turned up nothing. In the meantime, Parker, Gibb and Butterly had driven to Frankston where the stolen 4WD was waiting, hidden in a storage unit. They headed north. The following day at Latrobe Hospital at Moe, Gibb received treatment for a broken arm and Butterly had several deep gashes to his arm stitched and bandaged. Then they headed into the rugged bush of the north-east high country where it was all but impossible to find them if they were careful. But they weren't.

Even though they had enough supplies to last them in the bush for months until the heat died down, four days later they chose to stay at a hotel at the tiny township of Gaffney's Creek, about 200 kilometres north-east of Melbourne, where there was no TV or radio and no one had the faintest idea about the Melbourne breakout. Parker and Gibb joined the locals for dinner in the dining room and stayed for beers and a singalong before going to bed for a quick nap.

Soon after the trio vacated the hotel at around 1am and had moved on into the night, a fire broke out in their room and by first light the historic hotel, built in 1865, had burned to the ground. The fire brought police to the area, and a description of the tenants of the room where the fire had started soon had every officer in the district on alert for the escapees.

After finding the 4WD hidden in the bush 25 kilometres south of nearby Jamieson two days later, police tracker dogs picked up a scent and ran into the rainforest, to be met by intense shooting at the pursuing police. The shooting stopped and as Gibb and Parker tried to escape through waist-deep water in the Goulburn River, the dogs were let loose and were soon upon them. The lovers were quickly arrested and shackled. In nearby grass police found the body of Archie Butterly. He had been killed by a single bullet behind his left ear.

Parker and Gibb were charged with six counts of attempted murder and 23 other charges, including armed robbery, car theft, endangering life, using firearms to prevent arrest and possession of explosives. Although it was found that the gun that killed Archie Butterly was the one that the escapees had taken from the police officer during the breakout, and that he hadn't committed suicide, incredibly no one was ever charged with his murder. Three months later, Parker was granted bail on the condition that she live with her mother.

During the committal hearing and trial Heather Parker and Peter Gibb were like two lovesick teenagers, holding hands and gazing into each other's eyes throughout the proceedings. Even when they were both sentenced to 10 years, they pledged to wait for each other. And wait they did. In September 1997, Gibb, who had been released six months earlier after serving just four years (Parker did four-and-a-half), collected Parker from Deer Park Prison in a stretch limousine. They spent the night at Crown Towers. They moved in together and had two children, but with Gibb continually in and out of jail for a variety of offences, life was always going to be tough.

Then Heather Parker caught the old man playing up. She punched the girlfriend, bashed her arm repeatedly against a steel bench, hit her with stools and kicked her while she was lying on the ground. The poor woman was hospitalised for six days and had a metal plate put in her left arm, which was broken in the attack. In March 2007, Heather Parker was sentenced to 18 months' jail, suspended for two and a half years. With Gibb awaiting sentencing for burglary, the judge said she didn't want to see their two children go to foster homes.

The couple have since split up.

16 | THE SAINT VALENTINE'S DAY MASSACRE: WHEN THE GANGSTERS RULED CHICAGO

By late 1928, the street thug, bootlegger and murderer Al 'Scarface' Capone practically owned Chicago, one of the biggest cities in the USA, with a population of 3 million people. In a few short murderous years, Capone had expanded far beyond booze, gambling and prostitution. Capone's Mafia-affiliated organisation controlled at least 91 of Chicago's trade unions, which in turn controlled every aspect of normal life in the huge city. Capone's thugs collected union initiation fees and monthly dues and in return gave the employers protection from the unions and their right to strike against them. It was pay up or be killed. Everyone paid.

The cost to the public was mind-boggling. When Capone moved into the cleaning and dyeing industry, in order to get the protection money the merchants had to raise the price of cleaning a suit by 75 per cent. When Capone gained control of the kosher butchers, the price of corned beef went up by 30 cents a pound. In Chicago alone, the Mafia's control of the unions was costing consumers an extra $136 million a year. That was around an extra $45 for every man, woman and child.

But Al Capone was anything but unpopular. On the surface at least. Everyone knew him, and wherever he appeared a crowd would gather. And little wonder. From the huge roll of notes he produced he would peel off $10 tips for bell boys, $20 for hat check girls and $100 for waiters and maître d's. When an innocent bystander was severely wounded in a public shootout with Capone's men and opposition gangsters, Capone paid the woman's hospital bills and paid for repairs to the restaurant that was the backdrop to the gunfight. But given that in 1928 Al Capone's income was around $105 million per year, he could afford it.

But Al Capone had a pebble in his shoe that was annoying him enough for him to exact a terrible punishment, which has gone down in history as the most infamous gangland hit of them all. The pebble was an Irish bootlegger named George 'Bugs' Moran. As is the way of the Irish, Moran had fearlessly gone into competition against Capone in the grog distribution business and was hijacking Capone's trucks and setting them on fire.

Things really got out of control when Bugs' boys tried to muscle in on Capone's control over the garment unions. And Al wasn't all that impressed either when Bugs' assassins narrowly missed bumping off one of Capone's favourite henchmen, a terrible bit of work named Jack 'Machine Gun' McGurn. When Bugs took to calling Capone 'the Beast' in public and telling anyone game enough to listen, 'If you ask me, Capone's on dope,' Bugs was way past his use-by date.

By early 1929, with Bugs Moran becoming more of an embarrassment as each day passed, Al Capone had had enough. He took off to Florida where he conducted his business over the phone with his top aides, did a bit of fishing and enjoyed the anonymity. On the morning of 14 February, Capone had his customary morning swim and a long breakfast and then took himself down to the office of the Dade county solicitor, Robert Taylor, for a chat about what he had been doing in Florida. Truth be known, Capone was establishing a

The Saint Valentine's Day Massacre

watertight alibi for himself for what was about to happen back in Chicago.

So with Capone away in Florida, that morning Chicagoans rose to flowers and chocolates to celebrate St Valentine's Day with their loved ones. At the SMC Cartage Company garage at 2122 North Clark Street, members of Bugs Moran's gang were waiting for a truckload of whisky from a hijacker in Detroit. They were also waiting for the arrival of their leader who, as fate would have it, was running late. The gang members consisted of Johnny May, Frank and Pete Gusenberg, James Clark, Adam Heyer and Al Weinshank. With them was Reinhardt H Schwimmer, an optometrist and friend of Moran's who, although he was not a gangster, enjoyed the company of criminals. And there was a stray dog.

A long black Cadillac with a police bell on its running board and a gun rack behind the driver pulled up outside. Bugs Moran, running late for his appointment, spotted the car pull up and, thinking that he had just walked in on a police raid, turned and hurried away. Four men, two in police uniforms and two in civilian clothes, emerged from the Cadillac and disappeared into the garage while a fifth man stayed at the wheel.

One resident thought he heard the sudden clatter of a pneumatic drill going on and off in short bursts, then the sound of an automobile backfiring twice. Two neighbourhood women, drawn by the noise, looked out of their windows and saw two men in civilian clothes leave the garage, hands in the air, followed by two policemen with their guns drawn. They got in the Cadillac and drove off. It seemed as if it was just another raid. And then the dog emerged from the garage and started a sad and deathly howl as if it was mourning the dead. And it would not stop. Those who went to investigate fled to call the real police, sick to the stomach at what they saw. All the while the dog sat on its haunches, howling at the moon, as the gun smoke wafted from the garage.

As best as anyone could reconstruct it, the seven men in the warehouse had been disarmed, lined up against the wall and then cut down at close range by submachine guns and shotguns.

They were riddled with bullets and there was blood everywhere, on the floor and all over the brick wall against which they had stood. Miraculously, Frank Gusenberg survived, but lasted only a few hours. His dying words were, 'Nobody shot me. I ain't no copper.' But Capone's killers had missed their main man, and Bugs Moran let it be known who had slaughtered his gang. 'Only Capone kills like that,' he told the press, breaking the underworld's code of silence.

Although no one was ever charged with the St Valentine's Day Massacre, it was the beginning of the end for Al Capone. Vendetta followed vendetta and with at least 227 gangland killings from 1927 until 1930, law enforcement agencies decided to get rid of Capone no matter what. Unable to catch him on racketeering or murder charges, in 1931 Al Capone was found guilty of evading millions of dollars in tax and was sentenced to 11 years in Alcatraz, where he lost his mind from advanced syphilis of the brain and died after his release.

In 1936, Jack 'Machine Gun' McGurn, who had allegedly helped to orchestrate the St Valentine's Day Massacre, was murdered on St Valentine's Day with a note left in his hand that included a joke. Since Bugs Moran loved jokes, it is believed that he murdered Machine Gun in retaliation for the slaughter of his gang. In February 1957, Bugs died of lung cancer in prison, where he was serving a 10-year sentence for bank robbery.

17 | THE PERSECUTION OF HARRY 'THE HAT' BLACKBURN

It was no secret among detectives at Kogarah police station in the early 1970s that Detective Sergeant Harry 'the Hat' Blackburn was a dead ringer for the Georges Hall rapist, a disgusting fiend who had been raping women at knifepoint in Sydney's southern suburbs since 1969.

An identikit likeness of the rapist resembled Harry Blackburn because they both had similar, distinctive teeth. Blackburn heard that because of the alleged likeness, he was a suspect. Blackburn, a decent and straight cop, was aware of these rumours but as far as he could see there was no resemblance at all.

Other alleged evidence linking him to the assaults was a knife scabbard that was found in bush near where one of the rapes had taken place. On the scabbard were initials that matched two of Harry Blackburn's initials; a third letter was indecipherable.

At work, Harry Blackburn wasn't one of the boys. Rather than stay at the pub after work, he was a loner who kept fit by jogging or playing squash. A dedicated family man, he had no time for fools and chose his friends carefully. He was a tenacious investigator with a strong work ethic and a dedication to justice, and would not tolerate inefficiency. It was no secret that due to his forthright manner and being a stickler for the rules, Harry Blackburn had trodden on many toes within the police force over the years.

While the rumours persisted that Harry Blackburn was the Georges Hall rapist, it wasn't until almost 20 years later that anything was done about it. On 24 July 1988, outside the War Crimes Commission building in the city where the now retired 57-year-old Inspector Harry Blackburn worked as an investigator, seven police officers arrested him and took him away. Acting on a tip-off that 'someone big' had been arrested, there was a huge contingent of media waiting back at police headquarters to get their first glimpse of the multiple rapist who had eluded police for so many years.

Once there, in one of the most shameful acts in the history of the New South Wales police force, Harry Blackburn was paraded before the TV cameras before he was taken inside and formally charged with 25 offences, including rape, armed robbery, kidnapping and assault. Although he vehemently protested his innocence, for weeks on end Harry Blackburn was headline news. He lost his job and his pregnant wife miscarried as a direct result of the stress.

It seemed that a month earlier, in June 1988, Detective Sergeant Phil Minkley was investigating the latest attack by a new offender in the district, known as the Sutherland shire rapist. At that stage the new Sutherland rapes and the old Georges Hall rapes had not been linked. Minkley's task force comprised Minkley, Detective Kevin Paull, and other detectives under the supervision of DCI Jim Thornthwaite, the commander of the Tactical Intelligence Unit (TIU). Inspector Thornthwaite and Harry Blackburn had had a close association both personally and in the police force for several decades but they hadn't seen each other in recent years.

The Georges Hall rapes had occurred from 1969 to 1972. Then for 13 years there were no rapes of a similar nature until

The Persecution of Harry 'the Hat' Blackburn

they began again in Sutherland, from 1985 to 1988. The rapist's disguises included dark clothes and a red balaclava, beret or a kilt. He threatened his victims with a knife, pistol or sawn-off shotgun, and would usually lock the man in the boot and rape the woman in the car. He usually preyed on couples in lover's lanes and spoke with an authoritative Australian accent that led detectives to believe that he was either a policeman or an army officer.

The TIU gave Detective Minkley a photo of Harry Blackburn and told him that Blackburn was a suspect in the Georges Hall rapes. Relying solely on the photo, Minkley made what he regarded as a 'positive identification' of Blackburn from a witness to a Sutherland rapist attack that happened on 25 June 1988. By now the Georges Hall rapist and the Sutherland rapist were deemed to be one and the same, and the suspect photo ID had linked Harry Blackburn to both cases. He was arrested.

But as it would turn out, a twist of fate saw to it that Sergeant Minkley wouldn't see the drama unfold. In the early hours of the morning after Harry Blackburn's arrest, Phil Minkley was involved in a serious car accident and he wound up in hospital with brain damage, from which he would never fully recover.

With the alleged rapist in jail, once the Director of Public Prosecutions began to put together the Crown's case against Harry Blackburn, he was horrified to find on what flimsy evidence Harry Blackburn had been arrested and charged.

- There were two very dubious photo identifications, one from 19 years earlier and the other from the recent 'Sutherland Rapist' rape at Mascot. Several other victims had been shown photographs of Blackburn, but no one else identified him.
- The only DNA sample was not linked to Blackburn.
- The rapist's blood sample was found *not* to be of the same type as Blackburn's.
- Of the eight Sutherland attacks, Blackburn had watertight alibis for at least four of them and was able to prove that he was in Katoomba at the time of the most recent rape.

It was all so ridiculous.

In October 1988, three months after his nightmare began, the charges against Harry Blackburn were dismissed due to lack of evidence. But terrible damage had been done to him and his family. In a subsequent royal commission into the botched investigation, the brain-damaged Sergeant Minkley was described as:

> *. . . the person principally responsible for most of the problems that have arisen in this case. He is responsible for the lack of records. The suppression of records, we suggest, was done at his direction. There is no question that Sergeant Minkley behaved like an unprincipled scoundrel and almost all the list of deficiencies are his responsibility directly or under his direction.*

But in view of the severe brain damage Sergeant Minkley incurred in the car crash, the Commission did not recommend charges.

On 8 May 1990, at the same royal commission, Harry Blackburn wept when the 11 police officers who had investigated him apologised for falsely accusing him. Blackburn sued the NSW Government for defamation and was awarded an undisclosed amount, believed to be in excess of $2 million. Soon after, Harry Blackburn moved his family to Robina, on the Gold Coast, where he set up a private inquiry agency.

While the truth will never be known, there is more than one person who believes that Sergeant Minkley's accident and subsequent brain damage were a blessing in disguise. Had it not happened then, Phil Minkley may have been able to tell the truth as to who in the police force was really pulling the strings, and the real reasons behind the persecution of Harry Blackburn.

Police now believe that the Sutherland Rapist was in fact Ashley Mervyn Coulston, who was also known as the Gold Coast Balaclava Rapist when he terrorised that area in 1979–80. Coulston is currently serving multiple life sentences for the murders of three young people in Victoria in 1992.

18 | THE REAL-LIFE CANNIBALS

Hannibal Lecter, eat your heart out. Or someone else's. With some fava beans and a nice chianti, perhaps. In Thomas Harris' novel *Hannibal*, the author gives us a completely new perspective on eating human beings, making the unthinkable appear almost socially acceptable. The only problem, it would seem, is finding the flesh, murder being the obvious answer.

But as Tom would know only too well, considering that two of the role models for his serial killer in his previous book *The Silence of The Lambs* were real-life cannibals, people who enjoy eating human flesh have been around since the Stone Age (though surprisingly, there haven't been all that many) and some of them would make the rapacious Dr Lecter look like a vegan.

Harris' serial killer in *Lambs*, a charmer nicknamed 'Buffalo Bill' whose mission in life is to murder as many young women as it takes to make a dress out of their skin, was modelled partly on the life and times of one Ed Gein. Gein had a penchant for wearing human skin and making clothes out of the corpses of the females he had either murdered or dug up from the local cemetery. Among them was his mum. You will find the full story of Ed's exciting adventures in Chapter 20 of this book.

Harris' other role model for Billy Boy was 42-year-old army pensioner Gary Heidnik who, in Philadelphia, USA, in 1986, kidnapped women and kept them chained up in his cellar as sex slaves, eventually murdering some of them and eating their remains. The description of Heidnik's cellar is not unlike that of Buffalo Bill's in *Lambs*, though unlike Bill, who was monogamous, Heidnik kept as many as five women in his cellar at a time until one escaped and called the cops.

What police found defies imagination. Four young women who had been repeatedly tortured, raped and beaten, chained in filth and squalor in the dungeon, with a young woman's head in a pot in the kitchen and human ribs in a roasting dish that was presumably going to be theirs and Gary's dinner. Heidnik was executed by lethal injection on 6 July 1999.

But long before Ed and Gary shocked the world with their distinctly individual diets, people had been eating each other. Back in 1570, an evil bit of work named Peter Stump roamed the German countryside, faithfully aided and abetted by his mistress and daughter, in search of young women to tear to shreds to satisfy his bloodlust. Stump had also eaten a newborn baby that was the result of his incestuous relationship with his daughter. Urged on by the two women, in five years Stump murdered 15 women and children and ravenously ate their hearts while they were hot, along with other delectable body parts.

When caught, the law's retribution for the evil trio was almost as savage as their crimes. Stump's body was tied to a cartwheel and the flesh was pulled from his bones with red-hot pincers. Still alive, his arms and legs were then broken with a wooden hatchet and he was beheaded. His headless corpse was then burned alongside his mistress and daughter.

Australia's dark past isn't without a taste of human flesh either. In 1822, convict Alexander Pearce escaped from the Hell's Gates penal settlement in southern Tasmania with seven

The Real-life Cannibals

other prisoners. After a few days in the freezing conditions, three of the escapees returned to prison, leaving the others to systematically murder and eat one another to survive.

Finally it came down to two men, Pearce and Robert Greenhill, who stalked each other until Pearce outwitted Greenhill and killed him with an axe and ate him. Pearce was eventually captured and returned to prison where, incredibly, he was flogged for escaping but received no punishment whatsoever for the confessed cannibalism because the authorities refused to believe him and there was (understandably) no one left to back up his story.

But Pearce wasn't so fortunate the next time. He persuaded fellow convict Thomas Cox to escape with him, and once on the outside Pearce killed Cox and ate him too. Alexander Pearce was hung in Hobart in 1824.

The 'Werewolf of Hannover', Fritz Haarmann, delighted in killing his victims by biting through their throats while raping them, and gorging on the meat and blood. In cohorts with another depraved homosexual deviant, Hans Grans, the pair abducted, sexually assaulted and murdered as many as 50 transient young men in Germany between 1919 and 1924.

In his lucrative profession as a dealer in second-hand clothes and meat, Haarmann was in a perfect position to capitalise on Germany's recent crushing defeat in World War I by giving his starving fellow Germans exactly what they wanted . . . at a price, of course. His black-market meat customers, who were delighted with their lovely cuts of veal and hindquarters of lamb, must have wondered where they came from in such grim times, but not in their wildest dreams did they think that they were from the two youths a week that Haarmann and Grans were raping, murdering and cutting up for sale. Haarmann was beheaded in 1924.

From 1955 to 1976 Joachim Kroll murdered, mutilated and had sex with the corpses of at least 14 young women and children throughout Germany. After he had had his way with their bodies he would cook them up and eat them, the younger the better. When captured, he told police that he loved the meat of young children as it fell off the bone, and he said it was of much better quality than the meat available in the West German butcher shops.

When police searched Kroll's foul-smelling apartment, in the refrigerator they found pieces of human flesh on a plate. Scattered around the lounge room were putrefying bags of human flesh, stripped from his victims' bones with a butcher's knife. On the stove was a simmering vegetable stew with a tiny human hand in it.

Not surprisingly, Joachim Kroll was declared a mental defective and placed in a mental asylum, and authorities threw away the key.

Of all of the modern-day cannibal serial killers, by far the most prolific was 56-year-old Andrei Chikatilo, who, in a 24-year killing career in Russia, was responsible for the horrific deaths and cannibalisation of 53 victims, mainly children. Like Kroll, Chikatilo was a necrophiliac in that his victims had to be dead before he could have sex with them.

Blaming his lust for human flesh on the fact that as a boy he'd witnessed his younger brother being eaten alive by villagers in a famine, Chikatilo selected his victims from the runaways and young prostitutes that hung around bus and train stations. Once he had lured his victims into the nearby woods on the promise of a meal or money, he would set upon them and hack them to death, rape the corpses and then disembowel his victims and ravage the warm internal body parts.

The fact that Chikatilo was an average-looking school teacher allowed him to blend in with the crowds at the busy venues where he selected his victims, and even though he was questioned nine times about the murders, twice near the scene of a murder (once he was carrying a knife in his bag), incredibly, police let him go, as he was a card-carrying member of the Communist Party and comrades didn't do such things.

Chikatilo was eventually caught and executed with a single bullet to the back of the head in 1994. At his trial, people fainted in horror as he told in graphic details how he boiled and ate the sawn-off nipples and testicles of his victims. Chikatilo is the subject of the movie *Citizen X*.

The Real-life Cannibals

The best-known real-life cannibal of modern times is Jeffrey Dahmer, which isn't surprising. Dahmer was a monster beyond human belief. A handsome young man who wouldn't have had a problem acquiring any number of sexual partners, Dahmer was a necrophiliac serial killer and cannibal whose perversions most human beings would find impossible to comprehend.

His Milwaukee, USA, apartment was an execution chamber, bordello, abattoir and exclusive café with only human remains on the menu. The beverage of the day was always human blood.

From 1988 to 1991, Dahmer, a 28-year-old chocolate factory worker, slaughtered 17 young men, raped and mutilated their corpses and ate their body parts. When police arrested him after a young man escaped and led them to Dahmer's apartment, they were overwhelmed by the putrid smell that hit them when they opened the door.

Inside they found three bodies dissolving in acid vats in his bedroom, a man's head in the fridge, along with three other severed heads and seven skulls, hands, heads and fingers stored in the freezer. Scattered about the apartment were decapitated penises and used condoms. Dahmer admitted to having sex with the bodies of the dead men as well as their decapitated heads and mutilated torsos. He pointed out to police that he always wore a condom when having sex with his dead partners or their body parts. Better to be safe than sorry, he said.

Jeffrey Dahmer was sent to prison for 1070 years, where he was murdered several years later by another inmate.

But no crimes in history were more abhorrent than those of deranged 64-year-old house painter Albert Fish. Passing himself off as an innocuous, benevolent little old man, Fish abducted, molested, tortured, castrated and ate at least 16 children in New York and all over the USA between 1928 and 1934.

What made Fish's crimes so ghastly was that he was a prolific writer and his jottings included a letter to the parents of a little girl telling them in detail how he had murdered, dissected, cooked and ate their daughter. This letter would be his undoing.

The Australian Crime File 3

Born in 1870, Albert Fish was a devout Christian who married in 1898, fathering six children. When his wife eloped with another man in 1917, Albert's latent perversions came to the surface and he began indulging in coprophilia (eating human excreta), inserting alcohol-soaked cottonwool balls in his anus and lighting them, getting his children to beat him bloody with a nail-studded paddle and inserting needles into his genitals.

In 1928, in response to an advertisement, Fish, calling himself Frank Howard, called on the Budd family in New York, taking with him cheese and strawberries. While their 12-year-old daughter Gracie was sitting on the cuddly old man's lap, he was fantasising about eating her. Fish convinced the Budds to let him take Gracie to a local children's party. That was the last they would see of her.

Six years later, in 1934, the Budd family received a letter, which read in part:

> *I took Gracie to an empty house in the country. I grabbed her and she said she would tell her mamma. First I stripped her naked. How she did kick, bite and scratch. I choked her to death, then cut her into small pieces so I could take my meat to my rooms, cook it and eat it. How sweet and tender her little ass was roasted in the oven. It took me nine days to eat her entire body. I did not fuck her though I could have had I wished. She died a virgin.*

The letter was traced to Fish and hardened police retched as Albert described to them how he had cooked and eaten another little boy's buttocks:

> *I put strips of bacon over each cheek and put it in the oven. When the meat was roasted for about a quarter of an hour, I poured a pint of water over for gravy and put in the onions. At frequent intervals I basted with a wooden spoon so the meat would be nice and juicy. In two hours it was nice and brown. I never ate any turkey that tasted*

half as good as his sweet, fat little behind did. I ate every bit of the meat in about four days.

Albert Fish was delighted to die in the electric chair, describing it as the 'ultimate experience in pain', and went to his death like a man going to a picnic, even helping the attendants strap him in.

And no doubt to Albert Fish's eternal pleasure, the metal pins and needles self-embedded in his genitals and scrotum caused the electric chair to short circuit and the first charge failed to kill him. Amid wisps of blue smoke, Albert was sent smiling to his maker with the second charge.

19 | THE FINAL INDIGNITY FOR DARRYL RAYMOND BEAMISH

When the former death row inmate Darryl Raymond Beamish was granted an ex gratia payment of $425,000 in June 2011, it was the final indignity in a chain of events that had been going on for 52 years, during which Darryl Beamish had spent 15 years in jail for a murder he did not commit. Let's go back to the beginning.

At around 11.30pm on the evening of 19 December 1959, at a block of apartments at Cottesloe, a fashionable seaside suburb of Perth in Western Australia, a peeping Tom got lucky. While peering into a bedroom he watched as 22-year-old Jillian Brewer and her fiancé made love, before the man left at around midnight and left her naked on the bed, sleeping soundly.

Armed with a stolen hatchet, the peeping Tom crept silently into the bedroom and stood beside the bed. But as he gazed down on the young woman's nakedness, it wasn't sex he had on his mind. He was there to defile and murder her in protest that he could never have anyone such as her in his lifetime. Beautiful young socialites were strictly off limits for a facially deformed man such as him.

The man raised the hatchet and chopped at her throat, breasts, genitals, face and head, fracturing her skull and pubic bone and severing her windpipe in the frenzy. Then he attacked her lower body, her thighs, stomach and legs, with the flat side of the hatchet head until what minutes before had been a sleeping beauty was now unrecognisable. When the hatchet handle broke he stopped and listened to see if anyone had heard and, convinced that he was safe, picked up Jillian's sewing scissors and plunged them deep into her abdomen five times.

Exhausted, he sat on the bed beside his victim and pulled the bloodied sheet up to her chin as if to cover the massive wounds to her body, but leaving her battered face on display. He put a pillow across her chest, folded the sheet back over it and placed her left arm on the pillow as if she were sleeping peacefully. Happy with his work, the man calmly cleaned the apartment of prints and left via a window, which he closed behind him and threw the hatchet over the back fence as he went.

Next morning, Jillian's fiancé returned at 9am for golf to find the normally open front door closed. Using his key, he found the bedroom door was also unusually closed. He opened it to find the carnage. The police found the hatchet wiped of prints, as was the pair of scissors and everything else in the apartment. This bloke knew what he was doing. Ten months earlier there had been a similar murder of a naked woman in South Perth in the early hours of the morning, when an intruder had stabbed 33-year-old Pnena Berkman to death during a violent struggle in her waterside apartment and hadn't left a clue.

There was no motive as to why anyone would kill Jillian Brewer. The glamorous socialite and heiress to the MacRobertson Freddo Frog/Cherry Ripe confectionery fortune had only been in Perth 15 months, was engaged to be married in a couple of months to a young man beyond reproach, and didn't have an enemy in the world. And there was nothing missing, which ruled out a burglary gone wrong. The coroner and mortuary staff

The Final Indignity for Darryl Raymond Beamish

agreed that the murders of Jillian Brewer and Pnena Berkman could have been committed by the same person.

In a city that was more like a big country town where doors were never locked and keys were left in car ignitions, the citizens of Perth demanded an answer. Fourteen months later they found it in 19-year-old mentally impaired Darryl Raymond Beamish, who had convictions as a prowler and petty thief and crimes of a sexual nature against young girls. Mentally, Beamish was of an equivalent age to them. Darryl Beamish was also a deaf mute who could say only a few words and communicated by interpreter or writing. He was the perfect scapegoat.

It wasn't hard to cajole a confession to Jillian Brewer's murder out of Beamish. Had he not had a watertight alibi for the night Pnena Berkman was murdered, Beamish would have been charged with that as well. At his trial it was said that he confessed four times – twice through an interpreter, once in a statement and once in writing on the cell floor of the Perth lockup. There was no forensic or other evidence to connect him with the crime. On 13 August 1961, the bewildered Darryl Beamish was found guilty of murder and sentenced to death by hanging. Four months later his sentence was commuted to life imprisonment with hard labour.

Two years later police apprehended Jillian Brewer's real murderer, the social-outcast serial killer Eric Edgar Cooke. Over the previous eight months Cooke had held Perth under siege. A man and a woman were shot at in their car. Two men on separate occasions were shot at point-blank range as they slept in their beds. Another was shot between the eyes as he opened his front door. A young woman was strangled to death and raped. An 18-year-old babysitter was shot dead as she studied and listened to music in front of the fire. Cooke also admitted to the murders of Jillian Brewer and Pnena Berkman and running down and killing Rosemary Anderson in a stolen car, a crime for which another man was serving a 10-year sentence for manslaughter.

Although Cooke supplied knowledge of the Brewer and Anderson cases that only the killer would have known, police chose to ignore it; Cooke was found guilty of his other many crimes, and was hanged on 26 October 1964. Ten minutes before he was hanged, Cooke took the Bible in his hand and said: 'I swear before Almighty God that I killed Anderson and Brewer.'

The deaf mute Darryl Beamish spent 15 horrible, silent years in jail for a murder he did not commit, before being released on parole. Over the years he appealed his conviction six times and eventually, in the wake of the successful appeal of John Button, who was another man wrongfully convicted of one of Cooke's murders, was finally exonerated on 1 April 2005. Both men had been championed by Perth journalist Estelle Blackburn and you can find their stories in her books *Broken Lives* and *The End of Innocence*.

In 2010, 51 years after Jillian Brewer's murder, Darryl Beamish, now 70, lodged a claim for a 'meagre' $500,000 to 'make him and his wife Barbara comfortable in old age'. In light of the fact that John Button had been awarded $460,000 in 2003 for the five years he had wrongly served for one of Cooke's murders and another man, Andrew Mallard, had been awarded $3.25 million in May 2009 for the 12 years he spent behind bars after being wrongfully jailed over the 1994 murder of Perth jeweller Pamela Lawrence, you would consider this a reasonable request.

But no. In their wisdom, on 2 June 2011, the state of Western Australia decided that Darryl Beamish isn't worth that kind of money and have discounted his ex gratia request by $75,000 to just $425,000. Seems as though they intend to bully the scapegoat until the bitter end.

20 | THE REAL-LIFE *PSYCHO*: ED GEIN

Everything you've heard about Alfred Hitchcock's 1960 movie *Psycho* is true. It is a masterpiece of suspense. It was the first movie in the serial killer genre as we know it today; the music in the shower scene actually sounds like someone being stabbed to death. And yes, it was based on a real character. Well, sort of.

Truth be known, the 'real life' killer on whom Hitchcock modelled Norman Bates never owned a 12-room motel on a forgotten back road, complete with a big house on the hill. He was in fact a mild-mannered Wisconsin hillbilly named Ed Gein, who was as mad as a cut snake. On screen and in real life, the only thing that *Psycho*'s Norman Bates and Ed Gein had in common was their obsession with dead women.

Poor Norman had a problem with his dead mum sitting in the lounge room, who couldn't help herself when it came to murdering the guests. In Ed's case it was any dead woman he could dig up. And as if that wasn't a touch unusual, Ed used the skin from the female corpses he exhumed from the local graveyard

The Australian Crime File 3

and women he murdered to make clothing for himself, which he wore at night when he danced around in the backyard doing hillbilly jigs under the full moon. Ed was definitely a few chops short of a barbecue.

It all came to light when local farmer Ed Gein was seen loitering around the local hardware store in Plainfield, Wisconsin, on 17 November 1957, after it had been robbed and its owner, Bernice Worden, had gone missing. Police picked Ed up and decided to have a look at his farmhouse. Inside was like a rubbish tip, with rotting garbage and piles of junk almost up to the ceilings, making it all but impossible to walk through the house. The stench of rotting foodstuff was sickening.

In his torch beam in the darkened kitchen, sheriff Arthur Schley caught what he thought was a skinned deer hanging from a butcher's hook in a beam in the ceiling. The head had been removed and the carcass had been gutted. It didn't strike him as unusual, as it was deer season. But closer inspection revealed that the 'deer' was in fact the corpse of a woman. The missing woman, 50-year-old Bernice Worden, mother of his deputy Frank Worden, had been found.

But the body of Bernice Worden was merely the beginning. As dazed police fossicked through the grisly mess of Eddie Gein's existence, they realised that they had stumbled into a chamber of horrors. Ed's soup bowl was a human skull. His waste-paper basket was made with human parts covered with skin, as were the lampshades throughout the house. His favourite armchair was made of human remains, and scattered about the place were all manner of parts of the female anatomy. But the prize of them all was the suit made completely out of human skin.

It turned out that Ed Gein had grown up on the lonely farm with his domineering mother and older brother, who mysteriously died when beaten about the head in a bushfire that he was fighting beside his brother. The local police couldn't find any suspicious circumstances and dismissed any foul play.

After his brother's death, Ed became totally dependent on his mother's love and when she died in 1945 he was so distraught that he boarded off the rooms his mother had used the most,

The Real-life *Psycho*: Ed Gein

mainly on the upstairs floor and the downstairs parlour and living room, and turned it into a macabre shrine. Eddie had lost his only true friend and his one true love. He was now alone in the world. Desperately lonely, Ed found his female company in the local graveyard, where he exhumed bodies and took them home, chatting away to them and reading them nice things that had been said about them in the obituary columns.

Ed was fascinated with women and the power they held over men and decided he wanted to become one, so he fashioned women's clothing out of the remains, wearing them about the house and dancing about in the light of the moon. Fortunately for Ed, there were no close neighbours up there in Hillbillyville.

During the late 1940s and early 1950s, Wisconsin police had noticed a sharp increase in missing persons, including two young women, in the district. On 17 November 1957, after the discovery of Bernice Worden's body and the other gruesome artefacts in Eddie's house, police began an exhaustive search of the remaining parts of the farm and surrounding land. They believed Ed may have been involved in five more murders and that the bodies might be buried on his land. They were eight-year-old Georgia Weckler, Evelyn Hartley, 15, local tavern keeper Mary Hogan, and deer hunters Victor Travis and Ray Burgess, who had all disappeared under mysterious circumstances.

At first Eddie Gein did not admit to any of the killings. However, after more than a day of silence he told the horrible story of how he had killed Mrs Worden and where he had acquired the other body parts that were found in his house. Ed said that he had stolen them from local graves, but insisted that he had not killed any of the people whose remains were found, with the exception of Mrs Worden. However, after days of intense interrogation he finally admitted to killing Mary Hogan.

Ed Gein showed no signs of remorse or emotion when he talked about the murders and his graverobbing escapades. He spoke very matter-of-factly, even cheerfully at times. He had no concept of the enormity of his crimes.

The Australian Crime File 3

With investigators unable to prove that he killed the other missing persons, Ed Gein was convicted of the murders of Mary Hogan and Bernice Worden but later found not guilty on the grounds of insanity. Ed's nocturnal lifestyle inspired author Robert Bloch to write a book about the deranged motelier Norman Bates, a character based loosely on Ed, on which Hitchcock based his movie *Psycho*.

Until Ed Gein came along, the civilised world had never known of such depravities. *Psycho* made Ed a household name and he became a cult hero. He died behind bars in July 1984 and was buried alongside his mother, not far from the many graves he had robbed years earlier.

In 1991 Ed was the inspiration for another famous fictional serial killer, Buffalo Bill, in the screen adaptation of Thomas Harris' novel, *The Silence of the Lambs*. But this time the serial killer didn't have a passion for digging up dead women. Instead, Bill was inspired by Ed's dressmaking techniques and preference for using freshly murdered women's skin to make satin and silks for making garments for his winter dress collection.

21 | MR FROGGY AND HIS ILL-GOTTEN MILLIONS: THE PONZI FRAUDS OF KARL SULEMAN

The dot-com boom – and its subsequent dramatic bust – of the late 1990s and early 2000s was a strange time indeed. During those heady days, fortunes were earned virtually overnight – and often lost even quicker. At a time when the internet still seemed like something from the future to much of the Australian population, most investors had little idea what it was all about – but there were no end of regular folks willing to part with their cash in the pursuit of a quick and easy profit.

Of course, that also meant that there were no end of unscrupulous types eager to swindle everyday people, bamboozling them with talk of page imprints and brand growth, then quickly suggesting they could be part of this brave new world simply by handing over their hard-earned cash.

Of all those grifters, natural-born salesman Karl Suleman – founder of Karl Suleman Enterprises and Froggy.com – deserves special mention, not just for the amount he swindled, but for having the sheer audacity to blindly steal from his own people so blatantly. The majority of those Suleman rorted were fellow members of the tight-knit and hard-working Assyrian community who had migrated to Australia and lived mainly in and around the Fairfield district in Sydney's west.

With rumours quickly spreading that Froggy had a potential worth of $300 million, Suleman had little trouble finding investors – after all, he went to church with these people, he knew their children, he ate with them regularly. Then he robbed them blind. And once he had a few of his peers involved, it was no problem to get the rest.

By the end of his epic con, Suleman owned four palatial homes, a dozen apartments, several racehorses, a $3 million luxury cruiser, several Ferraris and Lamborghinis – even a private jet. In 2001, Suleman attended a fundraising dinner for the Australian Labor Party, where he forked out $150,000 in cash without blinking for the chance to sit beside guest speaker Bill Clinton.

Obviously enjoying the company of US presidents, he then organised for Froggy to host a lavish Melbourne Cup lunch just so he could have his photo taken with George W Bush.

To secure this fast cash, Suleman used the oldest scam in the book and one of the most basic – a pyramid scheme or, as it become known, a Ponzi scheme, after Charles Ponzi, who became notorious for using it throughout the USA in the 1920s.

The idea of a Ponzi scheme is to spruik a fantastic investment to those who will listen and then offer them a huge rate of return. To that end, Suleman was telling potential investors about an impressive 17 per cent per month – or an obviously unbelievable 204 per cent per annum!

Once the fish have taken the bait, you pay that interest with money grifted from new investors. They tell all of their friends that it is fair dinkum and then they all get in on the act. Then you have a terrific time spending the millions.

Of course, once the new investors run out, the funds dry up. But by then the conmen will normally have lined their pockets substantially – helping themselves to millions and transferring those ill-gotten gains into property deeds.

Mr Froggy and His Ill-gotten Millions

From there, the best idea is to sign the real estate over to your wife, send as much cash as you can into offshore accounts, then just tell the taxman you've gone bankrupt. At worst, you'll go to jail for a little while and live like the cat that got the cream once you get out.

Karl Suleman followed the blueprint to the letter – except he forgot about the last part and ended up with nothing. Still, he had a good run while it lasted. In just two years working his scam, Suleman conned more than $130 million from investors – and he did it all by word of mouth. All he had was a website, a few ideas and a good line of patter. He didn't even have a prospectus to show potential investors where their money would be heading.

Of course, Suleman spent about half of that cash – and most of that money has now simply vanished without a trace.

The whole thing began in earnest in 1999 when Suleman formed the Froggy Group under the umbrella of Karl Suleman Enterprises. It consisted of a mobile phone resell business, a music company and two internet service providers (ISPs). Suleman would later confess that he didn't even know what an ISP was.

At first, Suleman targeted relatives and friends that he knew had no knowledge of such matters to invest with him. They thought it sounded like he knew what he was on about – and more importantly, they trusted Suleman when he told them about the vast profits they were assured of. After all, an Assyrian ripping off another Assyrian for such a large amount of money was simply unheard of.

The news of potential easy money spread like wildfire among the community. Soon, local Assyrian organisations were supporting their countryman with his grand plan. Further support came when a bishop from a Catholic Assyrian church told his congregation that he was backing the young churchgoer. It seemed Suleman just had to sit back and admire the mountain of cash that was landing in his lap.

As word got out that Froggy could be worth as much as $300 million, Assyrian families in Fairfield started to borrow money to get involved. Many mortgaged their houses. There's one report that a friend of Karl Suleman turned up at the Froggy office with $100,000 in cash in a plain brown paper bag. He handed it over and left without even getting a receipt.

With so much money on hand, Suleman figured he should play the part – he soon became the local face of dot-com businessman made good. The first thing on his list was to move from his Fairfield flat to a far more salubrious residence. He chose a mansion in exclusive Point Piper, where he soon set about ingratiating himself to Sydney's eastern suburbs social elite.

With his staff basically only employed to write high-interest cheques for previous investors as their payments fell due, Karl Suleman did what every budding Bill Gates would do – he spent up big, adding to his property portfolio and filling his garage with luxury cars. And still the money rolled in.

Believing they could get an annual return of as much as 204 per cent, more than 2000 investors did anything they could to get on board Suleman's money train. Their life savings combined between 1999 and 2001 until Karl Suleman Enterprises had reaped $138 million. Included in that sum were 15 people who invested a whopping $3 million between them. That earned them a fortnightly return of $140,000 – all funded from the pockets of Froggy's most recent run of investors.

Of course, all these profits were built on a foundation of smoke and mirrors. The only real asset that Karl Suleman Enterprises had was a business responsible for collecting abandoned shopping trolleys. That venture brought in the grand total of $4000 a week in profit. You don't need a business degree to realise something was about to give – big time.

Acting on a tip-off, the Australian Securities and Investments Commission (ASIC) raided Suleman's premises in November 2001. Considering their target was a multimillion-dollar investment organisation, they were shocked to find almost no financial records. There was also a noticeable lack of cash receipt books and client contracts. The only information they could locate related to money being deposited in the bank, and the cheques being sent out. But after noting the massive withdrawals

Mr Froggy and His Ill-gotten Millions

Suleman was making to fund his increasingly extravagant lifestyle, ASIC shut the business down. That, however, didn't stop investors sending in money.

Considering how shonky the whole operation was, it's not a major shock that Suleman didn't hold an investment adviser's licence. His investment scheme wasn't even registered. ASIC froze Suleman and his wife's assets and set about trying to return as much of Froggy's investors' money as they could.

With Karl Suleman Enterprises and the Froggy Group in liquidation, the financial forensics team soon realised that around $65 million of investors' money remained unaccounted for. It was as if the vast sum had simply vanished – either gambled away, gifted to family or friends, donated or stolen.

During a court hearing in 2002, Suleman explained that he never kept a record of any transactions conducted by his companies. He said that once he had received a cheque for over $260,000 but couldn't remember what he had done with the money. The court action followed an investigation by ASIC, where it was alleged that in December 2000 Suleman gave a false bank statement in a bid to raise finance to buy a Ferrari. And three times between March and October 2001, ASIC claims, Suleman supplied false bank statements to finance brokers to finance a new-model Ferrari and a $3.3 million yacht.

Suleman was officially declared bankrupt in May 2002. He was also barred from assuming the position of director of a company for the rest of his life. In September 2003, he was committed to stand trial on four counts of fraud. Suleman pleaded not guilty. Rather incredulously, he explained that his frivolous spending had actually been intended to better mankind. After all, his plan was to set up an exclusive sailing, flying and driving operation for the benefit of the rich and famous. Suleman is likely to never join the ranks of either again. Infamous, definitely.

The judge found him guilty and sentenced him to 21 months in jail with a minimum of one year. To the people he had fleeced it seemed like a very lean sentence. But there was more to come.

In August 2004, liquidators announced that investors could expect about 20 cents in the dollar back from the $138 million they had invested.

Two days before his release from Junee Prison in March 2005, Suleman, then 45 years old, was served with 26 new charges relating to his shopping trolley business and obtaining more than $3 million through false statements, and was granted strict bail conditions.

On 1 May 2006, Suleman pleaded guilty to 15 counts of making false statements after ASIC's investigation found he induced 15 investors to enter into agreements and invest $3.185 million in KSE's supermarket trolley collection business between April 2000 and July 2001. Suleman also pleaded guilty to 11 counts of using false documents that induced one investor to invest $1 million in the business.

In January 2007, he was sentenced to seven years and four months in jail with a non-parole period of five and a half years.

While it still seems as though he got off lightly, Suleman's victims can take at least a small amount of solace in the fact that he wasn't smart enough to transfer anything into his wife's name or send any cash offshore. He has absolutely nothing left of their money.

Despised by his community in Sydney, he'll be lucky if he can get a job driving a cab. And if he does and his passenger is one of the people he robbed and recognises him, let's hope they dud him on the fare. That's about all they'll ever be able to get back from the man known forever as Mr Froggy.

22 | WHO POISONED BOBBY LULHAM?

Throughout the 1940s and 1950s in Australia, thallium poisoning was a popular method of murder. The cases of Sydney housewife Yvonne Fletcher, who murdered her two husbands with thallium-laced roast dinners, and Sydney grandmother Carolyn Grills, who did away with five family friends and relatives with Devonshire teas and thallium, were the most famous of the time.

But when it came to intrigue and drama, the 1953 case of the thallium poisoning of one of Australia's most famous and loved rugby league players of the time, Bobby Lulham, leaves them all for dead . . . if you'll pardon the pun.

Renowned for his lightning speed on the wing, Bob Lulham played for Balmain and had been good enough to tour England and France with the Australian rugby league team in 1948. Since his return he had been a prolific try scorer and an inspiration to his team. But, totally out of character for Lulham, in an important club game against Canterbury Bankstown on

18 July 1953, he repeatedly dropped the ball and even when he did gather it up he was quickly tackled by the opposition. There was clearly something wrong with the star Balmain winger and his teammates and fans were deeply concerned. Unable to offer an explanation, Bobby Lulham went home to bed.

The mystery of Lulham's poor form was revealed two days later when an anonymous woman sobbed into the phone to Dr Les Greenberg, the Medical Officer of the NSW Rugby League, that Bobby Lulham had been poisoned and that it was her husband who had put the rat poison Thall-Rat in Lulham's beer.

Two detectives from the CIB were sent immediately to Lulham's home, where they found the footballer very ill in bed. He told the detectives that he had been feeling increasingly crook over the past fortnight; the team doctor had told him that he was most likely suffering from an ulcer, and that with a lot of rest it would eventually go away, but it hadn't.

But as Lulham explained his symptoms – nausea, pins and needles in the toes and fingers, and pains in the chest – from their experience with similar cases in recent years, the detectives knew it wasn't an ulcer. To them there was little doubt that the Balmain legend had been, or was still being, poisoned with thallium. But by whom? It had to be someone close to him. It was now up to them to find out.

Bobby Lulham was rushed to the Royal Prince Alfred Hospital, where his hair began to fall out until in no time at all he was completely bald. The government toxicologist reported that he was lucky to be alive and it was most likely his perfect physical condition that had saved him. Lulham had ingested as much as 8 grams of thallium – more than enough to kill a normal person but a couple of grams less than it would take to kill a healthy athlete.

Two weeks later police charged Bobby Lulham's mother-in-law, Mrs Veronica Monty, with attempted murder. It seemed that Mrs Monty had admitted poisoning her daughter's husband – but by a terrible accident. She said that in a fit of depression she had intended killing herself and had heavily laced her bedtime drink of Milo with thallium, but then it had become mixed up

Who Poisoned Bobby Lulham?

with Bobby's mug of Milo and he inadvertently drank it instead and became ill.

But at Veronica Monty's trial for attempting to murder her son-in-law, held in November 1953, the prosecution would have none of it. The Crown steadfastly claimed that Lulham could not have drunk her cup of Milo by mistake as she didn't take sugar and Bobby did and he would have known the difference immediately. Apart from a lack of motive, it seemed an open and shut case. But no one was prepared for the bombshell that lay ahead.

The Sydney Central Criminal Court was packed to the rafters as the handsome footballer took the stand to give his evidence. Bobby Lulham told the court that in November 1951, he had married Judith Anne Monty. Soon after, his mother-in-law, Veronica Monty, had separated from her husband and moved in with the newlyweds at their Ryde home in Sydney's inner north-western suburbs.

Lulham said that he and his wife's mother became a little closer than perhaps they should have and on three separate occasions they had indulged in 'acts of intimacy', all of which were at Mrs Monty's instigation. At the revelation that her husband had been having it off with her mother, possibly in the marital bed, Mrs Judith Lulham had to be helped from the court for fear she would faint.

The following day at dawn there was a long queue of women with cut lunches and thermos flasks in string bags, waiting for front row seats in the court for what was shaping up to be the juiciest scandal Sydney had seen in years. As ten o'clock approached, police on horseback were forced to break up the huge crowds of women outside the court as they tried to get a glimpse of the players in the drama that was about to unfold.

The court heard that four days after her being charged with attempted murder and released on bail, Veronica Monty had taken an overdose of thallium and was admitted to hospital, where they saved her life. Her lawyers made mincemeat of the allegations that it was Mrs Monty who had seduced Bobby Lulham. They challenged the jury to try and believe that the much smaller woman had grabbed the huge footballer by the hand and dragged him to the bedroom, where she had had her way with him and deprived him of his honour against his will.

Mrs Veronica Monty looked a broken and pathetic figure – certainly one incapable of seducing a footballer – as she stood in the dock and pleaded her case from a written statement:

> *I am not guilty of this crime. I have never borne any ill feelings to Bobby in my life. I consider that I always have and always will more than like him.*
>
> *There were many things I had done that I know I shouldn't have done. There were many things I said that I shouldn't have said. But I want you to believe me when I say . . . and I say this quite deliberately . . . that I never gave Bobby thallium deliberately.*

A sympathetic jury found her not guilty.

But that was not the end of it. In a matter of days the whole sordid affair was back on the front pages of the dailies. Veronica Monty's husband, Alfred, announced that he was suing his estranged wife for divorce and naming Bobby Lulham as the co-respondent. Bobby Lulham's distraught wife, Judith, also announced that she was suing her husband for divorce and that she was naming her own mother as the co-respondent.

But it was not to be. In a tragic and final twist before any further courtroom dramas could take place, Veronica Monty committed suicide. Bobby Lulham made a full recovery and played one more season with Balmain. He eventually passed away in 1986.

23 | THE INJUSTICE OF COLIN CAMPBELL ROSS: A CENTURY TOO LATE

The only thing that Colin Campbell Ross had in common with Ned Kelly was that they were both hanged on the same gallows, albeit 42 years apart. The differences in their executions were that while Kelly died swiftly, Ross died in agony, and that while some may dispute Kelly's guilt, Ross was an innocent man railroaded to the gallows for a crime he didn't commit. Just before he was hanged, Colin Ross wrote to his family saying that one day his innocence would be proved. It was. It took 86 years.

One of Australia's most terrible murders took place on the afternoon of 30 December 1921, when 12-year-old Alma Tirtschke went missing while on an errand for her aunt. When Alma hadn't returned home by dark her family called the police, who searched unsuccessfully throughout the night. The following morning Alma's naked body was found in Gun Alley, a laneway along the way where Alma was on her errand, off nearby Little Collins Street. Alma had been raped and strangled.

The murder of Alma Tirtschke was sensationalised by the Melbourne press, who told the citizens that there was a madman in their midst who was likely to strike again soon. A reward of £1250 was instigated, one of the largest in Australia's history at that time. The papers called for an immediate arrest, and public pressure on the police grew. They had to come up with someone. Anyone. Colin Ross fitted the profile. The problem was that he had an alibi. But it was only a minor problem.

Ross, 28, had been in trouble with the police and was in the window of opportunity to murder the girl. In 1920 Ross had threatened his fiancée, and was sent to prison for two weeks and fined for carrying a firearm. In 1921, Ross and his two brothers bought a sleazy wine saloon in inner Melbourne. In October 1921, Colin Ross and an accomplice were charged with attempting to rob a customer at gunpoint. Ross' associate was sent to prison for six months, while Ross was acquitted.

The last time Alma was seen alive was between 2.30pm and 3pm near the lane where her body was found, at the corner of Alfred Place and Little Collins Street. Among the many men questioned was Colin Ross, who owned a nearby saloon and accurately described a girl matching Alma's description standing outside his bar. Several other witnesses confirmed his memory of the events. Despite the fact that several other witnesses confirmed that he had never left his saloon all afternoon, police decided that Ross was their man and, on 12 January 1922, he was arrested and charged with getting the girl drunk in his saloon and then raping and murdering her.

Colin Ross' trial was a joke from the outset, with the prosecution determined to deliver a culprit to appease the newspapers and the seething masses that turned up at the court every day. But Ross told his lawyers, family and friends that he had nothing to fear. He was an innocent man and justice would prevail. The prosecution's first witness was John Harding, Ross' cellmate and convicted perjurer, who testified that Ross had admitted his guilt to him in prison. After the trial, Harding's current sentence was reduced significantly for his testimony.

The Injustice of Colin Campbell Ross

A prostitute, Ivy Matthews, and a fortune-teller named 'Madame Gurkha', also testified that Ross had confessed the crime to them. The pair split the reward after Ross was found guilty. Six credible witnesses who were in Ross' wine bar with him all afternoon and a cab driver who heard what is believed to have been the girl being murdered while Ross was working were not allowed to testify.

Strands of hair from Alma Tirtschke's corpse were compared with hair found on a rug in Ross' possession by the government analyst, Charles Price, a trained chemist with little previous experience in the new field of forensic science. Price concluded that the hair from Ross' house was light auburn while Alma's hair was dark red, and concluded the diameter of the hairs were a different thickness. Mr Price testified that the hairs on Ross' blanket had most likely fallen from the head of a regular visitor, such as Ross' girlfriend, but then changed his mind and said that the hairs were 'derived from the scalp of one and the same person'. His contradiction was accepted by the judge without comment. The defence protested and requested that a further examination be carried out by a more qualified person, but the judge refused. The jury found Ross guilty of murder and he was sentenced to death by hanging. He was refused the right to appeal, as the judge stated that Ross' guilt had been proven beyond doubt.

Awaiting his execution, Ross received a letter from an anonymous man who admitted that he had killed Alma but was not willing to come forward as it would cause grief to his family. On the eve of his execution, a letter believed to have been written by the real killer was sent to Ross' lawyer. But it was all too late. Before his execution in his farewell letter to his family, Ross wrote: 'The day is coming when my innocence will be proved.' Colin Ross died the most horrible death. The noose didn't do its job in snapping his neck cleanly and his subsequent death by asphyxiation took as long as 20 minutes.

Over the years there were several attempts to exonerate Ross but the Victorian Government wasn't interested, and it wasn't until 1993 that schoolteacher Kevin Morgan took an interest in

The Australian Crime File 3

the case. From interviews and court transcripts, Morgan discovered information that had been kept from the court, including the testimony of six reliable witnesses who saw Ross inside his saloon the entire afternoon of Alma Tirtschke's murder.

Furthermore, a cab driver, Joseph Graham, had heard screams coming from a building in Collins Street at 3pm, while Ross was in his saloon. Graham's interview had been disregarded by police and he had not been called to give evidence. Kevin Morgan hit the jackpot when he found a file containing the original hair samples, which had been thought lost. Through DNA the Victoria Institute of Forensic Medicine found that the hairs did not come from the same person, thereby disproving the most damning piece of evidence presented at Ross' trial.

On 23 October 2006 the Victorian Attorney-General wrote to the Chief Justice asking to consider a plea of mercy for Ross. The subsequent pardon, granted on 27 May 2008, is the first case in Victoria's legal history of a posthumous pardon.

Alma Tirtschke's believes that Colin Ross' pardon does not go far enough and that he should be exonerated completely. In his book *Gun Alley: Murder, Lies and Failure of Justice*, Kevin Morgan says the true murderer may well have been a close Tirtschke family relative, George Murphy, a disturbed war veteran with paedophilic tendencies and a history of pestering Alma's sister Viola. Murphy was believed to have been seen in the vicinity of where Alma disappeared on the day she was murdered, but the police never investigated it.

On 18 October 2010, the remains of Colin Campbell Ross were handed back to his family at a service at the Old Melbourne Gaol so that he could be buried a free man. Little consolation for arguably the worst case of blind justice in Australia's history.

24 | THE WILLIAM MOXLEY MURDERS

We can only wonder what drives people to murder. The case in point is a fine example. William Cyril Moxley was a harmless petty criminal at best. Stealing was what he was best known for. Violence and assault were never part of his crimes. Yet, given the opportunity, William Moxley committed two of the worst unprovoked murders Australia has ever seen and then farcically went on the run while the police conducted one of the biggest manhunts in our history. And in the end, if it hadn't been so terribly real, it could have been straight out of the Keystone Cops.

According to the police reconstruction of the crime, on the afternoon of 5 April 1932, Moxley was gathering wood in his battered old truck near a notorious lover's lane at Holdsworthy, near Liverpool, in Sydney's west. A car pulled up nearby with 26-year-old newspaper compositor Frank Wilkinson and his girlfriend, 21-year-old Dorothy Denzel, inside. The couple, who were officially 'going steady', as was the term of the time, placed a rug on the grass beside the car and lay down and embraced, enjoying the sunny afternoon as they talked about whatever young lovers talk about.

Moxley, who had been watching their every move from nearby, burst from the bushes waving a shotgun and demanded that they hand over their money. But Frank Wilkinson would have none of it. He lunged at Moxley and tried to wrestle the shotgun from him; a desperate battle ensued until Moxley broke free and battered the younger man on the side of the head with the shotgun butt, knocking him to the ground unconscious. To make sure that Frank Wilkinson would give him no more trouble, Moxley belted his head a few more times with the shotgun butt as Wilkinson lay unconscious on the ground.

Moxley bound Miss Denzel to her unconscious partner, dragged them both into Frank Wilkinson's bright red Alvis motor car and drove to an empty house on the outskirts of Liverpool. Here he locked the still unconscious young man in a shed and turned his attentions on Dorothy Denzel, repeatedly sexually assaulting her throughout the afternoon and night. The following morning, Moxley dragged Miss Denzel out to the back shed to find that Frank Wilkinson had almost untied his hands and was just about to escape and call help. Moxley forced the distraught young lady to watch as he bashed Frank Wilkinson into unconsciousness with a shovel.

With that, Moxley tied the couple together and dragged them into Frank Wilkinson's car, where he concealed them beneath a blanket in the back and drove to bushland in nearby Milperra. Here he dug a single shallow grave and calmly executed the young man with a shotgun blast to the back of the head while Miss Denzel begged for her life. Moxley then set upon the dead man with a shovel and bashed his face beyond recognition before burying him. He then dragged the screaming young lady off into the bushes, where he executed her in similar fashion. Before he buried her body Moxley also battered her beyond recognition.

When the couple didn't arrive home that night, their families were quick to notify the police. They weren't the type of young people to elope or run away for no reason, so police could only

The William Moxley Murders

fear the worst from the outset. Frank Wilkinson's distinctive red Alvis was soon located in bits in a garage rented in the name of William Moxley. Fortunately for police, Moxley hadn't done a very good job at covering his tracks and good detective work eventually led investigators to a lonely patch of bushland at Milperra.

On the morning of 11 April, six days after the couple went missing, police came across the shallow grave of Frank Wilkinson. What they discovered shocked even the most hardened officers among them. The young man had been so badly beaten about the face that there was no way that they could confirm that it was Frank Wilkinson from the photos that his family had provided. About 500 metres away they found the body of the once beautiful Dorothy Denzel, who had also been beaten beyond recognition. But who would do such a thing? And more to the point . . . why? There must be a madman on the loose. Police warned all residents to lock their doors and windows at night until the culprit was caught.

By now police knew for certain who they were looking for. Moxley had been identified driving Frank Wilkinson's car around the district. The garage where they had found Mr Wilkinson's car was in William Moxley's name, and police had found a hessian mask with slits cut for eyes in the garage. They believed that Moxley had concealed his face with the mask when he first jumped from the bushes and confronted the young lovers. They couldn't imagine how terrifying it must have been for them.

Police wasted no time in letting the press know who they were looking for and the then-biggest manhunt in Australia's history was formed to bring Moxley to justice as quickly as possible before he killed again. But Moxley had fled the Liverpool district and was last seen heading north on a bicycle. A few days later, the *Daily Telegraph* reported that Moxley, whose mug shot was on the front page, had ridden his bicycle down George Street and straight across the harbour bridge, paying the threepence toll right under the noses of surveillance police.

The *Daily Telegraph* revealed that of an evening you would find Moxley riding his bicycle through the Mosman and Spit

Junction areas under the noses of police. The *Telegraph* claimed that twice Moxley had visited a picture show, where he had watched himself on the news and in a talkie of police telling picture-goers that he was on the run and very dangerous.

It was all getting a little hot for Moxley, so he used some axle grease from his bike to colour his eyebrows and painted a false grease moustache on his face to avoid further detection. It worked for a while but it couldn't last forever. With his eyebrows and moustache running from the sweat of riding his bicycle, an observant motorist noticed the clown-like fugitive and notified the police, and Moxley was picked up after a short chase on foot. His only defence was that he couldn't remember a thing and at his trial he pleaded insanity. But Moxley's cleverness at avoiding the police was proof enough that he was sane and a jury found him guilty in no time at all.

William Moxley was hanged from the gallows at Long Bay Gaol on the morning of 18 August 1932. The records don't indicate if there were any protestors to his execution at the gates of the prison. Given the circumstances, it would hardly seem likely.

25 | THE BTK SERIAL KILLER

In the mid-afternoon of 15 January 1974, 15-year-old Charlie Otero arrived home from school in Wichita, Kansas, where he lived in a quiet neighbourhood with his devout Catholic parents and four siblings. Inside he came across the dead bodies of his mother and father in their bedroom. His father Joseph, 38, was lying face down on the floor at the foot of the bed with his wrists and ankles bound together and a plastic bag tied over his head. Charlie's mother, 34-year-old Julie Otero, was tied up on the bed where she had been gagged and strangled. Charlie fled to a neighbour's house to get help, not realising that he had only witnessed the half of the horror. There was more to come.

The neighbour tried to call the police but the Otero home phone line had been cut. He went home and rang the police while Charlie waited outside. When the police arrived and searched the house they found Charlie's brother, nine-year-old Joseph Jr, face down on the floor in his bedroom. The boy's wrists and ankles were also bound and there were three plastic bags over his head. In the basement police discovered the dead body of Charlie's 11-year-old sister, Josephine. She had been sexually assaulted and strangled. Joseph Otero's watch was missing and Julie Otero's purse had been rifled and dumped nearby. Outside of that there was no evidence of a break and enter, robbery, or any sort of a struggle. After the murders, the killer had brazenly driven off in the Otero family car and parked it to be found near Dillons grocery store, only a few blocks away.

With absolutely nothing to go on, police dug deep into Joseph and Julie Otero's past. Joseph Otero was born in Puerto Rico and emigrated to the United States; he joined the military services, where he was a well-regarded flight instructor and mechanic. Joseph Otero was in peak physical condition and was an excellent boxer. He was a loving husband and father and well regarded in the community. The same could be said for his beloved wife Julie, who was a loving wife and devoted mother with lots of friends. Like her husband, she knew how to look after herself in the event of trouble after many years of training in judo.

So how could this possibly happen? Was it a contract hit? If so, why? There was no possible reason. Was it a random killing? If so, then why a whole family? To be carried out without so much as a living witness in broad daylight required surveillance, planning and precision timing. And how could one person subdue so many people who were skilled in martial arts? That's if it was just the one killer.

But it was just the beginning. After the Otero family killings, over the next four years three more women were brutally tied up, tortured, asphyxiated and murdered, unmistakably by the same killer. And, as the death toll mounted, the killer taunted police with a barrage of appalling poems of death and letters complaining that his murders weren't getting enough publicity. In the letters the killer said that he reasoned it was because he didn't have a nickname like other multiple murderers, and seeing as the local police or paper wouldn't give him one he would come up with one himself.

The BTK Serial Killer

After giving police such alternatives as 'the Wichita Strangler', 'the Poetic Strangler', 'the Wichita Hangman' and 'the Asphyxiator', the serial killer settled on BTK as the nickname for himself. It stood for 'bind, torture, kill', as this was how he murdered his victims. And then, in 1978, with seven murders to his credit, BTK disappeared without a trace or the slightest clue as to who he may be.

Wichita police never gave up the hunt for BTK, but every new investigation came to nothing. Then in 2004, almost 26 years after his last murder, Wichita police received a letter from BTK containing information that only the killer could have known, about another murder in 1986 in nearby Park City, which investigators hadn't connected with the BTK slayings.

Over the next 12 months BTK corresponded regularly with police and left packages all over town containing items that he had souvenired from each victim, along with graphic descriptions and Polaroid photos of each murder scene. Becoming more brazen as each week passed, BTK decided to use a computer for his correspondence and, in his ignorance of modern technology, in one of his letters asked the detectives if they would be able to read anything else on a disk other than the file he addressed to them, if he sent them a floppy disk. Naturally they said no in their response through the local newspaper's classifieds.

When the disk arrived and the investigators saw what was on it, they couldn't believe their eyes. Apart from the usual BTK diatribe of torture and death, there were other files relating to matters where the disk had originated from . . . the local Lutheran church. On 26 February 2005, Wichita police arrested 59-year-old Dennis L Rader, Wichita's ordinance inspector and dog catcher, former Boy Scout leader and President of the Wichita Lutheran Church congregation. Rader was a happily married, highly respected member of the city's religious community with two grown-up children. BTK had been living right there among them all of those years. Rader confessed to all of the BTK murders and another two murders in nearby Park City in 1985 and 1991, bringing his total to 10.

At the first day of his trial on Monday 27 June 2005, Dennis Rader pleaded guilty to the murder of 10 people. When Judge Waller asked if he had anything to say, such as apologising to the victims' families or asking for forgiveness, it was as if this was Dennis Rader's moment of glory and he wasn't going to miss a beat.

To the court's astonishment – and an audience in the tens of millions watching live on *Court TV* across America – Rader stood up and proudly described in horrific detail every murder he had committed, and the ones he almost had, which were equally as terrifying.

Prompted by the judge, Rader went on and on for hours with what must be the most extraordinary confession ever broadcast on live television anywhere in the world.

This is how Dennis Rader described the murders of the Otero family to the court:

> The Defendant: On January 15th, 1974, I maliciously, intentionally and with premeditation killed Joseph Otero.
>
> The Court: All right. Mr Rader, I need to find out more information. On that particular day, the 15th day of January, 1974, can you tell me where you went to kill Mr Joseph Otero?
>
> The Defendant: Mmm, I think it's 1834 Edgemoor.
>
> The Court: All right. Can you tell me approximately what time of day you went there?
>
> The Defendant: Somewhere between 7:00 and 7:30.
>
> The Court: This particular location, did you know these people?
>
> The Defendant: No, that was part of my – I guess my what you call fantasy. These people were selected.
>
> The Court: All right.
>
> The Court: You were engaged in some kind of fantasy during this period of time?
>
> The Defendant: Yes, sir.
>
> The Court: All right. Now, where you use the term 'fantasy',

is this something you were doing for your personal pleasure?

The Defendant: Sexual fantasy, sir.

The Court: I see. So you went to this residence, and what occurred then?

The Defendant: Well, I had – did some thinking on what I was going to do to either Mrs Otero or Josephine, and basically broke into the house – or didn't break into the house, but when they came out of the house I came in and confronted the family, and then we went from there.

The Court: All right. Had you planned this beforehand?

The Defendant: To some degree, yes. After I got in the house it – lost control of it, but it – it was – you know, in the back of my mind I had some ideas what I was going to do.

The Court: Did you—

The Defendant: But I just – I basically panicked that first day, so—

The Court: Beforehand did you know who was there in the house?

The Defendant: I thought Mrs Otero and the two kids – the two younger kids were in the house. I didn't realize Mr Otero was gonna be there.

The Court: All right. How did you get into the house, Mr Rader?

The Defendant: I came through the back door, cut the phone lines, waited at the back door, had reservations about even going or just walking away, but pretty soon the door opened, and I was in.

The Court: All right. So the door opened. Was it opened for you, or did someone—

The Defendant: I think one of the kids – I think the – Junior – or not Junior – yes, the – the young girl – Joseph opened the door. He probably let the dog out 'cause the dog was in the house at the time.

The Court: All right. When you went into the house what happened then?

The Defendant: Well, I confronted the family, pulled the pistol, confronted Mr Otero and asked him to – you know, that I was there to – basically I was wanted [by the police], wanted to get the car. I was hungry, food, I was wanted, and asked him to lie down in the living room. And at that time I realized that wouldn't be a really good idea, so I finally – The dog was the real problem, so I – I asked Mr Otero if he could get the dog out. So he had one of the kids put it out, and then I took them back to the bedroom.

The Court: You took who back to the bedroom?

The Defendant: The family, the bedroom – the four members.

The Court: All right. What happened then?

The Defendant: At that time I tied 'em up.

The Court: While still holding them at gunpoint?

The Defendant: Well, in between tying, I guess, you know.

The Court: All right. After you tied them up what occurred?

The Defendant: Well, they started complaining about being tied up, and I re-loosened the bonds a couple of times, tried to make Mr Otero as comfortable as I could. Apparently he had a cracked rib from a car accident, so I had him put a pillow down on his – for his – for his head, had him put a – I think a parka or a coat underneath him. They – you know, they talked to me about, you know, giving the car whatever money. I guess they didn't have very much money, and the – from there I realized that, you know, I was already – I didn't have a mask on or anything. They already could ID me, and made – made a decision to go ahead and – and put 'em down, I guess or strangle them.

The Court: All right. What did you do to Joseph Otero, Sr?

The Defendant: Joseph Otero?

The Court: Yeah, Joseph Otero, Sr. Mr Otero, the father.

The Defendant: Put a plastic bag over his head and then some cords and tightened it.

The Court: This was in the bedroom?

The Defendant: Yes, sir.

The Court: All right. Did he in fact suffocate and die as a result of this?

The Defendant: Not right away, no sir, he didn't.

The Court: What happened?

The Defendant: Well, after that I – I did Mrs Otero. I had never strangled anyone before, so I really didn't know how much pressure you had to put on a person or how long it would take, but—

The Court: Was she also tied up there in the bedroom?

The Defendant: Yes, uh-huh. Yeah, both their hands and their feet were tied up. She was on the bed.

The Court: Where were the children?

The Defendant: Well, Josephine was on the bed, and Junior was on the floor.

The Court: All right.

The Defendant: —at this time.

The Court: So we're – we're talking, first of all, about Joseph Otero. So you had put the bag over his head and tied it.

The Defendant: Mm-hmm.

The Court: And he did not die right away. Can you tell me what happened in regards to Joseph Otero?

The Defendant: He moved over real quick like and I think tore a hole in the bag, and I could tell that he was having some problems there, but at that time the – the whole family just went – they went panicked on me, so I – I – I worked pretty quick. I got Mrs O—

The Court: All right. What did you – you worked pretty quick. What did you do?

The Defendant: Well, I mean, I – I – I strangled Mrs Otero, and then she out, or passed out. I thought she was dead. She passed out. Then I strangled Josephine. She passed out, or I thought she was dead. And then I went over and put a – and then put a bag on Junior's head and – and then, if I remember right, Mrs Otero came back. She came back and—

The Court: Sir, let me ask you about Joseph Otero, Sr.

The Defendant: Senior.

The Court: You indicated he had torn a hole in the bag.

The Defendant: Mm-hmm.

The Court: What did you do with him then?

The Defendant: I put another bag over it – or either that or a – if I recollect, I think I put a – either a cloth or a T-shirt or something over it – over his head, and then a bag, another bag, then tied that down.

The Court: Did he subsequently die?

The Defendant: Well, yes. I mean – I mean, I was – I didn't just stay there and watch him. I mean, I was moving around the room, but—

The Court: All right. So you indicated you strangled Mrs Otero after you had done this; is that correct?

The Defendant: Yeah, I went back and strangled her again.

The Court: All right.

The Defendant: And that – and that – that finally killed her at that time.

The Court: So this is in regards to Count Two. You had, first of all, put the bag over Joseph Otero's head.

The Defendant: I don't know. I have no idea. Just—

The Court: What happened then?

The Defendant: I got the keys to the car. In fact, I had the keys I think earlier before that, 'cause I wanted to make sure I had a way of getting out of the house, and cleaned the house up a little bit, made sure everything's packed up, and left through the front door, and then went there – went over to their car, and then drove to Dillons, left the car there. Then eventually walked back to my car.

You can watch all of Denis Rader's confession on YouTube. Type in 'Dennis Rader Confession'. Be warned. It is not for the faint-hearted. And remember as you watch it that he is completely sane.

After the confession, Dennis Rader, the BTK serial killer, was taken away and locked up forever; he will die in jail. Although he would like visitors, no one comes, which surprises him as he feels as if he is a celebrity. The whole story of the BTK serial murders is available in the book *Unholy Messenger* by Stephen Singular. The movie *The Hunt for BTK* is available on DVD. Very scary stuff.

26 | THE CANBERRA COP KILLER: THE MURDER OF COLIN WINCHESTER

Born on 18 October 1933 and raised in a mining town a little way south of Canberra, Australian Federal Police Assistant Commissioner Colin Winchester holds the tragic and unfortunate distinction of being the most senior police officer to be killed in the line of duty in this country.

Sadly, it would take almost six years and one of the most intensive forensic investigations Australia has seen to bring the murderer to justice.

Two months after the assassination, the former Director of National Operations for the Australian Federal Police, Alan Mills, would go on record to say that 'Assistant Commissioner Colin Winchester's death is the end of the age of innocence for Australia'.

Colin met his violent demise outside the modest home in the Canberra suburb of Deakin he had bought in 1966, at around a quarter past nine on the balmy night of 10 January 1989. He died as a result of two bullets fired into his head at close range

The Australian Crime File 3

as he parked his car in the driveway he shared with his family's next-door neighbour.

The married father of two had joined the police force when he was 28 years old, and worked his way up the ranks from his initial role as a general duties constable. Popular and renowned for his sense of humour, he was considered honest and reliable by all those who worked alongside him. Colin was also admired by his colleagues for the lengths he went to in order to improve his work skills, through taking many and varied courses available to officers – from detective training to accountancy to advanced management.

That diligence and hard work paid off in 1984, when Colin attained the rank of Assistant Commissioner after 23 years on the job.

Just about everybody that came into contact with Colin Winchester – from either side of the law – considered him to be what is commonly known in this country as a 'good bloke'. Canberra solicitor Peter Crowley would later describe his good friend as being honest and compassionate in his job. A practical joker and dedicated family man, he was tough but fair, straight to the point and always ready to go an extra mile for the sake of the job. But even the most admired people in the world can find themselves on the wrong side of someone's opinion. For Colin Winchester, that someone was David Harold Eastman, an intelligent but highly disgruntled former public servant who seemed angry with the world in general, and eventually came to channel all of his dissatisfaction towards Colin.

At one point in his life, Eastman went to private school and had a strong future to look forward to. His father was a senior diplomat, held in high esteem by his colleagues. Eastman himself was dux of his year when he finished up at Canberra Grammar. He soon found himself working for the Treasury.

Somewhere along the way, though, Eastman seemed to develop a persecution complex, believing a variety of injustices had been carried out against him. He seemed to grow angrier by the day, sure that he was being conspired against, and he would show that anger by harassing anyone he felt had slighted him or held him back in any way – including the Australian Federal Police.

His rage wasn't isolated to law enforcement officers, though. Other public services copped Eastman's wrath, with accusations of corruption. It was also common for Eastman to pass his opinions on to the media.

Eastman left the Treasury after being overlooked for a promotion he clearly believed he should have received. The year was 1977 and he spent the next decade trying to get hired back into the public service. Feeling victimised, he also spent that time trying to convince anyone who would listen that the Treasury was corrupt. As the years dragged on, Eastman grew even more irate. There are stories that he would make direct threats to various reporters.

It's fair to say that Eastman was a difficult person to get along with, something that his neighbour Andrew Russo was becoming increasingly aware of. The two men became embroiled in an argument in December 1987 about where Russo had parked his car. Terse words were exchanged. The fight became so heated that Eastman and Russo ended up reporting each other to the authorities. The police sided with Russo, and Eastman found himself charged with assault. It was no surprise that he saw this as further persecution. He became convinced that the police had decided to conspire against him. He also believed that a police record would make it even harder for him to get back into the public service.

Concerned about his future, Eastman fought long and hard to have the assault charge against him quashed. The campaign saw him make repeated calls to the media. Once he got a reporter on the phone, it was hard to get him off, with the unfortunate journalist being forced to listen to an endless tirade revolving around conspiracies and persecution.

It was around this time that Colin Winchester was appointed regional chief of the Canberra police force. Eastman firmly believed that the new boss would be the man to help his cause. The men finally met in person at the police headquarters in

The Australian Crime File 3

December 1988. Colin had been asked by a number of politicians to look into the matter.

The meeting, though, wasn't a comfortable one. Eastman insisted that he had been attacked by his neighbour, that it was unreasonable that he had been the man charged by police for the incident. Colin Winchester listened to his version of the story passively. He then told Eastman that he would have the opportunity to defend himself when the matter went to court, and that he would investigate the situation himself.

Before that could happen, however, Eastman received notice from the authorities that the case would proceed within weeks. The date he got the news was 9 January 1989. In just a few more than 24 hours, Colin Winchester would be dead.

When Colin pulled in to his driveway at around 9.15pm on 10 January, his wife Gwen Winchester was waiting inside. She heard the car idle then stop, but the sound of his keys in the door never came. She did hear a couple of faint popping noises, but passed them off as children throwing small rocks or something similarly trivial.

Gwen had no way of knowing that, just as Colin had removed the key from the ignition and opened the car's door, he had been shot square in the back of the head. The bullet killed him on impact. A second shot above the right ear made sure the job was done.

Shortly afterwards, Gwen Winchester went outside to see what was going on. She was confronted with the sight of her loving husband still sitting in his car. With her mind racing, she was concerned he'd had a heart attack. Gwen bolted back inside to phone the emergency services hotline. After that, she went back outside. The light inside her husband's car was still on, and it helped her to see the blood pooling on the ground. Realising that something far more sinister was going on, Gwen ran back inside to call the police.

As would be expected when such a high-ranking member of their squad is concerned, a very large number of police were on the scene in no time at all. Still, besides two empty bullet

The Canberra Cop Killer

cartridges sitting in the grass next to the driver's side door of the car where Colin Winchester had been murdered, they could locate very little evidence.

Expert forensic investigator Robert Barnes was flown up from his home in Melbourne. He got to the murder site at close to 1am. He immediately noted that, due to the lack of solid evidence at the scene, they would have to rely on trace evidence. His first priority was to seal off the area to ensure absolutely nothing was moved or altered.

He then shocked the other investigating officers by having Colin Winchester's body taken out of the car and placed on a tarpaulin upside down so that he could examine it right there and then, rather than at a mortuary, which would have been standard operating procedure. His reason for doing this was that he believed there would be a huge loss of blood doing things the traditional way, which would have resulted in valuable trace evidence being washed away. His theory eventually helped put David Eastman into jail.

The detectives assigned to the case were the most senior and dedicated available. Their prime goals were to discover a motive for the killing and find any possible witnesses, as well as to locate the murder weapon.

One local couple told them that they had seen two cars driving away wildly on the night of the murder, and a woman who lived behind Colin and Gwen Winchester revealed that she had heard someone walking past her house around the approximate time that Colin was assassinated. She heard the sound again a few minutes later, going in the other direction. This time the footsteps were accompanied by a faint muttering. She then heard a car driving away.

Another neighbour told the police that she had seen a car parked nearby two nights earlier. It was blue and the driver had tried to hide his face as she got close. The man's behaviour seemed somewhat weird to her so she tried to remember the number plate. She told the detectives that it was possibly YPQ 038, but when the police followed that lead they found out the car had been nowhere near the crime scene on the night in question. David Eastman's number plate, however, was very similar – YMP 028.

Robert Barnes studied photos and sketches of the crime scene, taking special note of the position of Colin Winchester's body and the location of the spent bullet casings. He was then able to establish that Colin had been shot in the back of the head as he started to get out of his car. The second shot came after he fell back into the automobile.

Barnes also discovered that the hollow-point bullets used were a cheap Korean brand, PMC. They had been fired from a Ruger 10/22 self-loading carbine rifle, a common weapon in this country, often used for sports shooting. Further testing on Colin Winchester's body revealed that there were two separate types of gunshot residue – one, called chopped disc residue, was a heavily charred particle; the other was from two ammunition brands, neither of which was PMC.

There were suggestions in the media that Colin Winchester had been murdered by the Mafia, but Robert Barnes thought that those allegations were highly unlikely. A Mafia hit would have been done by a professional, and professionals wouldn't have left the spent bullet casings at the crime scene. Barnes also found that the murder weapon had been fitted with a silencer; anybody with even a casual knowledge of guns would have known that it would have been next to useless on such a powerful rifle.

Looking for any lead possible, the detectives assigned to the case began to interview anybody involved in Colin Winchester's recent work. Two officers visited David Eastman the day after the murder. Eastman made sure that his lawyer was there when he answered their questions. He then told the officers that he had been driving through Canberra by himself when Colin Winchester was murdered, but he couldn't tell them specifically where he had been, apart from suggesting that he had bought some takeaway food at around 8pm and arrived back at his flat in the suburb of Reid at about 10pm. He neglected to mention something that he would later admit in court – that he had gone to a brothel in the suburb of Fyshwick sometime around

The Canberra Cop Killer

11pm. The prostitute he hired that night later testified that his visit had been during the period from 11pm until 2am, but she couldn't pinpoint an exact time. Either way, it didn't help Eastman establish an alibi.

Eastman's story – or lack thereof – compelled the detectives to take a closer look into his background. It didn't take them long to realise he was something of a loose cannon. They soon uncovered circumstantial evidence that he had accused Colin Winchester of being corrupt.

The police were back at Eastman's flat a week later, to conduct a search of his Mazda 626 and residence. Robert Barnes noted that Eastman's car appeared to be very tidy – except that there was a large amount of partially burnt propellant and residue from gunshots on the door handle on the driver's side, on the steering column, and on the right-hand side of the rear-view mirror.

The locations and large number of fine particles indicated a right-handed person had shot a gun and then got into the car almost immediately afterwards. Barnes took samples to analyse, but it would take several years for the results to be determined, due to the substances being so miniscule and the limits of the technology available at the time.

Of just as much interest to Barnes was the fact that the charred chipped disc particle matched evidence found on Colin Winchester's dead body.

All this, as well as other forensic evidence Barnes assembled that confirmed the murder weapon used was a Ruger 10/22 rifle with a silencer attached, was enough to convince the expert that whoever had driven this particular Mazda 626 had killed Colin Winchester.

The police were also able to confirm that no other person besides David Eastman had driven the vehicle since the night of the murder. The police began watching their prime suspect very closely. Eastman's phone was tapped, as was his home. Surveillance crews followed him whenever he went out in public.

Not surprisingly, David Eastman declared to anyone that would listen that he was being harassed by the authorities. He made several calls repeating his claims to the media and various politicians.

The police, though, stayed right on his trail. They even arranged a recall of Ruger 10/22 rifles, ostensibly to exclude innocent owners as much to target David Eastman. They also started looking at gun dealers and struck pay dirt when they contacted a man by the name of Louis Klarenbeek – now deceased – from the Canberra suburb of Queanbeyan.

Klarenbeek told them he had sold a Ruger to a man a short time before Colin Winchester was killed. The only problem was that he couldn't tell them the name of the man who bought it. He gave them a description of the purchaser, but it was of little use to them. Interestingly, though, he told them that the customer had said that he didn't need the gun's telescopic sight – a strange decision for a sports rifle, unless the target you're aiming for is very near.

One thing that Klarenbeek was able to provide police with was spent cartridges from a quarry that the Ruger had been test-fired in. After comparing the markings on the shells found at the crime scene, Barnes was able to forensically prove that the weapon Klarenbeek had sold to the mystery customer was highly likely to have been the same one that was used to murder Colin Winchester. The authorities lucked into further valuable evidence when another customer of Klarenbeek's was able to identify David Eastman as a visitor to the gun dealer's house. A woman, too, told them that she had seen a car like the suspect's parked near the dealer's house.

With the case dragging on, a coronial inquest began in 1991; its aim was to establish the exact reason for the murder. It only took two weeks before David Eastman emerged as the only genuine suspect in the matter.

Still, there was no conclusive finding. All that the inquest really managed to do was remove any doubt that Colin Winchester was corrupt.

Nonetheless, David Eastman was arrested and charged with Winchester's murder shortly afterwards, despite the majority of the evidence against him being purely circumstantial.

The Canberra Cop Killer

Anyone familiar with the case and the accused would have been expecting David Eastman to cause a major commotion when the case finally went to trial on 2 May 1995, more than five years after the murder. They were proved right virtually from day one, with the judge, Justice Kenneth Carruthers, being insulted by the defendant. Eastman also made a big production of publicly firing his lawyers a number of times throughout the trial, only to rehire them days later. Perhaps inevitably, though, there came a time in the 85-day trial when he didn't request their services again, and he ended up representing himself.

Eastman's behaviour in court hit a low point the day he threw a jug of water across the room when he believed things were going against him. For the most part, the Crown prosecutor, Michael Adams QC, let Eastman go on with his histrionics while he continued to present his case. He declared that the accused's motive came down to the dislike he held for the police, and the fact that Colin Winchester had done nothing to help him.

The prosecutor presented all the evidence that his team had assembled, and put forward five hours of the thousands of conversations they had gathered on the tapes made of Eastman's phone and the bugs at his house. One of those tapes is reported to have captured Eastman saying that he had never killed anyone before, but that it was 'a beautiful feeling; one of the most beautiful feelings you have ever known'.

In his defence, the best David Eastman could do was say that the gunshot residue evidence found in his blue Mazda 626 may have been from guns he had bought out of fear following the argument with his neighbour, Andrew Russo.

Despite his vigorous denials, the jury had little trouble reaching a unanimous guilty verdict. David Eastman was sentenced to life in prison on 15 November 1995, for the cold-blooded murder of Australian Federal Police Assistant Commissioner Colin Winchester. He has since mounted several appeals, all of which have come to nothing.

David Eastman maintains his innocence to this day. He will never be allowed parole. He is currently serving his time in the 300-capacity multi-grade Alexander Maconochie Centre in the Australian Capital Territory.

27 | WHO KILLED ADRIAN KAY?

Back in the 1970s and 1980s when proper gangsters such as Paddles Anderson, George Freeman, Stan 'the Man' Smith, Lennie McPherson and Neddy Smith controlled the Sydney underworld, one of the underlings stood out among them for his style and class. His name was Adrian Kay, and, from humble beginnings in Sydney's inner western suburbs, he had started out selling secondhand cars in the early 1970s and from there his career mysteriously took off, enough to provide him with the luxuries in life to which he quickly became accustomed.

Always immaculately groomed and with his trademark yellow Rolls-Royce with the number plate AK 000 double-parked out the front, Adrian Kay was often seen in the best eastern suburbs establishments, wining and dining with a beautiful young lady on his arm or sipping champagne at the bar at Eliza's in Double Bay with other colourful characters of his ilk.

But it was said that Kay made his money from things a little more nefarious than selling used cars. It seemed as though his car yard was really just a front for a racket where he manufactured fake number plates and log books for imported luxury cars to avoid paying import duty, which, in those days, especially on Mercedes-Benzs, was about another half on the top of the cost of the car. Business boomed in those days before computers, before things could be checked out in a hurry, and Kay reaped the rewards and lived like a king.

It was never really certain whether or not Adrian graduated to drugs, but you could be forgiven for thinking that he was in it up to the eyeballs. By the early 1980s he was hanging with a bad crew, men who dealt in heroin and would kill you as soon as look at you if you did the wrong thing by them.

By now Adrian Kay's fortunes had seen him buy into a partnership in the trendy King Arthur's Court hotel at the top of William Street in the Cross, and he also allegedly had interests in a couple of pubs interstate. But both federal and state police believed that Adrian's real skills lay in importing and distributing heroin.

But whatever the case, Adrian Kay decided he needed a bodyguard, or a 'minder' as it was fashionable to call them in those days, thus becoming arguably the only car dealer and hotelier in Australia's history to do so. And, never one to do things by halves, he employed the services of one of Sydney's most notorious crooks of the time, a thug named Bob 'the Basher'.

The Basher was a big lump of a bloke with a record for assault, malicious injury, resisting arrest, false pretences, breaking and entering and numerous driving offences. He left Sydney's western suburbs in the 1970s and quickly infiltrated the lucrative eastern suburbs underworld by bashing whoever they wanted and collecting unpaid debts for SP bookmakers.

It wasn't long before the Basher became a force to be reckoned with throughout the pubs in trendy Double Bay, Woollahra and Paddington, and it seemed as though wherever the Basher was, there was trouble. Drunk, the Basher was the most obnoxious thug on the planet and you'd only have to look at him sideways and he'd want to belt you. Sober, he was a good bloke and could mix with the hardcore criminals and at the same time bask in

Who Killed Adrian Kay?

the notoriety feted upon him by the society fringe-dwellers who hung around the more notorious pubs for kicks.

In only a short time it was fashionable to have the Basher in your company and he was seen in the best of Sydney's restaurants, wining and dining with some of the eastern suburbs' better-known villains and socialising with the hangers-on.

And so, Adrian Kay, with the Basher driving the Roller, became an item around town, and to mess with the dapper car dealer was to mess with the Basher, and that wasn't a good look. But before long Adrian sacked the Basher, telling everyone that his minder had developed a reputation as a 'big time' brawler and it wasn't good for Kay's image. The pair became bitter enemies.

Six months later on 27 March 1986, the Basher was having a few drinks with friends at the most fashionable bar in Sydney at the time, Pronto, in Double Bay, when a yellow Rolls-Royce with the number plate AK 000 and dark windows pulled up out the front. The Basher walked from the bar at Pronto, sat in the back seat of the car and closed the door. Soon after he left the Rolls and, as the patrons stood aside in horror, went back to the bar, his shirt covered in blood, ordered a beer and collapsed from a bullet to the chest.

The Basher survived the shooting and proudly wore the bullet, which had just missed his heart and surgeons said was too risky to move, like a badge of honour. He later told a reporter, 'I didn't know I was shot until I looked down and saw the claret.' By being shot in public in a Rolls-Royce, the Basher achieved legend status throughout the underworld.

The occupants of the Roller, Adrian Kay and an associate, Bob 'the Blender' McIntosh, were charged with attempted murder and held without bail for a week. It was alleged that when the Basher entered the back seat to discuss his ongoing feud with Adrian Kay, the Blender shot him once in the chest from the front passenger seat with a .22 pistol.

But, as is the way of the underworld, the Basher didn't hold a grudge against his alleged would-be assassins and arrived at court a few weeks later driven by Adrian Kay in the yellow Rolls, where he said that he would be appearing in Kay's defence and that he had accidentally shot himself in the chest while he and his best mate Adrian were having a quiet chat. It was all a simple mistake. Case dismissed.

Two months later, Adrian Kay was found dead at his King Arthur's Court Hotel with two bullets to the chest and one in the head, in a classic contract hit. Naturally the police made Bob the Basher – who they found in a bar – their first port of call. The Basher had a watertight alibi and when he heard the news he burst into laughter and shouted for the bar.

As it turned out there were a lot of reasons why a lot of sinister people wanted Adrian Kay dead, the most likely being his involvement in the funding of a military coup in the Seychelles Islands with Australian-raised money. Perhaps Adrian Kay knew too much. A Vietnam veteran, Peter Drummond, was charged with the murder and found innocent. The case remains open.

Meanwhile, the Basher's run of bad luck with prestige yellow cars continued. On 3 August 1986, he left Eliza's restaurant at Double Bay with a male companion at around 1am in the other man's yellow V12 Boxer Ferrari. As they neared the King's Cross tunnel the Ferrari ploughed into a solid concrete substation at 100 miles an hour. The driver survived but the Basher was killed instantly. In the end the Basher went out in the manner in which he and Adrian Kay lived. In the very, very, fast lane.

28 | THE 'MISTAKES' OF JUSTICE MARCUS EINFELD

If you're going to tell a blatant lie, it's in your best interests to make sure it stands up to simple investigation – especially if you're a prominent member of society, the sort of person who could be deeply compromised if such a thing came out. But it's a basic lack of attention to detail that saw Marcus Enfield become the first Australian former superior court judge ever to go to jail. And all over a measly $77 speeding fine.

Marcus Richard Einfeld was born in Sydney in 1938. The son of respected state and federal politician Syd Einfeld – namesake of the Syd Einfeld Drive in Sydney's Bondi Junction – the younger Einfeld made the most of his upper-class heritage, and later followed in his father's high-achieving footsteps, becoming a Queen's Counsel and then Justice of the Federal Court of Australia and of the supreme courts of New South Wales, Western Australia and the Australian Capital Territory. He also held the title of President of the Human Rights and Equal Opportunity Commission, as well as being a UNICEF

Ambassador for Children. He was even named a National Living Treasure by the National Trust of Australia, and was awarded membership of the Order of Australia. If that wasn't enough, he was presented with a United Nations Association of Australia's Founders Award for his contribution to justice and human rights. But of course, all of that would become irrelevant after his spectacular fall from grace.

The trouble started when Einfeld's silver Lexus was snapped by a speed camera travelling through Mosman on Sydney's leafy lower North Shore doing 10 kilometres per hour over the 50 kilometre per hour limit on the night of 8 January 2006. The $77 penalty also came with the loss of three demerit points. In the long run, it really wasn't such a big deal. But Einfeld had contested such issues in court before and won. So, once again, he elected to not pay the fine and cop the points and instead challenge it in court, a place with which he was especially familiar.

Einfeld fronted Sydney's Downing Centre Court in the old Mark Foy department store building in Sydney's CBD on 7 August 2006, telling the presiding judge that it couldn't possibly have been him behind the wheel for the alleged offence as he was at Forster on the New South Wales north coast at the time in question. Besides, he added, he didn't even know his way around Mosman. It must have been the friend that he had loaned his car to – Florida academic Professor Teresa Brennan. Sadly, Professor Brennan wouldn't be able to answer the charge, though. The poor woman had already returned home to the US, where she had since died as the result of a hit-and-run car accident.

It was a tragic story, but very convenient for the retired superior court judge. And just in case anyone had doubts about the veracity of his tale, he had a signed statutory declaration on hand to back it up. Anyway, there was no way to determine who was actually behind the wheel at the time, so the case and fine were dropped. Einfeld was free to speed through upper-class suburbs with a spare $77 in his pocket once again.

The only problem was that, even in retirement, Einfeld had a modicum of notoriety. With the added detail of the friend being killed in such a timely and coincidental circumstance,

The 'Mistakes' of Justice Marcus Einfeld

the story was deemed newsworthy enough to warrant a three-sentence article at the bottom of page 11 of the *Daily Telegraph* newspaper the next day. Most people no doubt skipped such an inconsequential piece, turning to the racing form guide, comics or crossword instead. But Marcus Einfeld's run of luck had come to an end.

That day, a pair of *Daily Telegraph* journos – veteran news hound Michael Beach and young court reporter Viva Goldner – were scanning through the paper's pages. The tiny article piqued their interest. Something didn't quite gel. Besides, how much trouble would it be to enter the name Teresa Brennan into Google and check her out?

No trouble at all, it turned out – especially compared with that which Marcus Einfeld would find himself in before too long.

It transpired that Brennan had indeed been left critically injured by a car accident in Florida. She died two months later, which was obviously an unfortunate situation for her family. But what was unfortunate for Einfeld was the date of the accident – 10 December 2002, almost three years before he told the court his friend had borrowed his car and was snapped by a speed camera travelling through Mosman doing 10 kilometres per hour over the limit on the night of 8 January 2006.

The journalists didn't need to be Woodward and Bernstein to know that a story was brewing. Goldner found Einfeld's phone number and rang him at home. She couldn't believe that she was listening to a distinguished member of the judiciary virtually talk himself into an uncomfortable prison cell.

Goldner recounted the conversation the next day in the *Daily Telegraph*. It read:

> *I just rang him and said we needed to double-check that it was Teresa Brennan who was driving the car, and he said it was, and I told him that we'd checked on the internet and that the accident she was killed in happened before the speeding fine. He then went quiet and I asked him if he was there, and he said yes. So I asked him how it*

137

could be possible that she was driving his car if she was dead. And he paused and then said it was the other Teresa Brennan. I asked him if there were two of them, and he said yes. I asked if she was also from Florida as it said in his statutory declaration and he said, yes, yes, I think so, and then he said he wasn't sure if it was Theresa with an h, or Teresa, but that there were definitely two of them, he didn't know where she was now, and then he said 'I have nothing more to say' and hung up.

Going into damage control after the unexpected phone call, Einfeld issued a 20-page statement about the new Professor Teresa Brennan from the US who was behind the wheel of his car when it was clocked going 10 kilometres per hour over the limit through Mosman. What a coincidence that this professor also died tragically in a car accident – on a date *after* incurring the speeding fine.

It's probably not a great shock that research failed to unveil any information to back up Einfeld's claim. But for a moment it seemed the former judge had a guardian angel.

Angela Liata was a 55-year-old attention seeker. Unprompted, she came forward and declared that she had caught up with Teresa Brennan on the day she had been snapped by the speed camera in Einfeld's Lexus. She had even been for a ride in the car. Liata loved the notoriety the story brought her, but she soon came clean, admitting she had fabricated the tale in order to get in contact with the retired judge.

Liata had to stand trial in 2009 for perverting the course of justice. After turning up in a variety of designer dresses and posing for the press on the steps to the court, she was eventually sentenced to 200 hours of community service.

But that was nothing compared with the legal storm Einfeld was facing. While Liata's case was going on, it was found that the 2006 fine wasn't the first time he'd used the excuse that he hadn't been driving his car at the time to get out of a traffic infringement. There were also statutory declarations from 1999, 2003 and 2004 stating the exact same thing.

The 'Mistakes' of Justice Marcus Einfeld

As the plot thickened, the authorities searched Einfeld's house. They seized his personal computer. With the evidence gathered, they arrested Marcus Einfeld on 29 March 2007. He was charged with 13 offences, including perjury, perverting the cause of justice, various traffic infringements and making and using false statutory declarations.

Shortly before his trial on 31 October 2008, Einfeld pleaded guilty to seven of the offences. He was sentenced on 20 March 2009, with Supreme Court Justice Bruce James finding that he had committed 'deliberate, premeditated perjury' and 'calculating criminality' that was part of 'planned criminal activity'.

Justice James went on to say, 'Any lawyer, and especially a lawyer who has been a barrister and a judge, who commits such an offence is to be sentenced on the basis that he would have been fully aware of the gravity of his conduct.' James then sentenced Einfeld to three years in jail. A non-parole period of two years was set for knowingly making a false statement under oath and for attempting to pervert the course of justice.

Still, Einfeld denies he ever did anything wrong. 'I don't think I'm the slightest bit dishonest,' he insists. 'I just made a mistake.'

Despite landing him the dubious honour of being the first Australian former superior court judge ever to go to jail, that 'mistake' saw Einfeld's licence to practise as a Queen's Counsel revoked. He was also struck off the lawyer's roll, and his Officer of the Order of Australia was terminated by the Governor-General.

On 19 March 2011, Marcus Einfeld was released after serving two years in jail. He said he would devote his time to prison reform.

29 | LITTLE HAS CHANGED IN 100 YEARS: THE MOUNT RENNIE RAPE CASE

While we are quick to condemn the gang rapes in recent years by young men of Middle Eastern origin, it is easy to forget that the majority of our most heinous crimes and gang violations against women have been perpetrated by Australians whose families have been here for many generations. So hideous were some of these crimes that they are deep-etched into our culture forever.

For example, the 1973 torture, rape and murder of Mrs Virginia Morse after she was abducted from her lonely farmhouse in rural New South Wales by the beasts Allan Baker and Kevin Crump; the 1986 rape-murder of nursing sister Anita Cobby by five men in Sydney's western suburbs; and the abduction, rape and murder of bank clerk Janine Balding by a gang of teenagers as she made her way home from work in Sydney's western suburbs in 1988, come immediately to mind.

The killers had typically Anglo-Australian names: Murphy, Baker, Crump, Elliot, Blessington, Jamieson, Travis and Murdoch. And it's not news that vile crimes against women by packs of men have been going on since the new settlers began arriving. But among them, there is one crime that stands out for its initial ferocity and then, to pander to a public demanding justice, the punishment of some of its perpetrators. It happened a long time ago, more that 130 years ago in fact, in Sydney, and became known as the Mount Rennie Rape Case. Tragically, it seems as though little has changed in all those years.

On 9 September 1886, 16-year-old orphan Mary Jane Hicks left home on the outskirts of Sydney, headed for the city in search of work as a domestic servant. So innocent was Mary to the ways of the world that she had never been kissed by a boy, let alone being aware of what else went on between consenting adults.

When the child was offered a free ride by a hansom cabbie, Charles Sweetman, Mary thought nothing of going with him, as cabbies were trusted and respected members of the community. Not so Mr Sweetman. He pulled the cab over to the side of the road in the disused area of a rope factory in Waterloo, climbed down from his perch and sat next to Mary.

As Sweetman was attempting to assault the lass, a small gang of teenagers from the notorious local Waterloo Push arrived on the scene and saved her. Glad to be away from Sweetman, Mary was only too happy to go with the youths, who led her along a bush path heading towards Randwick Road. Once in the cover of the undergrowth, they threw her to the ground and while two of the teenagers held her down the others had their way with her.

A labourer working nearby, Bill Stanley, heard Mary's screams for help and as he ran through the bushes to her rescue, the gang fled. As Stanley was comforting Mary, covering her up and making her as comfortable as he could so he could carry her to help, he looked up to find the gang was back, only this time with a lot of their mates. Now there were about 20 of them.

Stanley did his best against the gang but he was beaten and kicked to the ground, where he was set upon and belted with rocks, tree branches, fists and boots. Mary was ripped from Bill Stanley's grasp and dragged screaming to a sandy hill nearby,

Little Has Changed in 100 Years

which stood in what we know now as the Moore Park Golf Course. The hill was the highest part of the reserve and was known as Mount Rennie.

When Bill Stanley, who had fled to the nearby Redfern police station, returned with help, they found Mary laying naked and covered in blood, battered, bruised, barely alive and soaking wet. It turned out that she had tried to commit suicide by drowning herself in a drain rather than face the humiliation of the brutal mass assault.

Mary was rushed to Sydney Hospital but was so badly injured both physically and mentally that it was almost a week before she could give police a full account of what had happened, descriptions of her assailants and the names by which they called each other. The police knew them all very well.

The police dragnet rounded up 15 teenagers who were charged with 'carnally knowing and ravishing' Mary. By the time police broke it all down as the youths gave each other up in an attempt to save themselves, 11 of them were charged and sent to trial.

In the meantime, the trusted cabbie, Charles Sweetman, was found guilty of attempted rape, given a public flogging on two separate occasions and sent to prison for 14 years.

Nine of the defendants claimed they were not at the rape scene and provided alibis. Two admitted having had sex with Mary but said it was with her consent. But the prosecution had little trouble identifying the offenders thanks to eyewitness accounts from Mary and the man who had tried so desperately to save her life, the brave Bill Stanley.

After a trial that lasted six days, during which the court heard from almost 100 witnesses, the jury retired and in just two and a half hours returned a guilty verdict on nine of the 11 charged, content that the other two had watertight alibis.

Mr Justice Windeyer was damning in passing sentence. 'This poor, defenceless girl, friendless and alone, is like some wild animal hunted down by a set of savages, who spring upon her and outrage her until she lies a lifeless thing before them . . . I warn you to prepare for death.' With that he sentenced all nine of them to be hanged and concluded with the words, 'You committed a most atrocious crime: a crime so horrible that every lover of this country must feel it a disgrace to our civilisation.'

All of the condemned men lodged appeals against the severity of the sentences and after their lawyers had lodged one appeal after another, five of the youths were successful and had their sentences commuted to life imprisonment.

The four that remained – George Duffy, Joseph Martin, Robert Read and William Boyce, all of whom were under the age of 20 – went to the gallows at Darlinghurst Gaol at 6am on the morning of 7 January 1887.

The remaining five rapists who narrowly escaped the noose were released after 10 years of hard labour. Little is known about what became of them except for one – Mick Donnellan – who devoted his life to social work in the Waterloo district near where the rape had taken place. Later in his life he became a city alderman and earned great respect among those who knew him and forgave him for his crime.

30 | MURDER INC.: THE MAFIA'S OWN PRIVATE DEATH SQUAD

Earlier in this book we took a look at Charles 'Lucky' Luciano, the grubby street urchin who murdered his way to the top of the American Mafia in the early 1930s. Once there, Luciano moulded the Mafia into a modern organisation comprising five main New York families, all going about their business and reporting back to the board of directors as any huge corporation registered on the stock market would do.

Soon the Mafia became the largest organisation in America and operated without the authorities having a clue that it even existed, until Joe Valachi started singing to a congressional committee 30 years later in 1963. It was only then that America heard the words Mafia, Cosa Nostra and the Syndicate for the first time.

In 1931 Lucky Luciano became the Mafia's first *Capo de Tutti Capi* or 'Boss of all of the Bosses', and eventually his power reached out across all of the Mafia families throughout every state of America. Luciano held ultimate power over every

Mafia member in America and to defy his orders invariably meant death, as murder was the only certain way the Mafia could guarantee the secrecy of their organisation.

In this chapter we are going to take a look at how Charlie Lucky maintained the Mafia style of law and order through an organisation that eventually became known to us as Murder Inc.

Once in supreme power of the Mafia, or the Unione Siciliane as he preferred it to be known, in order to keep it under control, Lucky Luciano set up an internal 'death squad' that would act upon every deadly whim of the Board of Directors, or 'the Commission' as they called it. The Commission consisted of the heads of the five New York families and non-Sicilian advisers such as the Mafia's Jewish accountant Myer Lansky and the Jewish assassin Benjamin 'Bugsy' Siegel, who later went on to create Las Vegas.

To head up the death squad, Luciano appointed his trusted friend and ally Albert Anastasia, a ruthless Sicilian crime boss who had bashed and murdered his way up from the docks to become the most feared enforcer in the underworld. Luciano's choice was a good one. Anastasia's specialty was murder. Over the years he had become infamous for the way he disposed of bodies and the feared 'one-way ride' and 'concrete shoes' were just a couple of Albert's colourful inventions.

Extremely honoured to be working so closely with the revered *Capo de Tutti Capi*, Mad Albert went about his new position with great enthusiasm. His first appointment was Louis 'Lepke' Buchalter, a Jewish gun for hire whose specialty was having anyone murdered for a price. Lepke, whose nickname came from an abbreviation of Lepkeleh or 'Little Louis' in Yiddish, had had a long association with the Mafia but had never been placed in a position of such trust before. After all, the orders came from the top and Lepke would be the one who was receiving them. It was a special place of honour.

But in their wisdom, the Commission placed strict guidelines on their death squad which must be adhered to at all times, otherwise the assassin could very quickly become the victim. First,

Murder Inc.

outside hits and civilians were out of bounds. Killing police, politicians and reporters would only bring down the heat, and that wasn't what the Commission wanted. They killed only other mobsters, in the belief that investigators would not bother to look too hard for the killer, rationalising that the world was a better place without the deceased anyway. What was another dead gangster, more or less.

Second, they killed other mobsters only for good business reasons. Personal disputes such as affairs of the heart and internal family squabbles were no business of the Commission. They also didn't encourage torture, just straight in and out killings that wouldn't attract any unnecessary attention to the fact that there was an organisation out there cleaning up its own backyard.

And third, they made sure that it would be exceptionally hard to trace back to who had actually given the orders for the hit. The hitman may be picked up and, having no good reason to be killing the target other than for money, should he decide to sing then the trail would never lead any further than the fellow soldier who had been instructed to give him the hit. And even though the orders for as many as 400 murders over the years came directly from the Commission, not once did their origin ever reach the ears of the authorities.

Outside of that, other factions of the Mafia didn't have to get any vendettas sanctioned by anyone other than their immediate local superiors. They could kill whoever they liked and run the risk of being caught locally. Lepke's death squad operated strictly at the behest of the Commission. While the Mafia knew of its existence, outside of that no one knew a thing.

Lepke chose his assassins well. Murderers who would be slipped an envelope full of cash and some instructions. Colourful characters with bizarre names such as Vito 'Chicken Head' Gurino, 'Blue Jaw' Magoon, Abe 'Kid Twist' Reles, Frank 'the Dasher' Abbandando, 'Pittsburgh Phil' Strauss and 'Happy' Maione.

Even when Lucky Luciano was arrested in 1936 and sent to prison for 50 years, the death squad kept on killing people. But with Luciano away, Anastasia started breaking the rules and suddenly all sorts of dead bodies began turning up all over New York, lots of them ordinary people who Albert had simply taken a disliking to. Anastasia was also openly associating with Lepke and his killers. Sooner or later something had to give.

It did when one of the top hitmen, Abe 'Kid Twist' Reles – who got his nickname from the way he habitually chewed on candy bars – was pulled in on suspicion of homicide.

On the promise that he wouldn't be prosecuted if he squealed, Reles told the police that he had taken orders to murder directly from Albert Anastasia and Lepke Buchalter in person. Reles then went on to confess to 49 murders in the Brooklyn district alone. The press aptly dubbed Kid Twist's employers Murder Inc.

With the Kid as their star witness, the cops rounded up Lepke and Anastasia and threw them in the slammer. But Reles was mysteriously killed when he allegedly tried to escape via his eighth-floor hotel window where he was under 24-hour, six-policeman guard. They could never explain how his body was found 20 feet off the building alignment.

But it was too late for Lepke. Others now had also given him up. Lepke and several of his associates went to Sing Sing's electric chair soon after. But with Reles dead, there was no case to answer for Albert Anastasia and he was set free. It was almost as though Albert had saved the biggest gangland hit of them all for himself. On 25 October 1957, as he sat in the barber's chair at the Park Sheraton Hotel in New York, two gunmen ushered the barber away and filled Albert Anastasia full of lead.

I guess he would have been proud of that.

31 | THE TWO LIVES OF AL GRASSBY

While many residents of the ACT complained bitterly about the unveiling of a $72,000 statue of the late politician Al Grassby at the Theo Notaras Multicultural Centre in Civic, Canberra, in 2008, many other citizens thought it was a terrific idea. They believed that if the statue was placed outside, the pigeons could now do to Mr Grassby what they had been wanting to do to him for years.

Preferring to be referred to as the 'father of multiculturalism in Australia' rather than an 'associate of the Mafia', Grassby was a flamboyant character notorious for his loud appearance and enthusiasm for immigration. But the implications of Grassby's association with the Italian Mafia weren't lost on his detractors, especially when Grassby endeavoured to incriminate an innocent woman, Mrs Barbara Mackay, in the murder of her husband, Griffith drug campaigner Donald Mackay. These false allegations made Grassby many more enemies than friends.

Albert Jaime Grass was born in 1926 in Brisbane to a Spanish father and an Irish mother. Later Al changed his name to Grassby – allegedly to make it sound more Irish – and spent his earlier years working as a journalist specialising in rural and agricultural issues before standing for, and winning, the seat of Murrumbidgee representing the Labor Party as Member of the NSW Legislative Assembly in 1965.

He served as Shadow Minister for Agriculture and Conservation between 1968 and 1969. The outspoken Grassby became popular for his views supporting country issues and was encouraged to enter federal politics. In the 1969 federal election, he easily won the rural electorate of Riverina for the Labor Party. This included the town of Griffith, which was the marijuana-growing capital of Australia and was controlled by members of the Calabrian Mafia residing in Australia.

Following Gough Whitlam's landslide victory at the 1972 'It's Time' election, Al Grassby was a natural appointment for Minister for Immigration. In his purple suits and colourful shirts and ties, Grassby became one of the highest-profile members of the Whitlam ministry. He was best known for encouraging multiculturalism through immigration from non-English-speaking countries and burying the White Australia policy. He also banned racially selected sporting teams from playing in Australia and repealed the law that required Indigenous Australians to seek permission before going overseas.

But let's not forget that he was still the Member for the Riverina. Among Al Grassby's numerous other achievements while in a position of power was to override decisions by immigration officers in Italy, allowing Mafia personnel to enter Australia. Mr Grassby also later used his influence to thwart a National Crime Authority investigation into the Mafia in Australia.

In the early to mid-1970s, Sydney was awash with good, cheap Griffith marijuana. A retail ounce of cultivated primo grass was $30, or it was $300 for a pound – 16 ounces. And there was no mistaking where it was from. Among many other names, it was known as Griffith Green or Riverina Rocket Fuel.

The Two Lives of Al Grassby

It created a new type of criminal – the 'amateur' drug dealer. Ordinary working people looking for a quick, consistent quid would buy a pound, bag it up into 16 ounce lots at $30 each and sell it for $480, making $180 on their investment. And it seemed back in those days as though there was no shortage of pounds *or* customers.

So to deny the existence of marijuana plantations in Griffith was like saying the sun wouldn't rise tomorrow. But that's exactly what Al Grassby did. Defending his constituents, especially the ones he had become openly friendly with and who had mysteriously gone from bankruptcy to Rolls-Royces and nine-bedroom palaces – or grass castles, as they became known – overnight, made Al Grassby look stupid.

Seeing an opportunity to get rid of Grassby to their own ends, the anti-immigration group the Immigration Control Association campaigned against Grassby and in the May 1974 election he was beaten by the National Party candidate John Sullivan by a handful of votes. One of the others to have campaigned against Grassby in that election was the anti-drugs campaigner and Liberal candidate Donald Mackay. It was Mackay's preferences that helped get John Sullivan over the line.

Three years later at about 6.30pm on Friday 15 July 1977, Donald Mackay left the Hotel Griffith and vanished. His bloodstained vehicle was located seven hours later in the hotel car park. Three spent .22 cartridges lay in blood on the ground nearby. It seemed that Mackay had passed on information to the Drug Squad in Sydney, which had resulted in a huge raid on a cannabis plantation on 10 November 1975 at Coleambally, where police found the largest single crop yet discovered in Australia.

The case did not come to court until 7 March 1977, when Mackay's covert role would have been revealed. Public indignation at the failure of the police to find Mackay's body led Premier Neville Wran to appoint Justice Philip Woodward royal commissioner to inquire into drug trafficking. Justice Woodward reported in 1979 that Mackay was murdered by a 'hit man' on behalf of the Griffith Mafia.

In 1980 Al Grassby was charged with criminal defamation when it was alleged that he had asked a New South Wales state politician, Michael Maher, to read in the NSW Legislative Assembly a document that imputed that Barbara Mackay and her family solicitor were responsible for the disappearance (and probable murder) of her husband Donald Mackay. Grassby maintained his innocence and fought a 12-year battle in the courts before he was eventually acquitted on appeal in August 1992. He was awarded $180,000 in costs.

In 1986 James Frederick Bazley was sentenced to life imprisonment for conspiracy to murder Mackay. Bazley had been commissioned by the Griffith Mafia. The report in 1987 of a special commission of inquiry into the police investigation of the death of Donald Bruce Mackay named police officers, politicians and 'the Honored Society' members.

Al Grassby died on 23 April 2005 aged 78, after suffering a heart attack. After Grassby's death, the media was told that the trial and libel laws had kept from the public the fact that Al Grassby had allegedly been paid $40,000 by the Griffith Calabrian Mafia to blame Mrs Mackay for her husband's death.

The Melbourne *Herald Sun* ran a series of articles alleging Gianfranco Tizzoni, a Mafia supergrass (informer), identified Grassby as being at the 'beck and call' of the Calabrian Mafia for at least 40 years and according to the National Crime Authority the Mafia funded Grassby's election campaigns.

Tizzoni also said that he had been present at a meeting in Griffith of the local Mafia with Tony Sergi, Tony Barbaro and Robert Trimbole, in which ways of getting rid of Donald Mackay were discussed. One of Al Grassby's closest associates was Tony Sergi, the man identified in court and in Parliament as the Mafia leader who ordered the execution of Donald Mackay.

But when all is said and done, Al Grassby can rest easy for eternity. For all of the allegations, no one ever laid a glove on him. He had two terrific send-offs after he died – one from Ellnor, his wife of 43 years, in Canberra and another a week later from Angela Chan, his girlfriend of 25 years in Sydney.

The Two Lives of Al Grassby

And although it will forever be controversial, his $72,000 statue with his arms outstretched as if welcoming newcomers to our country was placed *inside* the Multicultural Centre, well away from the pigeons.

32 | THE PERILS OF PAULINE HANSON

She may be best known these days as a contestant on *Dancing with the Stars* or the Australian version of reality TV show *Celebrity Apprentice*, but in the mid-1990s Pauline Hanson held the title of the most polarising politician in Australia, both revered and reviled for her opinions.

It was 1995 – the year the Oklahoma City bombing in the US killed 168 people, the year the DVD format of information storage was announced, and the year OJ Simpson was found not guilty of double murder – when Queensland fish and chip shop owner Pauline Hanson narrowly lost her seat as an independent on the Council of the City of Ipswich, about 40 minutes' drive west of Brisbane.

At that stage of her life, the independently wealthy 41-year-old had been married twice and had four children. Popular among her local community, Hanson joined the Liberal Party of Australia and was endorsed as their candidate in the Ipswich-based federal seat of Oxley. At that time, Oxley was a blue-ribbon Labor seat with a 12.6 per cent majority, making it the party's safest seat in Queensland. Political pundits believed Hanson was on a hiding to nothing.

But this was a woman blessed with natural charm and enthusiasm. She was a force to be reckoned with, always available to the press for interviews – when not out talking to regular Aussies on the street or taking her word to them with a door-knocking initiative, of course.

Despite taking a personal approach to politics, it was one interview that the *Queensland Times* conducted with Hanson that set her on the path to the infamy that would eventually see her sent to prison. In the interview, Hanson told the journalist that she believed the government should abolish aid to Aborigines above what was available to other Australian citizens. The Liberals couldn't believe one of their candidates would make such an inflammatory remark in a public forum. They disendorsed Pauline Hanson immediately – but they were too late.

It turned out that the Australian Electoral Commission had closed nominations. The ballot papers listing Hanson as the Liberal Party's candidate had already been printed. When it was time for voters to hit the polls, Hanson was set as the Liberal candidate. Not that it really mattered – everyone knew she didn't have a hope in hell of winning the staunchly Labor seat.

But Labor's credibility with the constituents of Oxley had been sliding downhill for a while, and they finally decided enough was enough. They obviously appreciated Hanson's rhetoric and proved it by voting her in with an astonishing 19.3 per cent swing. No one could believe it – least of all the Liberals, who Hanson was quick to tell where to go and what to do with their party. She entered Parliament as an independent while being labelled a racist.

When Hanson made her opening speech at 5.15pm in Canberra's Parliament House on Tuesday 10 September 1996, it was to a near-empty chamber – but still, she didn't hold back, and her message came through loud and clear. The headlines in the newspapers the next day were all about the fiery redhead's call for Australia's Asian immigration policy to be reviewed and multiculturalism to be abolished.

If that wasn't enough to ensure her instant notoriety around the country, she also called for the reintroduction of compulsory national service for all 18-year-olds, and asked for a review of Australia's membership of the United Nations. She said the government should end foreign aid and spend the money back home, as well as claiming that the government was providing far more money, real estate and opportunities to Aborigines than to tax-paying white Australians. It's no wonder she caused such a stir.

While Hanson airing her views on public record was a breath of fresh air for those who supported her beliefs but had kept their opinions to themselves for years in fear they would be branded as racist, the woman herself was quick to strongly deny that she was being racist. Instead, she insisted, she was merely being realistic. Pauline Hanson believed she was simply stating the facts.

Of course, everybody has their own opinion on Hanson's opening speech – and it definitely polarised the country. Though if you were to go through the hundreds of phone calls and faxes that arrived at her office, or you listened to talkback radio as thousands called in, jamming the switchboards, there were a hell of a lot of people who agreed with her. Pauline Hanson looked like becoming a political juggernaut.

One of the reasons for Hanson's growing popularity was her ability to stand by her beliefs, no matter who she was pitted against – and, thanks to her extreme stance, there was no end of opponents seeking to take her on. Minority groups, politicians, Aboriginal and Asian leaders, and all manner of general do-gooders tended to come off second best against her basic, unswerving redneck logic.

One televised debate between Hanson and Aboriginal leader Charles Perkins – known as a persuasive speaker – saw the studio audience of around 100 average Australians vote 97 per cent to three per cent in favour of Hanson.

After a while, it felt like barely a day went by that some newspaper or current affairs program didn't run a poll – and they generally showed that two-thirds of average Australians agreed that immigration had gone way too far. It seemed the consensus was that migrants took jobs away from honest, hardworking Australians.

Of course, not everyone was on Team Hanson – far from it. With the death threats growing more regular, she simply changed her address. Indeed, the one person who seemed to have little to say about Australia's most controversial new politician and her controversial ideas was John Howard. The country's Asian newspapers were quick to point out the Prime Minister's indifference to Hanson's criticism of Asian immigration. They openly questioned why he hadn't taken a public stand against Hanson's opinions. The nation's leader would only say that, while he didn't necessarily agree with what she said, he believed that if he was to speak out it would only cause further controversy, which would in turn just bring more media attention in her support.

The fact was, John Howard didn't need to do anything to turn the spotlight on Pauline Hanson – she was just fine doing what she was doing. And what she was doing in April 1997 was forming her own political party, One Nation, with senior adviser David Oldfield and professional fundraiser David Ettridge. Early polls indicated that One Nation had a massive nine per cent of the primary vote, though that pulled back to just above five per cent by September.

Still, support for One Nation was going strong when the Queensland election came around in June 1998. Premier Peter Beattie's Labor Government may have won by 12 seats, but One Nation secured 22.7 per cent of first preference votes, which landed them 11 seats and put them in second place for another 27. It was a more than impressive debut in the political arena for the fledgling party.

Four months later, it was time for the 1998 federal election. John Howard, of course, came out on top, though One Nation polled a massive 8.43 per cent for almost one million votes.

The Perils of Pauline Hanson

Despite that respectable showing, though, they failed to secure a single seat. Even more of a blow was the fact that Hanson – who had been billing herself as 'The Mother of the Nation' throughout the campaign – lost her seat of Oxley. The only thing One Nation had to cheer about in the wash-up was a single seat in the Senate.

When Hanson missed out on a seat in the Queensland Senate at the next federal election on 10 November 2001, she blamed her declining popularity on John Howard, insisting that he stole her policies. Having heard that, many of her now ex-supporters believed that her next career could be in stand-up comedy.

One Nation was up against the wall in the 2001 Queensland election as well, losing eight of its 11 seats. Hanson moved from her beloved Queensland in 2003, relocating to Sydney to have a shot at the NSW Upper House in the election. She lost by just a small margin to John Tingle of the Shooters Party. But 2003 had even worse news in store for Hanson.

On 20 August, Pauline Hanson and David Ettridge were convicted of electoral fraud in Queensland's District Court. They each received three-year sentences for falsely claiming that 500 members of the Pauline Hanson Support Movement were actually signed up to the political organisation Pauline Hanson's One Nation. The ruse was done so they could get registered as a political party in Queensland and thus apply for electoral funding.

Because of the charge, the registration was deemed unlawful. That put a serious question mark over the $498,637 of funding Hanson had received. As a result, she received two further convictions for dishonestly obtaining property. She was given a further two three-year sentences, though these would run concurrently with her first sentence.

'Rubbish, I'm not guilty,' Hanson responded, adding, 'It's a joke.'

Despite her protests, the former fish and chip shop owner was soon sitting in a maximum-security cell. Not that she had too much time to get used to prison life. Both Hanson and Ettridge

159

had their convictions quashed on appeal. They were released in November 2003, after serving just 11 weeks.

In 2007, the *Bulletin* magazine named Pauline Hanson one of the 100 most influential Australians of all time. That once revered bastion of news reporting – founded in 1880 – folded the following year, three years before Hanson's stint on *Celebrity Apprentice*.

Perhaps Pauline Hanson is getting the last laugh, even if it's not for her political views.

33 | THE SHOOTOUT AT DANGAR PLACE: WHEN DETECTIVE ROGER ROGERSON MET WARREN LANFRANCHI

It was long odds that Warren Lanfranchi was ever going to get the old age pension or collect superannuation. Lanfranchi was a bank robber, a heroin dealer who ripped off other heroin dealers, a standover thug and a man who tried to murder a police officer in cold blood. At just 23 he was well past his use-by date.

Tall, fair-haired and ruggedly built, Lanfranchi was raised in a decent Sydney family and there doesn't appear to be any valid reason why he went off the rails other than the attraction of the big money and the glamour of being a gangster. At age 17, Lanfranchi was sentenced to five years in Long Bay Gaol for his part in stealing a truckload of TV sets. It was here that he met the notorious gangster Neddy Smith and when he was released Lanfranchi became a distributor for Smith, whose couriers were bringing in huge amounts of heroin from Thailand.

Not content making a fortune from cutting Smith's high-grade heroin and selling it on at a huge profit, Lanfranchi began 'ripping off' other dealers. It worked like this: a deal was made with another supplier to buy a few kilos of heroin, a meeting place was arranged and both parties would turn up and make an exchange at a pre-arranged price. Once he had seen the heroin, Lanfranchi took it at gunpoint and left without paying.

In his last 'rip-off' Lanfranchi had bundled the sellers into the boot of their car, locked it and made off with $37,000 worth of heroin, which is about $250,000 in today's money. Soon after, Lanfranchi received a phone call from Neddy Smith telling him that the heroin was the property of a high-ranking police officer who had stolen it during a raid and had given it to his underworld contacts to sell on his behalf. He wanted it back. Problem was that Lanfranchi had already sold it.

In the meantime, Lanfranchi took up robbing banks. As he was sitting in the back seat of the getaway car speeding from a bank in Drummoyne with a bag full of cash from his fifth armed hold-up, a motorcycle cop drew alongside and demanded they pull over. Lanfranchi levelled his pistol at the police officer at point-blank range and pulled the trigger twice, but the gun jammed both times. The luckiest policeman on earth, Constable Ray Walker, later identified Lanfranchi from a photograph. Above all, police take grave umbrage at someone attempting to kill one of their own. Warren Lanfranchi had made a monumental mistake.

With Lanfranchi nowhere to be found, Sydney's toughest detective, Roger Rogerson, called in a favour with his old underworld informant, Neddy Smith, Lanfranchi's boss in the heroin business. Rogerson told Neddy to tell Lanfranchi that he wanted to have a chat and work out a deal that would be beneficial to them both. Having blind faith in Neddy Smith and aware of Smith's close relationship with influential police officers, Lanfranchi fell for it. His impression of coming events was that he was wanted for ripping off drug dealers and bank robberies and that $50,000 would make it all go away. But he had to talk to Roger Rogerson first to set it up.

For their meeting, Lanfranchi chose a narrow lane called Dangar Place near busy Cleveland Street in Chippendale, about five minutes' drive from the heart of Sydney. It would be easy to

The Shootout at Dangar Place

see if there were other police around, and there were plenty of ways out if anything went wrong. Lanfranchi had been instructed to come unarmed and not wear a coat. Rogerson would be alone and unarmed.

As Smith drove Lanfranchi to the meeting in a green BMW, 18 detectives were being deployed around Chippendale. At Rogerson's back were sergeants Graham Frazer and Brian Harding and Constable Rod Moore. Frazer, armed with a shotgun, was hidden in the back of Rogerson's green Falcon; Harding, also armed with a shotgun, was hidden in the back of Moore's old white Volvo nearby. Rogerson had a .38 revolver tucked in the back of his trousers under his cardigan.

About 2.50pm on Saturday 27 June 1981, Neddy parked in Boundary Street near the Britannia Hotel, and they got out. Lanfranchi saw Rogerson sitting on a green Falcon at the entrance to Dangar Place, about 40 paces away, and raised his arms, as though to suggest he was not carrying a gun. Lanfranchi crossed Cleveland Street and walked along Beaumont Street to meet Rogerson. Graham Frazer got out of the car and crouched at its rear with his shotgun. Neddy Smith retreated to the BMW.

The two men met about halfway between Cleveland Street and Dangar Place. According to Rogerson, Lanfranchi said: 'What's the score? Are we going to be friends or not?' Rogerson turned, and the two men walked together, with Lanfranchi on the right. They turned right into Dangar Place and walked past the Falcon. Lanfranchi didn't notice the crouched figure of Sergeant Frazer, clutching his shotgun, at the rear of the car. Nor did he seem to notice the white Volvo, with Constable Moore at the wheel, rolling slowly down Dangar Place from the other end.

Walking together in silence for about 30 seconds, Lanfranchi and Rogerson got to a point about 10 or 15 metres into Dangar Place. According to Rogerson, Lanfranchi said, 'I can't do any more jail. Are we going to do business?'

'There is no business,' Rogerson replied. 'We are here to arrest you.'

163

Lanfranchi spotted Graham Frazer and then Brian Harding, who was now sitting up in the back seat of the Volvo. 'You tricked me!' Lanfranchi said. 'This is an ambush!' He backed away a little from Rogerson as Rod Moore stopped the Volvo about 10 metres away and he and Harding got out. All four police present agreed later that Lanfranchi reached down the front of his trousers and drew out a silver-coloured gun, which he held in his right hand and pointed at Rogerson.

Rogerson drew his .38 revolver and fired two shots, both from about 4 feet. The fatal shot went through the right ventricle of Lanfranchi's heart and came out his back, killing him instantly. The other shot went into his neck below his left ear. All the detectives present agreed that Rogerson's first shot to the chest was the fatal one. Lanfranchi did not fire any shots. Later it was discovered that there were no fingerprints on his gun, which turned out to be defective in a way that made it impossible to fire more than one shot.

There was no formal police investigation of the killing; an inquest was held in front of a judge and jury. The judge explained that it was the jury's function to find, on the balance of probabilities rather than beyond a reasonable doubt, on the cause and manner of Lanfranchi's death. The judge supplied them with a number of options from which to choose. He also advised them that they could, if they chose, recommend commendations for bravery on the part of the police.

The jury concluded that Roger Rogerson had shot and killed Warren Lanfranchi 'while endeavouring to effect an arrest'. The jury had struck out the options of 'in self defence' and 'in the execution of his duty'. The jury did not recommend commendations for bravery for the police. Case closed.

34 | NOT A GOOD TIME TO BE NAMED JODIE: THE CRIMES OF JODIE HARRIS

It takes a certain level of guts, rat cunning and steely determination to pull a significant con job – let alone a few hundred of them, which included breaching a high-security police station with the sole intention of stealing official equipment so that you can pass yourself off as an officer of the law. But to do it all while still using your own first name requires confidence, brazen attitude and, some would say, being just plain crazy.

But that's exactly what attractive Queensland brunette Jodie Harris did through the late 1990s and up to the mid-2000s, when authorities finally caught up with her.

Often likened in the press during her three-state crime spree to Frank Abagnale Jr – the multitalented US con artist portrayed by Leonardo diCaprio that the film *Catch Me If You Can* was based on – Jodie had no problem passing herself off as a doctor or psychologist, flight attendant or rich business owner, or, her favourite, a policewoman.

It's safe to say that Jodie gave her own name a very bad name, even though she teamed it with a variety of surnames, including Harding, Pearson-Harding and Kilroy. There was even a point where it got so tricky for her fellow Jodies that an innocent woman found herself being hauled off an interstate flight and questioned by police just because her parents had decided Jodie was a nice name to christen her.

But that all happened when Jodie Harris was at the height of her infamy, living in luxury, a far cry from the situation in which she came into the world. Jodie's mother fell pregnant with her in 1978, at the age of 16, and wound up in Brisbane's notoriously rough Boggo Road prison when she was 17. It seemed the die was cast for Jodie from day one.

The future con artist had a fascination with police from a very early age. Indeed, it was this obsession that would eventually end her criminal career. Of course, she had no way of knowing that when she started a relationship with an officer of the law while still in her teens. That affair came to a sticky end when the pair were investigated for insurance fraud when Jodie was just 17.

She had been driving her older lover's car without a licence and crashed it. To keep herself out of trouble, she lied and said the boyfriend had been behind the wheel. When it looked like the real story was about to come out, landing both of them in trouble, the boyfriend decided it was time to remove himself from the situation. He fled overseas, but it was just the beginning of a life of sneaky crime for Jodie whoever-she-chose-to-be-at-the-time.

All those who knew her maintain that Jodie is a friendly woman – intelligent, with a strong way with words. Those are exactly the sorts of attributes that work well in the deceitful world of the con artist. Jodie was adept at getting people to like her; it was a skill that let her manipulate people seemingly at will. Her method was fairly basic – befriend a woman, steal any identification from her that she could, preferably a driver's licence, assume her identity, then pilfer as much as possible from her bank accounts. Then move on to her next victim.

Not a Good Time to be Named Jodie

As a result, Jodie soon became accustomed to a luxury lifestyle. If she was drinking, it would be the finest French champagne on the menu of the best restaurant she could find. Her hotels were five-star all the way. She draped herself in designer clothes, offset with the sort of jewellery most women only dream of.

When she decided she wanted a canine companion to suit her image, Jodie was obviously not going to settle for a simple chihuahua from a pet shop – she paid $1500 for a designer bichoodle. And of course, her Bichon Frise/poodle cross had to look good alongside its affluent owner, so Jodie decked the dog out in a diamanté collar and cashmere coat.

Obviously a life of such extravagance can't be maintained without regular financial incomings to match the excessive outgoings, so whenever her funds started bottoming out, Jodie would simply find herself a new victim and set herself up again.

One story goes that, while posing as a rich businesswoman in Victoria, Jodie stepped into a high-end boutique to indulge her passion for designer outfits. She endeared herself to the owner of the shop and took her out for coffee. While enjoying their lattes, Jodie distracted the storeowner long enough to pocket the licence from the wallet the woman had left on the table. Before long, Jodie had gone to the woman's bank and convinced them to let her withdraw $50,000. The boutique owner quickly realised that something was amiss and had her account frozen. No problem, though – Jodie simply rang the bank and explained that she wanted the account reinstated. She then pilfered some more cash and set about finding her next victim.

The constant nature of her one-woman crime wave was bound to draw attention, which meant that by late 2005 – at the peak of her run – it seemed that there was a media report about a con by a woman named Jodie – or a slight variation of it – almost every other day.

One of those stories was about a lady who had fallen over on the street. By a fortunate fluke for her, Jodie saw what had happened and took charge before any other bystanders really knew what had happened. She told everyone that, being a doctor, she was qualified to handle the situation. The kindly doctor Jodie then helped the flustered woman to her car and drove her to the nearest hospital. During the journey to seek medical assistance, Dr Jodie helped herself to the woman's driver's licence – and after she had seen the lady safe at the hospital she helped herself to $20,000 out of the woman's bank account.

But such opportunities didn't land in Jodie's quick-thinking lap every day, so sometimes she'd have to go out and create her own lucrative situation. More often than not, that involved hopping on a domestic flight and keeping an eye out for an easy mark. Once, on a flight from Melbourne to Brisbane, Jodie convinced the woman in the seat next to her that she was a qualified psychologist. After all, if you can't trust a psychologist, who can you trust? With her guard down, it was no effort at all for Jodie to snatch her driver's licence from her bag. Back on the ground and straight on the phone to her victim's bank, Jodie was soon $22,000 richer for less than a day's work – if you could call it that.

But all the tales of fast cash grabs pale in comparison to Jodie's most daring exploit – when she was just 20 years old and using the surname Pearson-Harding. In 1998, the young woman obtained a rental car that looked as much like a regular police vehicle as she could find.

Her aim was to gain access to the high-tech Brisbane Police Headquarters. It turned out their expensive security system wasn't all it was cracked up to be. Jodie breached security there, gaining access right through the electronic gates, four times in one month, procuring a new part of a uniform from the storeroom each time. Before long she had a complete outfit, including the badge.

Resplendent in her new outfit, Jodie moved south, where she set about convincing members of the Victorian police force that she had skills as an undercover drug ring infiltrator. With no real reason to believe anyone – especially someone with a police badge and uniform – would lie about such matters it was only a matter of time before she was enjoying the thrill of tagging along on drug busts, without having to go through all that

Not a Good Time to be Named Jodie

time-consuming training and working your way up the ranks of the police force.

It was around this time, as well, that the attractive young woman is alleged to have had affairs with several police officers, one of which would bring about an end to her criminal career.

With 100 or more Jodie frauds between October 2005 and June 2006 in New South Wales alone, her name, or variations thereof, spread through the Australian business community like a coastal bushfire fanned by a southerly. It was only a matter of time before police got a break. It came from a property leasing company on Sydney's upmarket lower North Shore. A woman fitting Jodie's description had tried to rent a property. When asked by staff to photocopy her references and documents relating to her previous renting history, the woman grew agitated and left as quickly as she could.

Now that they knew where she was, the authorities tapped into the mobile phone belonging to her fiancé – Andrew Twining of the Victorian police force. They got a line on her, and Jodie was soon arrested in the inner-city suburb of Ultimo.

Twining was also arrested, but was later released without charge. There is speculation that he helped his peers in the police force set up his fiancée, but that has never been confirmed. All that is known is that he was soon suspended indefinitely – on full pay.

A search of Jodie's apartment yielded more than 100 items of identification, including driver's licences, passports and credit, Medicare and SIM cards. They also found 10 wigs.

Pleading guilty to 43 of 124 charges of fraud and larceny in Sydney's Central Local Court in September 2006, Jodie was sent to jail for a minimum of three and a half years, and received a fine of $175,000. But that was nowhere near the end of the matter. On 19 December 2008, a Victorian court imposed a new sentence of five years and nine months with a minimum of four years and three months in respect to both the New South Wales and Victorian offences.

When Jodie eventually walks free in Victoria she should enjoy a few minutes of fresh air before the Queensland detectives

The Australian Crime File 3

waiting at the gates whisk her home to no doubt face another slew of charges.

Despite all this, Jodie has been angling for early release by offering to help the federal police to catch other con artists. Maybe she wants to be like the man the press compare her with, Frank Abagnale Jr, who after serving his time in jail continues to advise the FBI in fraud-related matters.

Or maybe she just hopes she can get a nice uniform out of the deal . . .

35 | DOUBLE JEOPARDY JUSTICE: AT LAST A MURDERER IS TRIED TWICE

In Britain in September 2006, a mother, Ann Ming, who helped change British law, finally won justice for her murdered daughter at the Old Bailey, as her daughter's killer, William (Billy) Dunlop became the first person in almost 800 years to be tried twice for the same crime. With her husband Charlie, Mrs Ming had waged a tireless 17-year campaign after their daughter, Julie Hogg, was strangled and mutilated by the violent drunk Dunlop.

In 1989 Dunlop was charged with the murder of the 22-year-old mother of one, but was formally acquitted and freed after two juries failed to reach a verdict in 1991. Under the 'double jeopardy' laws of the time Dunlop could not be tried twice, even though he smugly later confessed to the killing in the belief that he could never be found guilty of her murder. The double jeopardy rule dated back to the Magna Carta, which was drawn up in 1215, and was meant to protect the public against malicious and vindictive prosecution. While supporters argued that the principle was an important democratic safeguard, others claimed it sometimes protected the guilty.

Julie's tormented mother refused to let Dunlop get away with murder and doggedly fought for a change in the law. She lobbied successive Home Secretaries and argued her case before Attorney-General Lord Goldsmith. Changes to the law were proposed in 1993 and were backed by a committee of MPs in 2001. The principle was abolished in the Criminal Justice Act in 2003 and came into force in April 2005. Under the Act, the Court of Appeal has the power to quash an acquittal and order a retrial where there is 'new and compelling evidence'. The new and compelling evidence in the Dunlop case was his blatant confession to Julie's murder years later. The 43-year-old Dunlop became the first defendant to be tried under the new system.

Julie vanished from her home on 16 November 1989, and despite an extensive police hunt and week-long search of her home her body was not found. It was her mother who eventually discovered the decomposing remains in her daughter's home 80 days later. Recalling the horrific discovery, Mrs Ming said:

> I went to the bathroom. I was a theatre sister for years so I recognised the smell of death. I accidentally knocked the bath panel and it fell away. I looked down to find Julie's naked body wrapped in a blanket. Even though it was badly decomposing, it was clear that she had been sexually assaulted and her body mutilated.

Police questioned 21 men who knew Julie but Dunlop was quickly identified as the chief suspect. His DNA profile matched that found in her home. Her keys, with his fingerprints, were found under floorboards at his nearby lodging house. Dunlop was charged with murder and his May 1991 trial at Teesside Crown Court was told he had murdered Julie in a frenzy after she spurned his sexual advances.

But the jury failed to reach a verdict and he was discharged. At a retrial in October of the same year, a second jury also

Double Jeopardy Justice

failed to agree on a verdict. Mr Justice Ognall brought in a formal not guilty verdict and Dunlop, then 28, walked free. The main factor in the jury's division – despite the seemingly overwhelming circumstantial evidence – was that the exact cause of Julie's death could not be established because her body was so decomposed.

Afterwards, Dunlop protested that police should 'find the real killer' and even consulted a lawyer with a view to getting compensation for the 20 months he had spent in jail awaiting trial. Under the existing double jeopardy rule, Dunlop knew he could not be tried again. But he did not reckon on the iron will of Mrs Ming, who, with her husband Charlie, a retired Middlesbrough heavy goods fitter, campaigned relentlessly for the law to be changed.

In the meantime, Billy Dunlop's violent ways continued. In one attack he bashed a former girlfriend with a baseball bat and in 1997 was jailed for six years for assault. Though it was unrelated to Julie's case, the Mings made it their business to attend his every court appearance.

It was while in jail in 1999 that Dunlop slipped up, cynically boasting to a female prison officer he had indeed murdered Julie. His confession to Julie's murder, and that he had lied on oath at his murder trial, led to him being charged with perjury, and in April 2000 he had six years added to his assault jail term. But under the double jeopardy rule it looked as though he could never be convicted of murder.

Mrs Ming was eventually awarded £20,000 ($A50,000) in an out-of-court settlement against the police over their handling of the case, but it was bringing her daughter's killer to justice that preoccupied her most. After years of lobbying for the law to be changed, on 7 September 2006, Ann Ming finally saw her daughter's killer brought to justice.

In a tense 10-minute hearing, the stocky, ponytailed Dunlop pleaded guilty to Julie's murder. Mrs Ming clenched a fist, then wept as Dunlop uttered the word 'guilty'. After Dunlop was found guilty, detectives released the extract of the transcript of his police interview in 1999 in which, for the first time, he gave the gruesome details of the night Julie died, in the belief that he couldn't be tried again.

On 15 November 1989, Dunlop, a labourer who lived a few hundred yards from Julie and had had a brief relationship with her, called at her house in Billingham, near Stockton-on-Tees, at 2am, drunk and in a 'sexual frenzy'. He became infuriated when Julie, a pizza delivery girl who was separated from her husband and lived with her three-year-old son, poked fun at an injury Dunlop had sustained in a rugby club fight.

'I just lost it and got up and strangled her, with my hands,' Dunlop told detectives. Panicking, he realised Julie was dead because she had 'turned blue' and was lying in the living room very still. Dunlop said he stripped them both naked, claiming he was trying to avoid police obtaining forensic evidence from their clothes, and tried to carry the lifeless Julie up into the loft. But she was too heavy and he dropped her so he opened a panel behind the bath in the bathroom and forced her body inside.

Outside court, flanked by police and her 81-year-old husband, Mrs Ming described Dunlop as 'pure evil' and said, 'I knew Dunlop was responsible and Charlie and I were determined not to rest until he had been brought to justice.

'We made a promise to ourselves that Julie's killer would be punished. He has done everything he could to avoid justice, but his lying and scheming has eventually all been in vain.'

Billy Dunlop received an automatic life sentence and the judge set a 17-year non-parole period – which ironically, was exactly the same period it took to finally bring Julie's killer to justice.

36 | BORN TO STEAL: THE FACTS BEHIND THE AUSTRALIAN SHOPLIFTING INDUSTRY

His Honour had seen it all before. But while he could express no emotion at the sideshow before him, he had to concede that it was one of the best acts in town. And to the uninitiated, it was certainly convincing.

'Hydraulics' (they reckon he could lift anything) was doing his thing. Old Hydro was no stranger to the courts. Horses had won Melbourne Cups with less form than the old shoplifter. He had been lifting gear and getting pinched for it since 1955. He always maintained that he was in the iron and steel business: he said that his missus did the ironing and he did the stealing.

'I'm an old-aged pensioner, totally illiterate and almost blind,' the ageing conman pleaded to the magistrate, producing his pensioner's bus and rail card. 'I only took a couple of things to sell so I could feed myself and my sick wife. Give me a break, your Honour.'

The beak looked over his bifocals at the prisoner in his well-prepared court outfit – a ragged suit peppered with cigarette burns, crumpled shirt and unshined shoes without laces. He wasn't convinced. But he had to agree that Hydraulics certainly looked the part, though it in no way resembled the outfit he'd been wearing when he was nicked. The magistrate inquired:

> *If you have fallen on such hard times, then what were you doing in the possession of 10 Giorgio Armani suits, four Ermenegildo Zegna jackets, eight pairs of handmade Bally shoes and 30 Christian Dior silk ties when you were arrested?*
>
> *And I'm led to believe that you were wearing an outfit comprising of some of these expensive garments plus a bowler hat, a carnation in your lapel and you were carrying a gold-tipped cane. That's hardly the attire of a poor old pensioner.*

Amid protests that he was minding the gear for someone else and couldn't read the labels, Hydro was taken away for yet another lagging. He would be out in a few months and straight back on the job. It was all part of what Hydraulics did for a living and he accepted jail as part of his livelihood.

He was one of many members of an organised shoplifting gang that specialised in stealing only the best brand names, pooled and fenced their booty and split the profits. His associates would look after his family while he was inside, just like Workers Compensation.

But while these farces go on in the courts around the country daily, retailers are finding it less and less amusing as their profits dwindle because of an industry that now has a turnover in the vicinity of billions of dollars a year. And no matter what device the retailers come up with to discourage them, the thieves always seem to be one step ahead.

And there would appear to be no end to the folks who buy the hot gear. It is almost as though it's every Australian's God-given right to buy something that 'fell off the back of a truck'. And if you know where to look, like the local pub or club, there's always something on offer. The general public's willingness to buy hot goods is the lifeblood of the shoplifter.

One inner-city Sydney hotel had become so notorious for its clientele buying and selling hot goods that the cops warned the publican that if he didn't put a stop to it, they would close him down. At one stage it was almost impossible to get into the toilet for the guys in there trying on gear.

NSW Bureau of Crime Statistics show that by far the biggest losers are the department stores, with more than 29 per cent of the annual turnover of convicted shoplifters coming from their shelves. Next are service stations, with 11.2 per cent, and supermarkets, with 10.1 per cent.

Other regularly targeted businesses include clothing stores, milk bars, newsagents, bookshops, chemists, DVD hire outlets, laptop computer shops, hardware shops, jewellery shops and sex shops. Of the 2736 convictions of adults for larceny by shop stealing, from the most recent figures available, only 180 of them were sent to prison, while the rest were either fined (1536), granted recognisance without supervision or conviction (434), granted recognisance with supervision, periodic detention or community service order (146) or received no recorded conviction (250).

Curiously enough, the lowest of these figures is that of imprisonment – this gives a pretty fair indication of what the law seems to think of the great old Australian pastime of shoplifting.

Australians have the dubious reputation of being the best shoplifters in the world. This stems from the halcyon days of the early 1960s, when the notorious 'Kangaroo Gang' took to London like a plague of locusts and cleaned out the shelves and clothing racks of Harrods, Fortnum and Mason, Austin Reeds, Selfridges and the House of Dunhill for almost every bit of clothing and jewellery that they had. The gang consisted of about 20 Australians, most of whom had skipped bail back home, usually for shoplifting, and were lying low in the Bayswater district of London in places like the Court Club in Inverness Terrace.

A member of the gang described London in the early 1960s as an Aladdin's cave full of shops just waiting to be robbed. He says that the Poms were so naive to theft in those days that he went to Sotheby's prior to a jewellery auction to have a look at what there was to pilfer. As he was browsing, one of the ushers handed him a five-carat diamond ring to examine and walked on. He slipped it into his pocket and walked out. It was as simple as that.

From then on, Sotheby's became a prime target for jewellery. The gang's favourite method of shoplifting was called 'head pulling', where a female accomplice with large breasts would go in first and distract the male attendant while the gang moved in and nicked what they could from the display cabinets.

But it was the huge department store Harrods that copped the biggest hiding. The 'shoppies' used to run competitions and bet on who could get the most full-length cashmere coats out in one day. The winner got out eight in as many trips, at 200 quid a coat. All of the gear was fenced through the local cockney lads.

The Aussie shoppies ate in the best restaurants, drank the finest wines, had the best tables at the nightclubs and, naturally, wore the best clothes. Tales of the Kangaroo Gang are legend. Old timers will tell you that they got away with it because they were so brazen and willing to try anything, like stealing the up-market and rare animals that were for sale at the pet shop in Harrods. French poodles and chihuahuas were easy to pinch, as they would snuggle up under the shoppie's coat and avoid detection.

But the classic of them all would have to be the day they nicked the chimpanzee. An ex-army colonel had a private zoo in Sussex and he badly wanted a chimp but didn't want to pay the outrageous price that Harrods was asking. So he called in the shoppies. But how do you get a baby chimpanzee out of a department store without anyone noticing?

Simple. The same way you would get an ordinary baby out. In a pram. With a 'nanny' at the wheel, they opened the cage, slipped the chimp out, wrapped it in a shawl, stuck a bottle in its gob, put it in the pram and wheeled it out the front door.

Born to Steal

The little old ladies in the lift on the way down couldn't help but wonder if the beautiful little baby they admired in the pram was either a West Indian kid or a white one with whiskers and a suntan.

By 1970 no one with an Aussie accent could get into a department store (or any store for that matter) in London, so the rort came to an end. To the dismay of retailers in Australia, there was an influx of the best shoplifters in the world returning home. It was back to business as usual and that's the way it's been ever since.

But apart from the organised gangs, it seems that the most common reason for shoplifting is good old-fashioned greed. 'It's something that's been around forever,' said a store detective who preferred not to be named. 'Kids from wealthy homes do it, so do mothers and fathers, poor folk and rich, old and young, country and city folk. Everyone seems to have shoplifted something at least once in their lives. Outside of the pros it's like one big national pastime and the retailer is the loser.'

According to the NSW Bureau of Crime Statistics and Research, only about one in 50 shoplifters are ever detected and even fewer are brought to the attention of the police. The reasons for this include fear of litigation for false arrest, bad publicity, losses associated with the removal of staff from the shop floor to deal with shoplifters, and subsequent proceedings and dissatisfaction with the manner in which courts deal with the offenders.

Based on Victorian findings, less than a third of detected shoplifters are referred to the police by retailers. Instead, retailers deal with thieves directly by demanding payment for goods, banning them from the shop, notifying parents or taking no action whatsoever.

Most of the professionals in Sydney and Melbourne work in gangs, usually about four to a team. While the big department stores are their bread and butter, they are now targeting more of the specialised clothing and electrical stores and pinching only the top-brand gear like Reebok, Toshiba, Gucci and YSL. They have found over the years that the top clobber moves quicker, and, at only a third of the ticketed price, it's the best bargain a punter will ever get.

The professional shoplifters take their livelihood seriously and actually pay tax as a self-employed 'whatever' to avoid an unpleasant confrontation should they have to explain their income down the track. Most enjoy 'non-working' holidays just like the rest of us, and they often take the family away from it all for a couple of weeks.

The female professional shoplifters are always well groomed and the men look like company directors. One notorious elderly shoplifter made a practice of fleecing a huge department store in the heart of Sydney so often that the unsuspecting staff got to know him and chat with him. As he was always immaculately groomed in three-piece suits and did actually buy things from time to time, he was able to pass himself off as a retired doctor who was lonely and was looking for something to do.

After some time, the staff convinced him that he would make the perfect store detective. So he applied for the job and got it, more on the staff's say-so than his fabricated credentials. It was like letting Jack the Ripper loose in the Touch of Class. It took the store about three months to realise that most of their gear was disappearing from under their noses. By then, the 'doctor' and his associates had taken off, along with a hefty amount of very expensive merchandise.

The better individual shoplifters make up to $1000 a day, as they are a lot more selective than your average shoppie. These are the cream of the shoppies, who will steal on order. Their clients pick out an item that they like – a cashmere cardigan, Louis Feraud suit or designer-label jacket – and tell the shoppie where it is, and the shoppie goes and steals it for them.

This usually costs about 30 per cent of the ticketed price, so it is one hell of a saving on a suit that costs $2000. These more exclusive shoppies will often employ a 'casual' as a deterrent and pay him or her a daily wage, the same as a restaurant would pay a casual waitress.

An oft-told story is about the guy who was whining down at the pub that he had found the right Christening dress for his tiny daughter, but the shop wanted a staggering $1200 for it. One of the shoppies was back in 10 minutes with the dress down the front of his pants for a third of the ticket price.

Some stores will go to any lengths to deter the shoppies. Like the manager of the big department store in Sydney's Bondi Junction, who was so sick of being ripped off that he had a life-sized cardboard cut-out cop erected in the store. When the pilfering persisted, he decided that the cop wasn't aggressive enough so he had another made a foot taller, and this time with a giant scowl on its face.

Someone stole it.

37 | FINAL JUSTICE FOR MERSINA HALVAGIS: SERIAL KILLER PETER DUPAS GETS HIS JUST DESSERTS

In November 2010, there was a favourable conclusion to a development in one of the highest-profile murder cases in Australia's history.

But let's start from the beginning.

It's a strange irony that one of Melbourne's one-time hotshot defence lawyers would be the undoing of one of Australia's most evil killers. There was a time when Andrew Fraser would defend the likes of Peter Norris Dupas. But if it wasn't for Fraser's testimony in the Melbourne Supreme Court at Dupas' murder retrial, police admit that Dupas could never have been found guilty of one of Victoria's most enduring murder mysteries. Without Andrew Fraser's evidence police had no forensic evidence, no eyewitnesses, no confession and no case, even though they knew Dupas was their man due to a mountain of circumstantial evidence.

There was a time when Andrew Fraser was the Johnny Cochrane – that's *the* Johnny Cochrane, who defended OJ

183

Simpson – of the Melbourne courts. His clients included underworld hitmen, disgraced sporting stars, alleged cop-killers and drug dealers. Anyone who had a profile, a lot of money and a problem with the law wound up on Andrew Fraser's doorstep. And they got their two bob's worth. Fraser was notoriously ruthless and would stop at nothing to get his clients the best deal. And in doing so he made a million enemies in the courts and throughout the police force. So when Andrew Fraser fell from his five-star perch and crashed and burned in the worst possible way, there were very few tears.

Seems as though apart from the mansion and Mercedes-Benzs, Fraser was sticking about a grand's worth of cocaine up his nose every day. Apparently he started out having a social snort 10 years earlier, got the taste and eventually couldn't wait to get out of court quick enough to have a line.

Then, uncharacteristically, Fraser jumped the fence from user to supplier and in December 2001 he was sentenced to a minimum of five years after pleading guilty to trafficking cocaine, being knowingly concerned with its importation and possessing ecstasy. He was struck off and bankrupted, and his wife left him.

Given that he had no previous record and it was a non-violent crime, Fraser expected to do his time in a low-risk prison. But it was payback time, and someone, who Fraser believed was from within the Victorian police force, had decided that Fraser would do it tough. They fed into the system that there was a hefty price on his head and that his time would be best served in protective custody. That's how he wound up in Sirius East, the maximum-security protection section of Port Phillip Prison that housed only Victoria's worst of the worst. That's where Andrew Fraser met convicted murderer Peter Norris Dupas.

Twenty-five-year-old Mersina Halvagis was ambushed from behind and stabbed to death in a maniacal attack on 1 November 1997, as she tended her grandmother's grave at Melbourne's Fawkner Cemetery. Police described it as one of the most violent deaths they had ever seen. Her body had almost 100 injuries, which included some horrifically unusual mutilations. Police

Final Justice for Mersina Halvagis

interviewed hundreds of people and eventually narrowed it down to one man – Peter Norris Dupas.

In November 2005, an inquest into Mersina's death concluded that while Peter Dupas was the only person of interest, there wasn't enough evidence to charge him. Police held back the fact that at the time she was murdered Mersina was leaning over her grandmother's grave. It was something that only investigators and the killer knew. The decision not to charge Dupas with Mersina's murder was heartbreaking for the Halvagis family, who had set up the gravesite where she was killed as a shrine and had relentlessly hounded the press for publicity so that her memory would never die and the search for her killer would go on.

In the meantime, police found additional new witnesses who put a man answering to Dupas' description in the cemetery at the time of the murder. Acting on a hunch, Senior Detective Paul Scarlett rang Andrew Fraser, who had been shifted to a minimum-security prison at Sale. Scarlett knew that Fraser had spent a lot of time in the same unit as Dupas and wondered if he could help them. Given the rough time that Fraser had had in prison, he doubted it. Expecting Fraser to hang up in his ear, Detective Scarlett was surprised when Fraser said, 'What took you so long?' and arranged an interview for the following day. Jackpot.

It seemed that Fraser and Dupas had formed an odd alliance in jail – the intelligent university graduate and the withdrawn, nerdy serial killer with the basin haircut and glasses. After a while Dupas confided in his new friend, perhaps in the misguided belief that it was lawyer/client privilege – Fraser wasn't a lawyer and Dupas wasn't his client – and told Fraser things and even re-enacted the murder of Mersina Halvagis in only a fashion the killer could have known.

Fraser agreed to give evidence against Dupas if he could get a reduction on his sentence. Police knew that despite his shortcomings, Fraser's testimony would be credible as it was coming from a trained legal professional with 30 years' experience. It would be Dupas' undoing. They waited a year and Fraser was released two months short of finishing his time.

185

At Dupas' trial, the mountain of circumstantial evidence placed him in the cemetery at the critical time, and the court heard that Dupas' maternal grandfather was buried just 130 metres from the death scene. To make the jurors aware of the circumstances of Fraser's testimony, all they were told before the trial was that Dupas had been convicted of two murders. That's all.

What the jury wasn't told was that Peter Dupas was among Australia's most depraved serial killers. Born into a loving home in 1953, at 15 years old, Dupas repeatedly stabbed the lady next door with a knife. From then on his list of convictions included offensive behaviour, housebreaking, stealing, abduction, assault with a deadly weapon, attempted murder, multiple rape and serial murder. Dupas was currently serving two life sentences without the possibility of parole for the murders of two Melbourne women in almost identical circumstances to that of Mersina Halvagis' murder. The police were also questioning Dupas about three other murders of Melbourne women with similar unusual mutilations.

Andrew Fraser's chilling re-enactment during the trial of Dupas stabbing Mersina Halvagis to death was the clincher and in August 2007, Dupas was found guilty of her murder. But that wasn't to be the end of it. Dupas appealed his conviction, arguing that the judge erred in some of his directions during the trial, and in 2009 he was granted a retrial. The Halvagis family was utterly crushed after having tirelessly campaigned for years to have their daughter's killer brought to justice, only to have it taken away and then have to go through the ordeal of a another trial, looking at a smirking Dupas, all over again.

But they saw it through and a Victorian Supreme Court jury convicted Dupas of murdering Mersina Halvagis near her grandmother's grave at Fawkner Cemetery in 1997. Ms Halvagis' family and supporters stomped their feet, clapped and cried when the verdict was read. As Dupas was led away, Mersina's mother Christina told him to 'rot in hell'.

He will.

38 | WHERE IS PETER FALCONIO?

On 14 July 2001, English tourists Joanne Lees and Peter Falconio, both from Huddersfield, Yorkshire and in their late twenties, were heading up the Stuart Highway for Darwin in their 30-year-old Kombi, which they had bought in Sydney specifically for touring the outback. They had been travelling the world together for six years and had been in Australia for about six months, starting their trip with a working stint in Sydney where they had both made many friends. It was their intention to drive to Darwin and on to Brisbane, where Peter would fly out to Papua New Guinea and Joanne would go back to Sydney to catch up with friends. They would meet up again in two weeks and travel on to New Zealand, Fiji and the US.

A couple of hours earlier they had taken a break from listening to music while cruising the lonely highway, sharing a marijuana joint at a stop called Ti Tree and cuddling and watching the sun set spectacularly over the desert. But in a couple of hours their plans would change forever in the worst possible way.

The Australian Crime File 3

Their orange Kombi was about 10 kilometres north of Barrow Creek when a white Toyota Land Cruiser ute overtook them and the driver waved his hand to flag them down, indicating that there was something wrong with the back of the vehicle. Joanne didn't want to stop but Peter was driving and pulled over to the side of the road, where he got out and went to the back of the Kombi with the stranger while Joanne stayed in the cabin with the engine running. A few moments later she heard a bang like a car backfiring and then the man appeared at her window holding a silver handgun.

The tall, thickset stranger got into the driver's side of the Kombi, pushed her forward and, despite her violent struggling, tied her hands together behind her back. He dragged Joanne out of the Kombi, loosely bound her feet, threw her into the back of his ute and left her there, she wasn't sure for how long.

Realising that her partner had most likely just been murdered and soon it would be her turn, Joanne managed to untie her feet and with her hands still tied behind her, she dropped from the back of the ute and fled into the pitch-black undergrowth along the side of the highway until she stumbled into a large bush and hid beneath it, not daring to breathe. There she stayed, curled up and crouching forward with her head on her knees, terrified to make the slightest sound, as the killer frantically searched for her. Time and again he passed nearby and she could hear his dog panting. She heard him dragging something along the ground. She saw the headlights of a vehicle scan the bushes in search of her. That the reflector strips on her shorts were never caught in the headlights and the man's dog never smelt her fear is a miracle.

Almost five hours later at about 12.45am and still not certain whether the killer had gone, Joanne plucked up enough courage to run in front of a road train and was rescued by driver Vince Millar and his co-driver Rod Adams. Almost in disbelief at finding a distraught young lady in the middle of nowhere telling a tale of murder and abduction, the truckies cut the hand-ties from Joanne's wrists and drove her to the nearby Barrow Creek pub, where they rang the police.

Where is Peter Falconio?

When the police arrived several hours later they found Peter and Joanne's Kombi driven off the road and blood on the highway where Joanne said she had heard the shot come from. Joanne was able to give them a positive description of the man who had apparently killed her partner in cold blood and then attempted to abduct her. Seeing as the man had made no attempt to cover his face, they could only assume that she would also have been murdered, after he had had his way with her. Joanne Lees also had some tiny specks of blood on her T-shirt that could not be eliminated by DNA testing and it was assumed that they belonged to the killer.

Within months a Broome diesel mechanic, 43-year-old Bradley John Murdoch, came under suspicion, as several people told police that Murdoch had gone to great lengths to change the appearance of his vehicle, had shaved off his distinctive Merv Hughes moustache and also shaved his head. Police questioned Murdoch but he claimed that he had been hundreds of kilometres away on his way home from a marijuana drug run in South Australia. They couldn't disprove this but the times and places he provided didn't quite add up as the perfect alibi.

Unfortunately for the police investigating the case, the law of the Northern Territory at the time didn't allow for them to forcibly take Murdoch's DNA, the results of which would allow them to either charge him with murder or not pursue him any longer. Then they got the break they desperately needed. In August 2002, Bradley Murdoch, who was said to be highly agitated about the search for Peter Falconio's killer and couldn't stop telling people that he was a prime suspect, was arrested and charged with the abduction and multiple rapes of a woman and her 12-year-old daughter in rural South Australia.

After a 25-hour drive in which the females were chained together and repeatedly assaulted at gunpoint, Murdoch dumped them at a Port Augusta service station, gave the mother $1000 and told them, 'You could make some money out of this if you went to the media.' The woman eventually went to the police, who arrested Murdoch on 28 August 2002 in a nearby

Woolworths store. He was carrying a loaded gun in a shoulder holster and another in the waistband of his trousers.

Aware that Murdoch was a prime suspect in the Falconio case, the South Australian police legally took his DNA and sent it on to the Northern Territory. The DNA from the blood on Joanne Lees' T-shirt and the sweat on her hand-ties was *150 quadrillion times* more likely to have come from Murdoch than any other Northern Territory person. They had their man. Trouble was, he looked liked spending the next 20 or so years in a South Australian prison for the abduction and assaults on the mother and daughter. Incredibly, that was not to be.

Murdoch was acquitted of all the South Australian charges on the questionable grounds that the woman, a former prostitute, and her daughter did not go to the police earlier. Murdoch was immediately extradited to the Northern Territory, where he was charged and tried for the murder of Peter Falconio and the attempted abduction of Joanne Lees. When asked if the man who'd assaulted her was in the court, Joanne Lees pointed to Murdoch and said, 'Yes. I'd recognise him anywhere.'

Despite driving 1800 kilometres in the 18 hours following the incident to create an alibi, the DNA and other evidence was too overwhelming and in December 2005, Bradley John Murdoch was found guilty and sentenced to life imprisonment with a non-parole period of 28 years. All avenues of appeal have since been exhausted. The remains of Peter Falconio have not been found to this day.

39 | THREE STRIKES AND GONE FOR GOOD: JUSTICE AT LAST FOR JOHN LESLIE COOMBES

Many times on our radio show, *Crime File*, we have looked at – either individually or collectively – the numerous killers in our history who have committed murder and been sent to prison, only to be released to commit murder again. Those who come immediately to mind are Barry Hadlow, who murdered a kiddie and was released 25 years later to murder another child; Robert Theo Sievers, who served 12 years for the shooting murder of his estranged wife and eight years later stabbed his girlfriend to death with a carving knife; and Eric Thomas Turner, who murdered his girlfriend and her father and after serving 22 years behind bars was released to murder his mother-in-law and his 11-year-old stepson.

But until just recently, only once in our history has anyone ever been found guilty of murder and sent to prison, released, then found guilty of murder again and sent back to prison, and then released *again* to commit yet another murder. But before we look at this latest case of multiple murder, which has left family and friends of the victim asking why the killer was allowed back on the streets, let's go back and look at the first landmark case.

Rodney Francis Cameron was born in Kew, Victoria, in 1955. By the time he was a teenager he had a shocking history of attacks on women. The children's courts said it was only a matter of time before he killed someone. In 1974, 18-year-old Cameron was working as a trainee nurse in the Queen Victoria Nursing Home at Wentworth Falls in the Blue Mountains, where he shared a platonic friendship with nursing sister Florence Edith Jackson, who he sexually assaulted and strangled to death in her home.

A week later, 19-year-old bank clerk Francesco Ciliberto picked up Cameron as he was hitchhiking towards Victoria. Cameron bashed Ciliberto with a boulder and then strangled him with a football sock and threw his body off a cliff. Cameron was eventually arrested in Queensland on 21 February 1974, after abducting a mother and daughter. Cameron told arresting detectives he 'had to kill three'.

Cameron was found guilty of murder and served nine years in New South Wales prisons. When he was released in 1983, he was arrested and taken back to Victoria to face the charge of murdering Francesco Ciliberto. Diagnosed as a 'psychopath not fit to be in society', Cameron was sentenced to life, with the recommendation he should remain in jail 'for the term of his natural life'. In other words, Rodney Cameron should have spent the rest of his life in jail without the possibility of parole. But no. On 12 March 1990, Cameron was released after a successful appeal against the length of his sentence. It was believed he had been fully rehabilitated. He had served just 16 years for the two separate murders.

Ten weeks after he walked free, on the evening of 26 May 1990, Cameron called a lonely hearts program on Melbourne's radio station 3AW, describing himself as a teetotaller marine biologist from Castlemaine. He added that he was a Gemini who played squash and basketball, had no hang-ups and was searching for a soul mate 'willing to share his happiness and enjoy a

Three Strikes and Gone for Good

good, quiet life'. Maria Goeliner was one of the nine women who rang expressing an interest in meeting Cameron.

On 23 June 1990, at the Sky Rider Motor Inn at Katoomba, New South Wales, not far from where Cameron had murdered Edith Jackson 16 years earlier, Maria Goeliner was found strangled. A week after the murder, Cameron, now dubbed 'the Lonely Hearts Killer', gave himself up. In sentencing Cameron to life imprisonment with the recommendation that he die in jail, the judge said that only 'old age or infirmity' would stop Cameron from carrying out his 'homicidal desires'. Cameron has since also confessed to the murder of an elderly lady in Sydney.

You would think that authorities may have learnt something from the case of the Lonely Hearts Killer. But apparently not.

John Leslie Coombes was a seriously rotten person. After a dysfunctional childhood, he married in Melbourne in 1975 and had two children. His family were regulars at the local hospital because of his beatings, with his wife suffering broken ribs on several occasions. He shot the family cockatoo because it was squawking and strangled the family cat in front of his kids. He also killed the family's adored German shepherd, which had followed his daughter everywhere, disembowelled it and hung it on the back fence.

On the night of 16 November 1984, Coombes took a kitchen carving knife to Henry Desmond Kells and violently stabbed him to death as Kells lay unconscious in a drunken stupor after an altercation with Coombes. With his wife Sandra as the main witness against him, Coombes was found guilty of murder and sentenced to life in prison with a minimum of six years. While in jail, Coombes was charged with stealing and escaping from legal custody and given another six months' imprisonment on each count. He ended up serving 11 years of his life sentence.

While Coombes was in prison police began investigating the suspected murder of Michael Speirani, 20, who was last seen in Coombes' company and went missing almost a year before he murdered Henry Kells. Released in 1995, in 1998 Coombes was charged with Speirani's murder, again based on the testimony of his now ex-wife, who told the court that Speirani came to their home to sell his car to Coombes.

To test the car, Speirani, Coombes and another man towed a boat to Port Phillip Bay, where there had been an argument; the two men had thrown Speirani into the water and repeatedly run over him and sliced him up with the boat's propeller. She said that he told her that they had dragged Speirani's body to the side of the boat and had sliced it up so that the fish could finish the job. Coombes made his wife scrub the blood and flesh from his boat. In April 1998, Coombes was sentenced to just 15 years in jail with a minimum of 10 years, after being found guilty of a violent murder for the second time. The other man received eight years for his part in the murder.

Released on parole in early 2007, in August 2009 the squat, grey-bearded Coombes, now 56, strangled 27-year-old early learning teacher Raechel Betts, at Phillip Island, dismembered her body in a bathtub and threw the body parts off various intervals of the Newhaven Jetty. Raechel Betts was an attractive and decent young lady who was the carer for two teenage girls. With Coombes' encouragement she had fallen into the drug trade and Coombes had become her supplier. Her terrible end became evident when, among other body parts, her easily identified tattooed foot was found washed up not far from the jetty. It led police to Coombes, who pleaded guilty at his trial.

In sentencing the ex-soldier Coombes to life in jail without the possibility of parole on 26 August 2011, Justice Geoffrey Nettle told him that he believed that if he was given the opportunity he would 'kill and kill again'. Justice Nettle concluded that Coombes had a 'frightening predilection for homicide', that 'the nature and gravity of your offending places it in the worst categories of murder', and 'you should never be released to be among decent people again'.

Seems as though someone finally got it right.

40 | THE YORKSHIRE RIPPER

According to medical evidence presented to Britain's High Court in April 2011, Peter Sutcliffe, aka the Yorkshire Ripper, now 63, was wrongly convicted of his crimes in 1981 as he was suffering from paranoid schizophrenia at the time of the murders; he will be safe to be released when his recommended time of 30 years in prison falls.

Kevin Murray, a consultant psychiatrist at Broadmoor secure hospital, where he has treated Sutcliffe since 2001, said it was the unanimous view of his colleagues that the Ripper suffered from paranoid schizophrenia at the time of his crimes. Dr Murray's report from 2006 concluded that his treatment has had 'very considerable success' and if he continues with it the Ripper poses a low risk of offending.

Judge John Mitting told the High Court that a psychiatrist's report might also form the basis for Sutcliffe to appeal against his murder convictions. The Ripper has been accused of 'hoodwinking' psychiatrists into believing that voices from God had ordered him to kill prostitutes. Judge Mitting said that the report should be disregarded.

Given the nature of Sutcliffe's crimes, we can only conclude that it is the doctors recommending his release who need psychiatric help and that any judge who lets England's second-worst serial killer back on the streets will be deemed to be crazier still. It simply won't happen.

What became known as the Yorkshire Ripper killings began with the murder of Emily Jackson, 42, a prostitute and mother of three, who was found on a cold January morning in 1976 by workmen in a derelict site in Leeds. She had been stabbed, bitten, bludgeoned and strangled to death. Her death was then linked to the earlier murder of another streetwalker named Wilma McCann.

In May 1976, Marcella Claxton was attacked with a hammer in Leeds and survived. In February 1977, Irene Richardson's body was found. Two months later, Patricia Atkinson was killed in her bedsit in Manningham, West Yorkshire. Then the Ripper no longer confined himself to murdering prostitutes. Jayne MacDonald, a 16-year-old shop assistant, was savagely stabbed, bitten and bashed to death in Leeds in June 1977.

As the body count rapidly rose, the women of the north of England were under siege and stayed home at nights. Female police officers worked undercover as prostitutes and put their lives in grave peril, should they go with a man in a car only to have to reveal their true identity and be stabbed to death if police did not back them up.

The biggest manhunt in England's history saw as many as 250,000 names of questioned people on file. Thirty thousand statements were taken and hundreds of thousands of number plates in red light areas were registered. But checking all of them out in those times before modern technology was an impossibility and nothing led to so much as a suspect.

Had it been these times of cross-analysis by computer, then one name, Peter Sutcliffe, a local lorry driver, would have been a rash across their screens. Sutcliffe's car was seen at red light districts 60 times. As a result, he was interviewed nine times. He

The Yorkshire Ripper

always had an alibi – he was at home with his family. Despite being on a list of 300 names connected to a £5 note, traced to his employment, from the purse of one of the murder victims, Sutcliffe was never strongly suspected.

Then in 1979 a tape and a letter arrived at Task Force Headquarters, which was believed to be genuine. But the voice belonged to a hoaxer who convinced West Yorkshire Assistant Chief Constable George Oldfield he was the killer. He said, 'I'm Jack. I see you've no luck catching me.' Delivered in a Sunderland lilt, the voice was played across the north-east of England, in pubs, clubs and football grounds. The public could hear it by calling a special number.

In a blunder of monumental proportions, Oldfield was so convinced that the tape was genuine that he switched their hunt to the north-east and anyone without a local accent was immediately eliminated. A month after the recording arrived, Peter Sutcliffe was being interviewed for a fifth time but walked free because his voice didn't match that of the hoaxer. Although they may have been close to at least suspecting Sutcliffe at the time, the real Ripper was freed to kill again and again.

By the end of 1980, police had spent more than two and a quarter million hours hunting a killer who had killed 13 women, and savagely attacked seven more who were lucky to escape with their lives. Twenty-three children were without a mother. At the time, the Yorkshire Ripper was the most prolific serial killer in England's history. And he was still at large. But not for long. And his capture had nothing to do with good detective work.

On the evening of 2 January 1981, two uniformed officers approached a Rover in a factory driveway frequented by prostitutes and their clients. In the car they saw a man and a prostitute who was known to them. The man said his name was Peter Williams and that he needed to go to the toilet. They watched as he walked along the driveway into the darkness and heard him relieve himself and walk back.

They rang the Rover's registration through, to find that the plates were registered to a car in a local scrapping yard. At the Hammerton Road police station the man confessed that

197

his name was really Peter Sutcliffe, and that he had stolen the plates so his wife wouldn't find out. It was his first time with a prostitute. During the interview he asked to use the toilet, where he hid a knife in the cistern.

Given the fact that Sutcliffe answered the description of the man who had bashed the survivors and had a gap in his teeth that matched the bite marks on the victims, police returned to where he had relieved himself the night before to find a hammer and a knife. In Sutcliffe's pocket they also found a length of rope.

All of a sudden it seemed blatantly apparent that the lorry-driving family man had been calmly murdering under their noses while they chased one red herring after the other.

After 48 hours of interrogation and with a mountain of circumstantial evidence piled up against him, Peter Sutcliffe sat calmly back in his chair and confessed to being the Yorkshire Ripper. For the next two days he confessed every crime in minute detail. Hardened detectives were sickened at the obvious pleasure he got from it. The only emotion he showed was when discussing the murder of 16-year-old Jayne MacDonald. Sutcliffe's excuse for his crimes was that he had been rejected by a prostitute when he was young.

When his wife Sonia was allowed to visit him for the first time, still unaware of the monster she had been living with, he confessed to her: 'You know all those women who were killed by the Yorkshire Ripper. That was me. I killed all those women.'

To the police officer's astonishment, after considerable debate, she replied, 'Peter, what on earth did you do that for? Even a sparrow has the right to live.'

The Yorkshire Ripper was given 20 life sentences, with a recommendation he serve a minimum of 30 years in prison before consideration for parole.

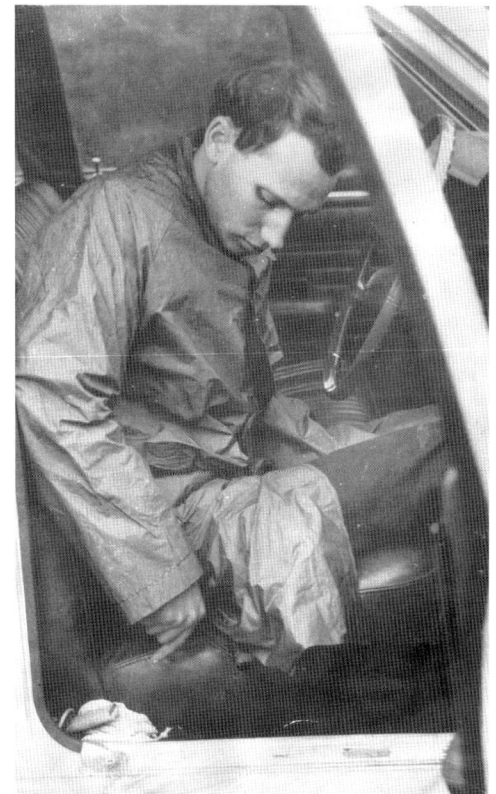

Above left: **Where is Jodie Larcombe?**
Although no body was ever found, Daryl Francis Suckling was found guilty of the murder of Melbourne woman Jodie Maree Larcombe and sentenced to life in prison.

Above right: **Is Derek Percy the Wanda Beach Killer?**
There is little doubt that 19-year-old Derek Percy murdered four children. He was convicted of one and sent to an insane asylum for the rest of his life. Percy was also in the vicinity at the time of the Wanda Beach Murders.
Newspix

Charles 'Lucky' Luciano, the Founder of the Modern Mafia
Luciano set up a criminal organisation that became the biggest business in the USA. In doing so Luciano became one of *Time Magazine*'s '100 Most Important People of the 20th Century'.

The Murders of Bruce Burrell
Burrell was convicted of murdering two women on separate occasions. No trace of either body has ever been found.
Newspix

The Sef Gonzales Family Murders
Twenty-one-year-old Sef Gonzales (front) lay in wait for his parents and sister to arrive home separately and then murdered them and attempted to make the killings look like a home invasion gone horribly wrong.
Newspix/Mark Williams

The Mysterious Disappearance of Samantha Knight
The face of the beautiful girl in the urchin's cap became familiar on posters around Sydney's Bondi Beach soon after Samantha Knight went missing.
Newspix/Chris Hyde

The John Christie Murders of Notting Hill
John Christie looked harmless but he murdered six women and a baby and hid them in his house. An innocent man went to the gallows for one of Christie's crimes.

Above left: **The Wales-King Murders**
For their kindness Mathew King repaid his mother, Margaret Wales-King and her new husband Paul King, by bashing them both to death to get his hands on his inheritance. All he got was a prison cell.
Newspix/Ben Swinnerton

Above right: **The Murder of MP John Newman: Australia's First Political Murder**
It was no secret that John Newman's political rival, Phuong Ngo, was out to get rid of him. But would the evidence lead to Ngo's involvement?
Newspix/Rachel Simpson

HIH: The Cash Cow for Corporate Crooks
Rodney Adler, the heartless corporate crook who bled HIH Insurance dry for his own greed and left thousands of decent hard-working Australians on the breadline while he lived the good life.
Newspix/Brianne Makin

The Love-struck Jailer: How Heather Parker Helped Peter Gibb Escape
When they told prison guard Heather Parker to keep a close eye on the bank robber they didn't mean to give him a good-morning kiss and help him escape.
Newspix

The Final Indignity for Darryl Beamish
After serving 15 years for a murder he didn't commit, deaf mute Darryl Raymond Beamish was finally awarded compensation 51 years later. But it was nothing like he expected.

The Saint Valentine's Day Massacre Seven men lay dead in a Chicago garage. All were gunned down in cold blood by Al Capone's assassins on Saint Valentine's Day, 1929.

Above left: **The Real-life *Psycho*: Ed Gein**
The mild-mannered Wisconsin farmer turned serial killer who liked digging up bodies from the nearby cemetery, was the real life inspiration for the movies *Psycho* and *The Silence of the Lambs*.

Above right: **Mr Froggy and His Ill-gotten Millions: The Ponzi Frauds of Karl Suleman**
Karl Suleman sucked his investors in by offering outrageously high returns to his friends in the Assyrian community. Instead he spent the millions he collected on himself.
Newspix/John Grainger

Who Poisoned Bobby Lulham?
Bobby Lulham, the handsome and super-fit Balmain and international footballer was being poisoned. But by whom? And why?

The Injustice of Colin Campbell Ross: A Century Too Late
Colin Campbell Ross was charged with the murder of 12-year-old Alma Tirtschke in 1922. He was hanged but widely believed to be innocent. Efforts were made to clear his name and finally, in 2008, he was pardoned by the Governor of Victoria. Alma Tirtschke is pictured (left) with her grandmother and sister in about 1916. Gun Alley, below, off Melbourne's Little Collins Street, is where her body was found in 1921.

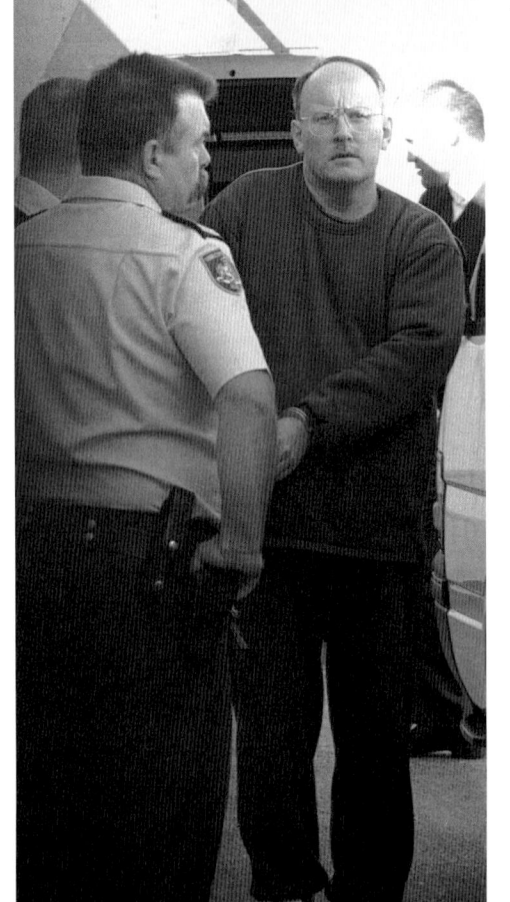

Above left: **The BTK Serial Killer**
When local dog catcher and serial killer, Dennis Rader, failed to get a nickname for his murders he anonymously wrote to the local papers and complained suggesting they name him 'The BTK Killer' which stood for his method of murder: Bind, Torture, Kill.

Above right: **The William Moxley Murders**
Petty criminal Moxley uncharacteristically committed two terrible murders and then eluded police by riding his bicycle around right under their noses.

**The Canberra Cop Killer:
The Murder of Colin Winchester**
For apparently no less than a grudge, David Harold Eastman lay in wait for Australian Federal Police Assistant Commissioner Colin Winchester and gunned him down as he left his car. This carned Eastman the privilege of becoming the only 'never to be released' prisoner in the ACT.
Newspix

Little Has Changed in 100 Years
Some of the nine young men who were found guilty of the Mount Rennie Rape Case. Four of them – all under the age of 20 – went to the gallows.

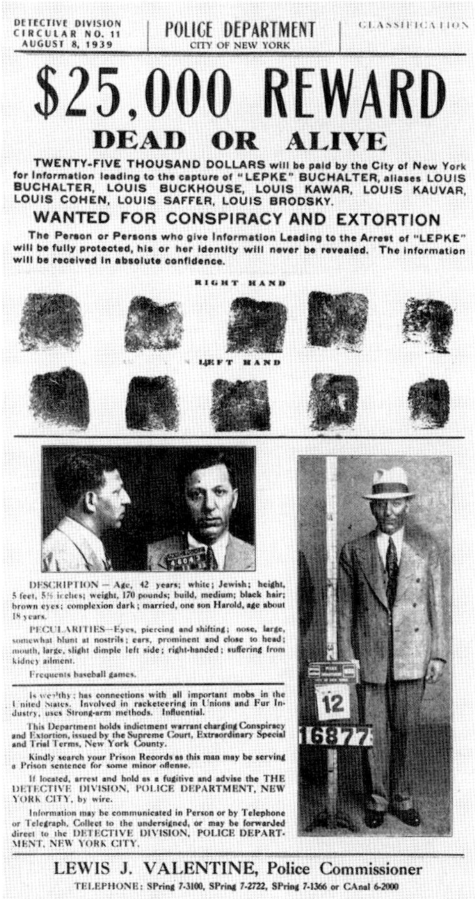

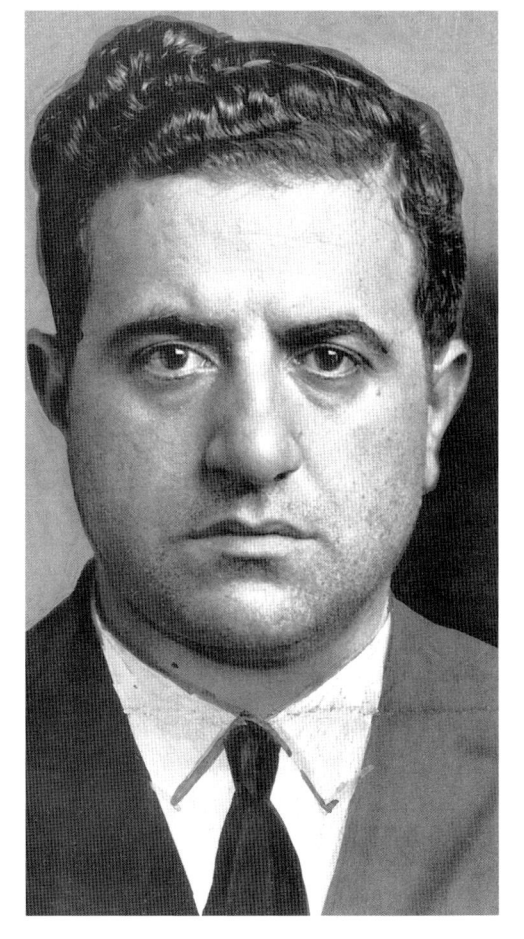

Murder Inc.: The Mafia's Private Death Squad
Left: The Wanted Poster for Murder Inc.'s number one assassin, Louis 'Lepke' Buchalter, who was directly responsible for the murders of as many as 400 people.

Right: Albert Anastasia ran the business of murdering people the same way anyone would run a normal business.

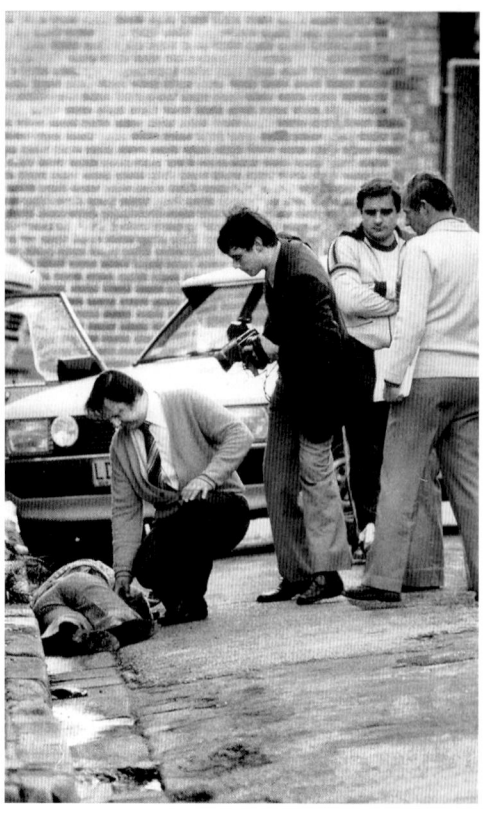

Above left: **The Two Lives of Al Grassby**
A colourful Labour politician who was really an associate of the Mafia, Grassby lost all credibility when he blamed murdered anti-drug campaigner Donald Mackay's wife for the disappearance of her husband. From then on he was despised.
Newspix

Above right: **The Shootout at Dangar Place: When Detective Roger Rogerson Met Warren Lanfranchi**
Warren Lanfranchi lies in the gutter after being shot dead by Roger Rogerson (far right) after he allegedly pulled a gun on Rogerson and the detective defended himself.
Newspix

Right: **Not a Good Time to be Named Jodie: The Crimes of Jodie Harris**
Con-woman Jodie Harris (middle) had so many aliases beginning with Jodie that anyone unfortunate enough to have the same first name was suspected of being her. One poor innocent Jodie was dragged from an aeroplane!
Newspix/Bill Hearne

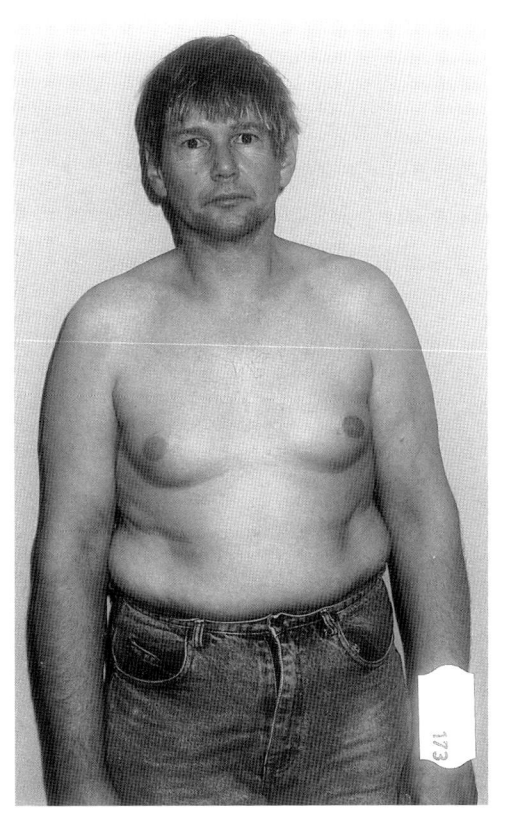

Final Justice for Mersina Halvagis: Serial Killer Peter Dupas Gets His Just Desserts
At long last signature serial killer Peter Dupas has been convicted of the 1997 murder of Mersina Halvagis. Dupas was already serving double life, never to be released, for two other murders. Police believe he has done at least three more.
Newspix

Where is Peter Falconio?
Although Peter Falconio's body has never been found there is absolutely no doubt that Bradley John Murdoch murdered him given that DNA from the murder scene proved to be 150 quadrillion times more likely to be Murdoch's than anyone else's.

Below left: A reward poster for the whereabouts of Peter Falconio.

Below right: Joanne Lees, who was almost also murdered by Murdoch.

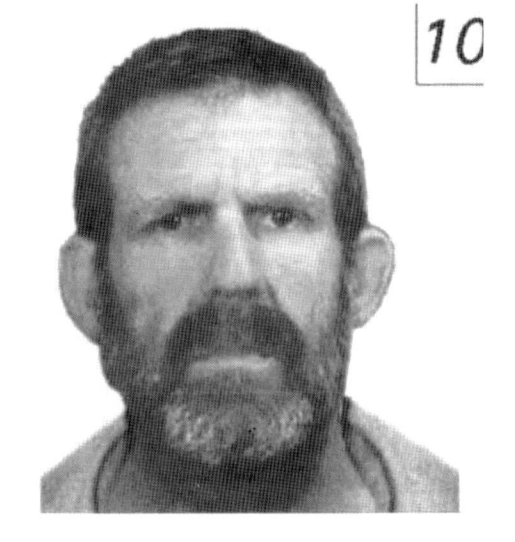

Three Strikes and Gone for Good: Justice at Last for John Leslie Coombes
How is it possible for someone to commit murder and be released, commit another murder and be released again to commit a third murder? But it happened and this time they got it right. John Leslie Coombes won't ever be released to kill again.
Newspix/Mike Keating

The Yorkshire Ripper
Peter Sutcliffe on his wedding day. He went on to murder 13 women and almost kill another 7 more. Psychiatrists believe he is safe to be released.

Death on Bondi Beach: The Bizarre Death of Roni Levi
A re-enactment of the shooting death of Roni Levi. Surrounded by police with weapons drawn and aimed at him, the obviously deranged Roni Levi waved his knife at police and was shot dead in front of bystanders. The police had a lot to answer for.
Newspix

Peter Foster: Australia's Dumbest Conman
Looking like he could use a 44-gallon drum of his famous Bai Lin slimming tea, conman Peter Foster seems to be contemplating what might have been as he is taken away by the police yet again. He says he is writing a book of his life. But who cares?
Newspix

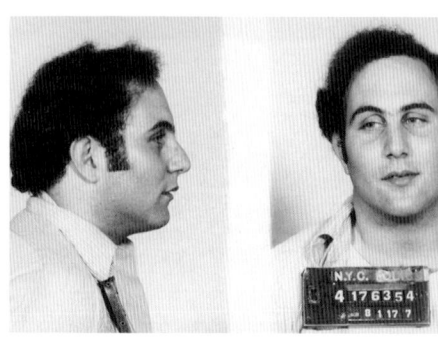

Above: **Son of Sam**
By day David Berkowitz was a New York postal worker. By night he was one of the most infamous serial killers the world has known, murdering couples with his Bulldog .44 handgun as they sat in their cars. When captured, Berkowitz said that it was his neighbour's dog who told him to kill.

Left: **Dr Death**
The crimes of Dr Jayant Patel were that he harmed and killed people under the guise of being a competent medical practitioner. Despite complaint after complaint, his employers let it go on until a nurse chose to blow the whistle and pay the consequences.
Newspix/Glenn Barnes

Below: **London's Notorious Kray Twins**
Ronnie and Reggie Kray, the most notorious gangsters in London's history, still managed to control their empire for many years from prison.

The Jury's Still Out on Sir Joh
Without any doubt Joh Bjelke-Petersen was Queensland's most controversial premier. But was he a crook? Many things would indicate he was, but if so each time the finger was pointed in his direction he managed to wriggle away. You judge for yourself.
Newspix

The Adventures of Captain Moonlite
Our most flamboyant bushranger of them all, Captain Moonlite surrounded himself with young men. His dying wish was that he be buried near his great friend Jim Nesbit, but that didn't happen until more than a century later.

Who Framed the Mickelbergs? The Story Behind Western Australia's Biggest Gold Heist
It was the most brazen heist with a huge amount of gold bullion stolen from the Perth mint and not a shot fired or an angry word spoken. The Mickelberg brothers (Ray left, Peter right in white shirt) went to jail for a crime they didn't commit.
Newspix/Ian Cugley

The Devil Made Me Do It
Multiple rapist and sex murderer Darren Osborne, is led from the court to spend the rest of his life in prison after being convicted of just some of his crimes.

America's Worst Serial Killer Ever: Pogo the Killer Clown
There was nothing funny about the other side of Pogo the clown. While the kids thought he was beaut at parties, at night he lured young men into his home and killed more victims than any other serial killer in America's history.

41 | DEATH ON BONDI BEACH: THE BIZARRE DEATH OF RONI LEVI

When you think of Bondi – Australia's most iconic beach – you think of sun, sand and surf and young blond-haired men surfing the famous rip at the Tamarama end. And beautiful women (some topless) lazing around on towels, burly lifeguards rescuing drunk backpackers and children with ice-cream dripping off their chins.

If you're a local, you might think about how hard it is to get a park on the weekend, but mostly it's the sort of place people go for a good time and pleasant memories. Visiting Sydney and not visiting Bondi Beach is like going to Paris and not seeing the Eiffel Tower.

With a strip packed with places to eat, drink and dance, or just a place to stroll around hoping to be seen, the last thing you think about is a mentally unbalanced man being gunned down on the sand not long after sunrise by two police officers – one a confirmed drug abuser. But that's exactly what happened to 33-year-old Frenchman Roni Levi on the morning of 28 June 1997.

The story of how Bondi resident Levi came to be surrounded by six uniformed policemen at 7am on that cold winter's morning, wet, bedraggled and confused, clearly in the grip of some sort of breakdown, brandishing a 21-centimetre-long Wiltshire StaySharp kitchen knife, began the evening before – but its roots lay even earlier than that.

Levi had come from a good family. He didn't drink or smoke, and he wasn't a drug user. He was married for a while, but that didn't work out. Following his divorce, he studied at TAFE and earned money as a photographer. But friends noticed differences in Levi after he moved to Bondi earlier in the year 1997. They say his personality changed. It's been said his mental health went into a sad decline.

Not long before he died, Levi had become involved in a difficult situation where a man insisted that he owed him money for some sports clothing. The man had been threatening Levi with violence if he didn't pay up right away, phoning Levi constantly. No one can say for sure if this is what tipped Levi over the edge, but it's unlikely that it helped matters. Either way, on the night of 27 June 1997, Levi was at a dinner party with friends. His behaviour seemed even more off-kilter than usual. It was so concerning, in fact, that his friends decided it was best to take him to St Vincent's Hospital in nearby Darlinghurst for observation.

Levi waited around at the hospital but eventually became too agitated to remain there. He walked out at 4.30am. He was back at his flat by 6am – his nose smeared with blood as he stood sweating and panting and arguing with his flatmate. He grabbed the StaySharp knife and ran out the door shortly before 7am, heading for the beach.

Once there, he bolted across the sand towards the famous surf break, wading into the icy winter water while waving the knife around as if he intended to stab himself. Six uniformed police officers arrived soon after, as a crowd mainly comprising the early-morning exercise set gathered on the promenade bordering the beach, watching on in disbelief. Levi ran back up the beach and across Campbell Parade, the main road that hugs the

Death on Bondi Beach

beach. He then bolted back down to the beach and waded into the water. When he got out, he was soaked and freezing.

Grouped in a semi-circle around him, the police officers spent half an hour trying to persuade an obviously disturbed Levi to drop the knife. It was no use. He was acting erratically and showed no sign of calming down. He ignored the demands of the six officers surrounding him, telling him to disarm himself.

Then he is said to have started to approach two of the officers – Constable Rodney Podesta and Senior Constable Anthony DiLorenzo. They both shot Levi twice at relatively close range, with all four bullets hitting him. Roni Levi was rushed back to St Vincent's Hospital but passed away two hours later.

There was an understandable uproar at what seemed a senseless and unnecessary slaying. The media and public alike questioned why six trained police officers couldn't subdue one distressed man. After all, Levi was of average build and hardly operating at his peak. And even if shots had to be fired, why not simply aim for a shoulder or leg?

Bondi police station was besieged with phone calls for two days, asking those same questions. But still, there was no official statement forthcoming from NSW Police. Quite the contrary; it seemed like the authorities were growing irate at the public for questioning their methods. They felt it had been a life-threatening situation – how could the public make a judgement as to the best course of action? A drastic decision had to be made, they contended, and the two officers in question had made it.

The general public weren't appeased. And then photos of the tragedy surfaced and the story took on a whole new life. French professional photographer Jean-Pierre Bratanoff-Firgoff had been on the scene that early morning, snapping away. The results were both enlightening and disturbing. They show Levi at varying distances from the six police officers, none of whom look to be in any serious danger. Then Podesta and DiLorenzo open fire right in front of the victim, only about 3 to 5 metres away.

Bratanoff-Firgoff's photos seem to show that Levi was shot even though it could have been avoided. It appears that the victim has a jacket wrapped around his arms and back. It doesn't look like he's in any position to harm anyone. When questioned about the photos by journalists, Bratanoff-Firgoff said that on hearing the shots he couldn't believe police had gunned the man down. The photographer had thought it must have all been a mistake.

Either way, Levi's parents were understandably shocked by what had happened. They demanded Podesta and DiLorenzo be suspended immediately. But the force wasn't ready to take such action. Instead, the two officers took extended sick leave, but remained on call. For a while there was talk that they might face charges regarding Levi's death, but the Director of Public Prosecutions ruled that there was a lack of evidence.

Constable Rodney Podesta resigned from the force a few weeks later. Senior Constable Anthony DiLorenzo was arrested in April 1998 on suspicion of supplying or possessing drugs; he denied that he had offered protection to a known drug dealer in exchange for illegal substances. DiLorenzo was kicked out of the force 14 months later. Not long after that, Podesta was charged with attempting to receive drugs for supply. He admitted that he had been using ecstasy and cocaine in 1997 and 1998.

That was enough for the Police Integrity Commission to re-open the Roni Levi case. The new Commission of Inquiry kicked off in November 1999, determined to find out if Podesta or DiLorenzo had been under the influence of drugs or alcohol the morning they shot and killed Levi.

Even though he had earlier claimed to have never used drugs before shooting Levi in June 1997, it was found that Podesta had made more than 120 phone calls to a drug dealer in the months leading up to Levi's death. Not only that, but according to phone records, the dealer had called Podesta five times on the day Levi was shot.

Podesta's girlfriend also gave evidence that he had been using a serious amount of cocaine in the early months of 1997. She added that he had visited her at about 10pm the evening prior to Levi's shooting. He had been wearing his police uniform. He was also allegedly high on cocaine at the time.

Podesta was later sentenced to 16 weeks' periodic detention after pleading guilty to one count of attempting to receive 3.5 kilos of cocaine for supply.

Another inquiry was launched in February 2000. It was critical of the initial Levi investigation, making particular note of the fact that the officers involved in the shooting were never tested for drugs or alcohol in the aftermath. That finding led to a ruling that there must be random testing for police officers involved in critical incidents. Capsicum spray is now deemed a better option in such circumstances as Roni Levi's than shooting the offender. These steps have been brought in to reduce what has been termed 'suicide by police'.

Let's hope it works.

42 | SYDNEY'S FIRST 'CHICAGO-STYLE' GANGLAND HIT: THE PUBLIC DEMISE OF PRETTY BOY WALKER

Back in the good old days in Sydney, long before drugs were the main source of income for the underworld, tough men fought over the huge profits from prostitution, sly grog, extortion, starting-price betting and the illegal casinos, all of which were allowed to flourish under the most corrupt police force and state government in Australia's history.

And so, like the Mafia, crime became organised with the top crooks having the top cops and politicians in their pockets. They saw to it that everyone got a share of the spoils and all ran smoothly. Any pimp, bookie or casino operator who didn't make their contribution, either to the Organisation's debt collectors or, in some cases, directly to the police, was put out of business and their illegal assets confiscated.

The man at the top was Lennie McPherson, a notorious Balmain criminal who over the years with fists, knives and a gun had fought his way to the top of the street crooks in Sydney. The mere mention of McPherson's name was enough to make anyone go yellow with fear and pay up. Naturally, being the Boss, Lennie didn't do much of the collecting himself, so he surrounded himself with Sydney's hardest men, who would maim, break, injure or kill at his command.

But while being at the top of the organised crime pile was very lucrative, it was also fraught with danger, with the possibility of any one of the ambitious underlings who had seen the spoils fancying having it all for himself. One such crook was Robert 'Pretty Boy' Walker, and although Walker would die in a manner the likes of which has never been seen in Australia before, or since, it wasn't ambition that was his undoing. It was the oldest trap in the book: a fight over a woman who eventually gave him up to save herself.

The 26-year-old 'Pretty Boy' Walker lived up to his name. He looked more like Ricky Nelson than a violent, psychopathic ex-stevedore turned pimp and debt collector for Lennie McPherson. Walker's stock in trade was prostitutes, and if he had to belt them around from time to time to keep them awake on the job, then that's the way it was.

So it came as a bit of a surprise when the Pretty Boy took umbrage when someone belted one of his ladies in the Woolloomooloo Bay Hotel while he and a team of Lennie's blokes were having a drink. It seems that he got terribly upset, resulting in one of the men, Barney Ryan, winding up with a broken leg courtesy of Walker. It was a bad mistake on Walker's part and he knew there would be reprisals.

The even-up came soon after, on 6 May 1963, when five of the most fearsome men in Sydney turned up on Walker's Paddington front door to 'pay him a visit'. A quick peak out the window and Pretty Boy knew he was in a lot of bother. And he had every reason to be terrified. Among the men were the notorious gunman 'Ratty' Jack Clarke, and Lennie McPherson's lieutenant and right-hand man, and arguably the most feared man in Australia alongside McPherson, Stanley 'Stan the Man' Smith.

Having had the foresight to arm himself with a .303 army service rifle, Walker fired several shots through the door before

Sydney's First 'Chicago-style' Gangland Hit

the murder squad could break it down and beat him to death. One of the shots hit Stan the Man in the upper chest, seriously wounding him. Smith was very lucky not to be killed, and spent several weeks in hospital. It would have been best for Walker if Stan Smith had died.

Police charged Walker with the shooting, but given the circumstances he was released on bail. Too stupid to go and live in darkest Africa until the heat cooled down, Walker secretly shacked up in nearby Randwick with the same prostitute who had been bashed in the pub and with whom all the drama began.

Instead of laying low and shutting up, Walker let it be known throughout the underworld that he was now the new tough guy in town and anyone who came near him would get the same as Stan the Man got. The story goes that his friends advised him not to bother watching any serials.

Lennie McPherson spread the word among Walker's hookers that it would be in their best interests to let him know where Walker was holed up. Fearing for her life, the trusted prostitute Walker was living with couldn't make the phone call quick enough to give him up. Now it was just a matter of time. And they had something special in mind for the Pretty Boy.

Seemingly oblivious to the fact that he was Sydney's most hunted man, in broad daylight on the afternoon of 8 July 1963, two months after he had shot Stan Smith, Walker emerged from a block of flats next to the Labor Club in busy Alison Road, a main thoroughfare in Randwick that runs around the racecourse. He was on his way for a beer at the local, apparently without a care in the world.

If he had been concerned for his safety he would have only had to look over his shoulder to see a car pull out from the kerb and follow him as he walked down the footpath. According to eyewitnesses, the car drew alongside Walker and a gun with its barrel protruding from the back window opened fire, with a continuous barrage of shots that seemed to go on for minutes.

And little wonder. The bullets were coming from an Owen submachine gun. When the smoke cleared the car was long gone and Pretty Boy Walker lay dead, cut in half by the barrage. The bullets had sprayed parked cars and nearby buildings. No other citizens were hurt. The stolen murder car was found abandoned about a mile away, clean of prints.

Although all of the usual suspects were hauled in over Walker's assassination, it has never been established who the shooter was. But according to the underworld scuttlebutt there is little doubt who pulled the trigger, and that the driver was a psychopathic killer named Ducky O'Connor, who revelled in the notoriety of being the wheelman for Sydney's most notorious hit. But he was never charged. Ducky became a dead duck in 1967 when he was shot dead in Sydney's Latin Quarter in an incident that became as infamous as the shooting of Pretty Boy Walker.

At a subsequent coronial inquest into the murder, the city coroner, Mr JJ Loomes, said, 'This killing leaves a feeling of abhorrence at the thought this is the first of its type in this state. It will, I am sure, engender in the minds of sober-minded citizens a feeling of revulsion and a hope for ruthless measures to combat this type of crime.'

Lennie McPherson went on to become the undisputed Mr Big of Sydney's underworld. Happy to play a less-conspicuous role, his trusted lieutenant Stan Smith took over the role after McPherson's death of old age in 1996. One of the most highly regarded and respected figures in the Australian underworld, 'Stan the Man', a deeply religious, successful legitimate businessman, died of a heart attack in 2010. He was 73. With him died the title of Mr Big.

43 | PETER FOSTER: AUSTRALIA'S DUMBEST CONMAN

The great news photograph for 2006 was of the handcuffed, pudgy Australian conman Peter Foster dressed only in his underpants with a bandage on his head, after he jumped into the river in Suva, Fiji, to avoid apprehension. Foster had been on the run for weeks when police finally caught up with him. Officers commandeered a fisherman's boat and Foster was struck on the forehead by the boat's propeller.

More used to a Mercedes than a police paddy wagon, Foster was carted off to hospital in his undies. When Foster recovered from his miniscule head wounds he faced charges for immigration violations, mortgage fraud and corporate sabotage. But what was new? It was just another chapter in the corrupt life of Australia's dumbest conman.

At 14, while all of the other kids at his school in Surfer's Paradise were doing homework, Peter Foster was leasing pinball machines and promoting theme nights at the local disco. At 17 he promoted an elimination world title fight on the Gold Coast between Australia's Tony Mundine, father of Anthony 'the Man' Mundine, and the British light heavyweight champion Bunny Johnson. Mundine won on a TKO in the tenth and everyone made a lot of money. The young promoter *Penthouse* magazine christened Kid Tycoon was on his way.

When 21-year-old Foster was staying at Muhammad Ali and his wife Veronica's Los Angeles home while making a documentary on Ali, Veronica showed Foster a packet of Bai Lin tea and told him of its wonderful slimming powers. What Mrs Ali, with her hourglass figure, must have omitted to say was that to make it work you just drank Bai Lin tea and didn't eat. But why bother with such trivialities? Foster purchased the Australian rights and using Mrs Ali's endorsement watched it take off. Next he purchased the Bai Lin distribution rights for England, South Africa and Europe, moved to England, and smooth-talked some very suspect high-profile celebrities into endorsing it.

Fergie, 'the Duchess of Pork', at that time the Queen's daughter-in-law, gave up eating altogether, drank only Bai Lin, and the weight fell off. 'It's amazing,' she said. As did one of the world's skinniest men, champion jockey Lester Piggott, who was notorious for endorsing anything if there was a quid in it. I would love to have seen 51-kilo Lester saying 'Drink Bai Lin tea and be like me' in his falsetto voice. Foster also had a highly publicised affair with the model Samantha Fox, whom he had employed to promote his tea. Business boomed.

But when government testing proved that Bai Lin was just ordinary black China tea with no more slimming powers than Twinings or Bushells, Foster's empire crumbled. Samantha Fox and the Bentleys had long gone and in 1994 Foster was fined £21,000 for a trading standards offence over Bai Lin tea, and in 1996 he was jailed for breaching laws regarding his distribution of slimming granules. Nine months later he absconded while on day release from open prison and went to Australia, where he was subsequently re-arrested and extradited back to England to finish his sentence.

Out of jail, Foster promoted a similar product, Chow Low tea, in the United States where they take grave umbrage to

Peter Foster

shonky promoters with fake products and toss them in the slammer until they get the message. After running ads in newspapers across the US that claimed that the tea lowered cholesterol levels, Foster was convicted of a trading standards offence and jailed for four months.

In September 2000 he was jailed in England for using fraudulent documents to obtain credit for a company that sold thigh-reduction cream. Upon release he returned to Australia, where he became a worldwide marketer of fake lotions and potions, pills and patches and spray-on hair, sold as health and beauty products.

With Foster back in England in 2002, the Prime Minister's wife, Cherie Blair, unwittingly made the mistake of asking her 'lifestyle guru', Carole Caplin, who was in a relationship with Foster (she had been told Foster was a genius on such matters), if he would help her out with some real estate advice. Foster secured a better deal on two properties in Bristol for Cherie Blair, and momentarily the ex-jailbird and international conman and the Blairs became friends.

Foster was even invited to No. 10 for dinner on the night of his 40th birthday. When the Prime Minister's advisers informed him of his wife's new best friend's track record, they couldn't distance themselves quick enough, but the incident achieved headlines worldwide.

To repay the Blairs' kindnesses and his pregnant girlfriend Carole Caplin's love for him, Foster later claimed that he believed his partner was pregnant with Tony Blair's child (which she lost prematurely), the product of a longstanding extramarital affair. It was proved to be an elaborate hoax and Carole Caplin said: 'This is just a new way for Peter to get attention. He is just a fantasist and these absurd stories shouldn't be given any credibility.'

In 2002, Peter Foster was living in Ireland and selling alleged slimming pill Trimit franchises for €200,000. Foster was deported from Ireland to Australia in 2003 because of a two-year prison sentence for fraud imposed in 1996 in Britain. Back in Australia in 2004, Foster, ever in search of publicity, foolishly appeared on

Andrew Denton's TV show *Enough Rope* and was literally eaten alive by the clever interviewer as he tried to pass himself off as a likable scoundrel. Instead, Denton showed him up to be the liar and fool that he really was. Fool, that is, for having anything to do with the considerably smarter Denton in the first place.

And so, he turned up in trouble yet again in 2006, this time in Fiji in his undies, where he was interviewed about presenting a falsified police clearance certificate to immigration authorities in Fiji to obtain a work permit, obtaining loans from the Federated States of Micronesia using lease documents and impersonating a rival developer to discredit a resort development by telling the press that it was going to be a nude hideaway for gay men.

Foster pleaded not guilty on three charges: forgery, uttering forged documents and obtaining a work permit on forged documents, and was released on bail the following day. On 10 January 2007, Fiji Television reported that Foster had disappeared.

On 14 January, Foster was arrested in nearby Vanuatu and was charged with illegal entry into the country on a yacht without a valid visa. On 2 February 2007, Foster was sentenced to six weeks' imprisonment and fined $A1400. He was released after three weeks and deported to Australia, where police were waiting at the airport for him. In 2007 Foster pleaded guilty to forging documents related to $300,000 that he obtained fraudulently from the National Bank of the Federated States of Micronesia. After serving 18 months of a four-and-a-half-year sentence, he was released on parole at the start of May 2009.

Although he denies being a 'conman' and now prefers to be known as 'an international man of mischief' – try explaining that to all of the people who bought franchises in his shonky companies – over the years Foster has been charged with false advertising, conspiracy to supply under a false trade description, operating a company as an undischarged bankrupt, travelling on a false passport, assaulting police, resisting arrest, absconding while on bail, failure to appear in relation to charges on counts of deception, failure to appear at extradition proceedings and uttering false documents, and has been jailed in three countries for fraud-related matters.

Apparently, his latest venture is a book of his life. That's a case of seeing is believing. For openers, it's hard work writing a book, and he doesn't like work, and it's doubtful there would be a word of truth in it. Besides, who's interested in his rotten life of robbing and conning people?

And it's doubtful that any publishers will be offering him a cash advance.

44 | SON OF SAM

'Signature' serial killers are the rarest of all multiple murderers. They are called this because on or near each victim they leave their unmistakable 'calling card', or signature, so that their pursuers know that the killing is the handiwork of the same offender. Signature serial killers are also among the best-known killers in history.

To name a few, Jack the Ripper's mutilations of his victims were unmistakable from one unfortunate prostitute to the next. The Boston Strangler, Albert de Salvo, tied the underwear of his 13 victims in a sailor's knot around their necks. Peter Sutcliffe, the Yorkshire Ripper, stabbed his victims up to 50 times with a screwdriver and finished them off with a hammer.

Australia has only ever had two true signature serial killers. The first was William 'the Mutilator' Macdonald in Sydney in the early 1960s, who specialised in voraciously stabbing derelicts to death in very public places and then souveniring their private parts with the skill of a Macquarie Street surgeon. As the bodies mounted up, police had no problem in assuming it was the work of the one deranged killer.

The other was a beast who became known as the Granny Killer. John Wayne Glover's specialty was bashing little old ladies to death with a hammer and then strangling them with their underwear in broad daylight in the Sydney Harbour foreshore suburb of Mosman. From the outset, it was obvious the style of killing and type of victim were without doubt the work of the same killer.

But of all of the few signature serial killers throughout history, there is one that has gone down in infamy as the most brazen of them all. His name was Son of Sam.

Late one night in July 1976, a man pulled a .44 calibre Charter Arms Bulldog revolver from a brown paper bag and shot and killed 18-year-old Donna Lauria, wounding her friend Jody Valenti, as they sat in Valenti's Oldsmobile in New York's Bronx district. To the police it was just another random killing in a city with a murder rate of 30 per week.

When a young couple cuddling in a car were shot and seriously wounded three months later at 1.30am in nearby Queens, police didn't link the two incidents. They still didn't connect the crimes a month later when two young women standing underneath a street light in Queens were seriously wounded by a stranger with a handgun. Police finally took notice when 26-year-old Christine Freund and her boyfriend John Diel, 30, were shot at 12.40am on 30 January 1977 as they sat in Diel's Pontiac Firebird. Diel escaped injury but Christine died later in hospital.

And then, at about 7.30pm on 8 March 1977, 19-year-old New York Columbia University student Virginia Voskerichian was murdered by a single shot to the forehead. The shot penetrated the school books she had used as a shield against the gunman, whom she must have confronted as she walked home from school near where Christine Freund was killed.

At last police announced that there was a maniac on the loose. The papers labelled him the .44 Calibre Killer. But the killings continued. A month later, as police examined the bullet-

Son of Sam

riddled bodies of students Valentina Suriani and her boyfriend Alexander Esau, who had been executed in their car at 3.00am in the Bronx, they found the first of what would be many teasing notes from the serial killer.

He complained that he was being badly treated by the press, who called him a woman-hater. 'I am not a woman-hater. But I am a monster. I am the Son of Sam. I am a little brat. Sam loves to drink blood. "Go out and kill" commands father Sam. I am the monster. Prowling the streets for fair game.' Then came the words that filled police with dread: 'I'll be back. I'll be back!' Yours in murder. Mr Monster.

From then on the letters kept coming to the New York Police Department and newspapers, taunting authorities to catch him before he killed again. When *New York Times* columnist Jimmy Breslin began publishing Sam's letters and then replying to them through his column in an attempt to draw him out into the open, incredibly, Son of Sam responded. 'Hello from the gutters of NYC which are filled with dog manure, vomit, stale wine, urine and blood. Hello from the sewers of NYC which swallow up these delicacies when they are washed away by the sweeper trucks.'

And in what Breslin described to his readers as 'the letter from hell,' when he asked Son of Sam, 'Will you kill again?' the killer responded, 'Mr Breslin, sir, don't think that because you haven't heard from me for a while that I went to sleep. No rather, I am still here. Like a spirit roaming the night. Thirsty, hungry, seldom stopping to rest.'

On the night of 29 July 1977, all of New York stayed indoors in anticipation that Son of Sam would strike again on the first anniversary of his reign of terror. But it didn't happen. Instead, as New York was breathing a collective sigh of relief, at 2.35am the following morning he murdered 20-year-old Stacy Moskowitz and seriously injured her date, Robert Violante, also 20, as they sat in his car near a city park in Brooklyn.

But time was fast running out for Son of Sam. Police checking out parking tickets in the vicinity of the Moskowitz crime scene noted a 1970 Ford Galaxy had been booked for parking too close to a fire hydrant 30 minutes before the murder. When repeated phone calls to the owner went unanswered, on 11 August 1977, detectives called at the address and found the Galaxy parked in the street. Inside they saw a rifle and found a letter addressed to the leader of the Son of Sam task force, which the killer had obviously intended leaving at the scene of his next murder.

Son of Sam was arrested that night as he left his apartment to kill again. A brown paper bag in his hand contained a Bulldog .44. He simply smiled and said, 'Okay. You've got me. What took you so long?' Instead of the deranged, ranting maniac police had anticipated, Son of Sam turned out to be a 24-year-old mail-sorter, David Berkowitz, who had the cherubic looks of an angel and the demeanour of a kitten. Chances were that the dozens of Son of Sam letters he had posted to the authorities had passed through where he worked.

Berkowitz proudly confessed to the murders and blamed his killing spree on his inadequacies with women. He explained that he could not approach a woman as a man would do and date her or have sex with her. He found sexual gratification in killing them instead. He also explained that he couldn't have done it of his own volition. Berkowitz said that 'Sam' was in fact his neighbour Sam Carr, and Carr's labrador retriever, Harvey, was possessed by an ancient demon, and the demon issued irresistible commands that Berkowitz must kill people. Son of Sam was in fact a black dog.

David Berkowitz was found sane and guilty of six murders and seven attempted murders; he was sentenced to 365 years in jail. Although he became a born-again Christian in jail, each time his parole comes up for review it is rejected. Son of Sam will die behind bars. And not soon enough, I hear you say.

45 | IS ARTHUR BROWN AUSTRALIA'S WORST CHILD KILLER?

It was one of Australia's most controversial murder trials. In December 1998, 86-year-old Arthur Stanley Brown was tried for the murders of Judith and Susan Mackay, aged five and seven, in Townsville, Queensland, on 26 August 1970. Brown's arrest came about when his name hit the headlines in 1998, after a woman broke a 30-year silence to tell police Brown had molested five children related to his first wife. Brown took the children and molested them where the Mackay sisters' bodies had been found.

At the time of the murders, Brown had owned a car with one odd-coloured door, matching the description of a car driven by a man seen near the abduction site on the day the girls went missing, which had never turned up in the investigation. Arthur Brown's relatives now came forth and told police that Brown had removed the odd-coloured door shortly after the murders and buried it. They thought nothing of its relevance at the time.

These revelations opened the floodgates of Brown's paedophilic activities over the years. Somehow he had managed to fly under the radar and had got away with molesting family and local children all of his life. Now Brown's unchallenged activities asked another far-reaching and much more sinister question: had Brown abducted and killed other children over the years – not just in Queensland, where numerous cases remained open, but also in other parts of Australia?

A thin-faced man answering to Arthur Brown's description was seen in the vicinity of Adelaide's Glenelg Beach on 26 January 1966, the day that the Beaumont children, Jane, nine, Arnna, seven, and Grant, four, disappeared; they have never been seen again. And was it just a remarkable coincidence that the middle-aged man with a thin face and gaunt features, who abducted four-year-old Kirste Gordon and 11-year-old Joanne Ratcliffe from Adelaide Oval during a football game in August 1973, had an uncanny resemblance to Arthur Brown?

A thin man with the build of a runner, Arthur Stanley Brown was born in Queensland in 1912 and worked mainly as a carpenter in Townsville until he retired in 1977, aged 65. He married into a family of six sisters and it was believed that over the years he had affairs with at least three of them apart from his wife. When Hester, Brown's wife of 34 years, died in mysterious circumstances after falling in the bathroom and hitting her head, Brown encouraged the family doctor to write out a death certificate without examining the body, which was cremated immediately. Brown married his wife's younger sister, Charlotte, soon after.

Convinced that Brown had murdered their sister Hester, family members began talking among themselves about matters that the family solicitor had advised them many years ago were best left unsaid. It turned out that Brown was also a paedophile who had molested at least five young girls in his wife's extended family over the years. No one said anything until 1982, when one victim told her parents that Brown had molested her when she was a little girl.

Is Arthur Brown Australia's Worst Child Killer?

Other victims in the family came forward and as the truth came out it seemed likely that there wasn't a female member of the family, adult or child, who hadn't been molested or confronted by Brown at one time or another. The oldest sister, Milly, also told the family that Brown's wife Hester had confided in her that 'it wasn't just big girls that Arthur liked – it was little girls too'.

Under family pressure and following legal advice, Brown's victims did not declare publicly what had happened. It was reasoned that it would be too traumatic for the victims to recall the incidents in court. The allegations remained a dark, unspoken family secret and Arthur Brown became the family pariah.

But while it was a family secret, Brown's adolescent philanderings in the local neighbourhood hadn't gone unnoticed by his intended victims. A family relative recorded in her diary that she was once walking a group of State Ward children to nearby Strand when Arthur Brown drove by. The children shouted 'rock spider, rock spider' at him. The children then explained that 'rock spider' was a very serious slang term used in prison for a child molester. Such was Arthur Brown's reputation among the children of the district.

The murder of the Mackay sisters was one of the most terrible crimes in Queensland's history. On the morning of 26 August 1970, seven-year-old Judith Mackay and five-year-old Susan left their home in Aitkenvale, Townsville, and walked to the nearby bus stop to catch the bus to school. From there they vanished. Two days later their bodies were found in a creek bed 25 kilometres south-west of Townsville. Both girls had been assaulted and murdered.

A huge investigation was launched, but all the police had to go on was the makes of two cars seen in the abduction area or near where their bodies were found. One was an FJ Holden and the other a blue Vauxhall Victor with an odd-coloured driver's side door. They were unable to locate either car. Outside of that, police had nothing. The local paedophile, Arthur Brown, though unknown to police, had a Vauxhall Victor sedan with an odd-coloured driver's door. No one ever bothered to tell police and he was never a suspect in the case. Eventually the case went cold.

In 1998, a woman who had been molested by Brown at around the time the Mackay sisters were murdered came across an old photo of Brown in a family album. She was one of the many who were persuaded at the time to say nothing about him, but she had always suspected that he was capable of murdering the two little girls. The woman rang police, who by coincidence were conducting a cold case investigation into the Mackay sisters' murders at the time. The police were very interested in what she had to say and frustrated that none of this had come out sooner.

Police interviewed the entire family and charged Brown with 45 sexual offences, going back years. The odd-coloured door from his Vauxhall, which he had removed and buried soon after the murders, Brown's fixation for neatness, the fact that the little girls' clothes were neatly folded and placed beside their bodies, and Brown's alleged confession to two associates that he had murdered the girls, were just some of the mountain of circumstantial evidence against him. The police charged him with murder in 1998 and he was sent to trial.

At Brown's trial for the murders of Judith and Susan Mackay, which began on 18 October 1999, things did not go well for the Crown. Much of their evidence was considered as hearsay and inadmissible. The jury couldn't arrive at a decision and another trial was ordered. Before his second trial in July 2000 was due to start, Brown was declared unfit to stand due to advanced dementia and Alzheimer's disease, and the trial was abandoned.

In July 2002, Arthur Stanley Brown, an innocent man in the eyes of the law, died alone, aged 90, in a local nursing home. He left strict instructions that there were to be no funeral notices placed in the paper and that he was to be buried in secret, ensuring that he would take his grim secrets with him to the grave.

46 | DOCTOR DEATH: THE CRIMES OF DR JAYANT PATEL

From the day we're born, brought into the world with the help of a raft of doctors, nurses and midwives, we're taught that we can trust the medical profession. After all, they're the ones we turn to when we're sick and at our most fragile. They make the lives of our dying friends and family as comfortable as possible. They even have a seemingly endless supply of lollipops for unwell children. And when they have to deliver bad news, they know just how to frame it.

Sure, they make mistakes – after all, they're only human, albeit very well-paid humans. But it's generally impossible to imagine a family member or loved one dying in hospital not because of complications, but because of the incompetence of their trusted medical professional – that was, until Dr Jayant Patel hit the headlines for all the wrong reasons.

The Indian-born US citizen allegedly contributed to the deaths of as many as 87 patients while practising in Australia, as well as regularly instigating unnecessary amputations, mutilating healthy organs and leaving surgical instruments inside patients after sewing them up. It's fair to say the moniker Doctor Death was a well-earned one for Patel.

And the next time you complain about the cost of medicine, health insurance or even a simple visit to a general practitioner, think about this – while Patel was earning his murderous nickname, he was pulling in $200,000 a year as the Director of Surgery at the Bundaberg Base Hospital in Queensland.

He secured the job thanks to an incredibly strong résumé – not that his credentials were ever checked. They were, however, as you would probably expect, all dodgy. But Bundaberg Base Hospital wouldn't have even had to check his quoted accomplishments with the Royal Australasian College of Surgeons – a simple Google search would have uncovered an unfortunate history of gross negligence through US hospitals where he had been employed.

Indeed, Patel had also been banned from performing surgery in his home country. In a perfect world, he would never have even been granted a second interview – let alone been accepted for a job with such responsibility. But the medical industry in Australia isn't perfect, and they needed a surgeon in Bundaberg. Sadly for his victims and their families, Patel was it.

No matter how many complaints they received about their Director, though, the hospital ignored them. Then one day, one nurse became so fed up with the situation that she had no choice but to go public. After telling of the scrappy workmanship she had witnessed, the brave healthcare provider was threatened with jail and temporarily blacklisted from her profession.

Thankfully, things eventually turned around for Toni Hoffman. She may have found herself unemployed for a time, but the nurse was eventually made an Australian of the Year 'Local Hero' in 2006, and a Member of the Order of Australia in the 2007 Queen's Birthday Honours List.

Of course, the story really starts when Patel turned up for work at Bundaberg on 1 April 2003. Things began to go very wrong not long afterwards. Hospital administration started to receive complaints from senior medical staff that the new

Dr Death

Director of Surgery wasn't following proper procedure. They noted a general lack of care, and cited poor knowledge of normal surgery skills. Disturbingly, they also complained that he was trying to run the hospital like a conveyor belt – getting patients in and out as quickly as possible, with little concern for their condition. There were even issues with basic hygiene procedures – Patel was known to not wash his hands between operations at times.

Still, nothing was ever done about the ongoing complaints. Hospital administration seemed to be of the opinion that as long as the money was coming in, it was best to turn a blind eye to the problems. After all, Patel was bringing in much-needed profits – and no one can argue with good cash flow. Though the victims of Patel's incompetence probably wouldn't really care too much about how well lined the coffers of the hospital became.

In his two years at Bundaberg Base Hospital, Patel performed almost 900 operations – and the results were far from spectacular. Indeed, many of the botched procedures sound like the stuff of horror films. One time, Patel is said to have tried to drain fluid from a sac near a patient's heart by stabbing him 50 times in the chest. The unwarranted frenzy had his fellow medical staff fleeing the scene traumatised. Another story sees a surgical procedure going wrong and Patel cutting a hole in the patient's chest to drain fluid – without the use of anaesthetic.

On another occasion, Patel allegedly decided that a patient's life support system should be switched off simply because he needed the bed for another patient. Internal bleeding caused the death of another patient, who passed away after Patel bungled a procedure he claimed to have performed many times before. To witnesses, though, it was obvious he didn't have a clue what he was supposed to be doing.

These bungles were sadly the rule rather than the exception, and they went on for almost two years, until February 2005, when Queensland Health realised they simply had no choice – they had to do something about the constant complaints from staff and relatives of patients who had either died or suffered serious repercussions as a result of Patel's poor performance.

The situation came to a head when Toni Hofmann went to the press, frustrated that the ongoing complaints were falling on deaf ears. This resulted in the National Party's Rob Messenger bringing up the matter in Parliament. From there, the case finally received the attention it deserved. Patel was about to be investigated – theoretically.

But two years to the day after he started work at the hospital, on 1 April 2005, Patel flew business class home to the US at the expense of the Bundaberg Base Hospital. In his luggage he had a reference from his bosses and a letter of thanks from Queensland Health for his devoted service to the sick, as well as the blessing of then Queensland Premier Peter Beattie.

Leaving a path of death, misery and despair in his wake, it seemed Patel had got away clean of at least a dozen deaths and many more allegations of professional neglect. The police hadn't even tried to detain him, let alone confiscate his passport to stop him leaving the country until an investigation could be mounted.

Patel had been out of the country, seemingly home free, for a month before Queensland's Public Hospitals Commission of Inquiry started looking into the man the newspapers now referred to as Dr Death. It was May 2005 and their job was to determine if Patel had contributed to the deaths at Bundaberg Hospital. They also wanted to know why authorities failed to check the dubious credentials he presented, and why it took so long to act on the numerous complaints. The facts presented to the Commission left everyone involved in shock.

In pure numbers alone, the 87 deaths linked to Patel in his two-year tenure at Bundaberg was enough of a concern – not to mention the vast number of serious injuries. But once the gruesome details of the stories came out, that shock turned to revulsion.

The Commission heard about a young man left impotent and urinating through his rectum thanks to a 30 centimetre surgical clamp embedded in his abdomen, and a 15-year-old boy whose leg had to be amputated as a result of Patel's poor judgement. Other gut-churning tales included Patel simply performing the wrong operations and leaving patients damaged for life. Nurses had even gone as far as to hide patients they knew personally – be they family or friends – from Patel so that he couldn't injure their loved ones. In short, the Commission heard that Patel wasn't just bad at his job – he was a threat to the life of any patient he came in contact with.

The Commission wrapped in November 2005, after seven months of inquiry. It found that Patel had contributed to the deaths of 17 patients, and declared that he should be charged with manslaughter, grievous bodily harm, assault and fraud. As a result, warrants were taken out for the arrest of the multimillionaire Patel currently living a life of luxury in a mansion in the US city of Portland, Oregon.

An Australian extradition order was taken out and Patel was taken into custody in March 2008. Two Queensland police officers escorted him back to Australia in July 2008. But despite facing 13 charges including manslaughter, grievous bodily harm and fraud, Patel declared that he had no case to answer. He was then ordered to surrender his passport before being released on $20,000 bail.

The trial of Dr Jayant Patel began in July 2010 in the Brisbane Supreme Court. After 14 weeks of evidence and summations, the 60-year-old was sentenced to seven years' jail for each of three counts of manslaughter, and three years for grievous bodily harm. Sadly for the families and loved ones of the dead and butchered, all of the terms are to be served concurrently. That means Dr Death could spend as little as three and a half years behind bars.

No one has ever been held fully responsible for not checking out Dr Patel's alleged credentials before he was let loose on the unsuspecting patients of the Bundaberg Base Hospital.

47 | BALI JUSTICE FOR SCHAPELLE CORBY

On 7 October 2005, Schapelle Corby, a 27-year-old sales assistant in her family's fish and chip shop on Queensland's Gold Coast, packed her bags to fly to Bali the following day to celebrate her sister Mercedes' birthday. The story goes that her father Mick was present as she packed and he replaced a plastic strip that was missing from her boogie-board bag before the board went in. Mick Corby stated later that 'she didn't have a bloody thing', referring to drugs in her bag.

That afternoon, Schapelle left for her mother Ros' house and picked up her friend Katrina Richards along the way. There were four travelling companions to Bali: Schapelle and Katrina, another girlfriend, Ally McComb, and Schapelle's 18-year-old brother James. They planned on staying at Ros Corby's house overnight so she could drive them to the Brisbane airport at dawn.

As they congregated in the garage at 4.30 the following morning, in full view of all of the others, Ally gave Schapelle a pair

The Australian Crime File 3

of flippers and Schapelle opened the boogie-board bag and put them inside with the board. They would all later testify that the garage was fully lit and that the only thing they saw in the bag was the yellow boogie board.

At 5.33am, airport cameras observed the group check in their luggage and the boogie-board bag at Brisbane airport for a total weight of 65 kilograms, and then fly to Sydney and transfer to the International Airport, where they boarded a Garuda Airlines 747 and flew off to Bali at 9.30am.

When the plane arrived at Denpasar Airport at 2.30pm Bali time (or 4.30 EST), the boogie-board bag was set aside from the other bags, which were on the carousel. The customs officer asked James if it was his boogie board and he replied 'Yes' but Schapelle said 'No, it's mine' and placed the boogie-board bag on the counter to be examined.

Inside the bag, on top of the yellow boogie board and under the flippers, the officer found 4.1 kilograms of high-grade hydroponic marijuana in two plastic bags, one in the other, the size of a pillowcase.

Mercedes Corby, Schapelle's Bali-based sister, rushed to the airport and warned her sister not to sign anything. What happened from then on could only be described as a sham. It seemed as though there was a standard set of rules for customs all over the world and a completely different set of rules for Bali.

Customs officers pored all over the bag of drugs with unprotected hands, thus eliminating any incriminating fingerprints – which very well may have been Schapelle's – from evidence. If Corby's prints were on either the external bag that held the bag of drugs or the internal bag in which they were vacuum-sealed, she was condemned. If not, she was a chance of having been framed. But we shall never know as they were never printed.

The Australian Federal Police confirmed that Schapelle had no criminal record. Queensland police could not connect her to drugs. And besides, where would a woman who worked in a fish and chip shop get the money to buy 4.1 kilograms of primo ganja at $8000 a kilogram? Surely there must be a mix-up? Surely smugglers in Australia must have used her boogie-board

Bali Justice for Schapelle Corby

bag to smuggle the drugs from Brisbane to Sydney and then lost the bag, and it went on to Bali and poor innocent Schapelle was pinched.

But despite numerous requests to have the luggage, including the boogie board, weighed at Denpasar to compare with its combined weight in Brisbane, nothing came of it. Amid headlines around the world that a young woman could be the innocent victim of internal drug smuggling in Australia, Schapelle Corby was charged with attempting to smuggle 4.1 kilograms of marijuana into Indonesia, found guilty and thrown in a filthy 24-person Denpasar prison cell, left to rot for the next 20 years. Despite numerous appeals she is there to this day, still vehemently maintaining her innocence.

Like the Lindy Chamberlain case, Schapelle Corby's fate polarised Australians. She either did it or she didn't. There didn't seem to be any middle ground. Until, that is, an old drug runner got out of jail and decided to clear his conscience and spill the beans.

Almost three years after Corby's arrest, in interviews in June and July 2008 for the Nine Network documentary *Schapelle Corby: The Hidden Truth* and Melbourne's *Sunday Age* newspaper, Malcolm McCauley, a 60-year-old convicted South Australian drug smuggler, confessed to supplying the marijuana that Schapelle Corby attempted to smuggle into Bali in October 2005.

Malcolm McCauley said he and Schapelle's late father, Mick, who had since died of bowel cancer, were involved in a long-standing drug-running racket in which he supplied the marijuana and Mick organised for it to be smuggled into Bali, accompanied by $US1000 in cash to bribe Indonesian customs officials. McCauley said that Schapelle knew all about the trafficking, and, while he didn't know if *she* put the drugs in her boogie-board bag or not, she certainly knew about her father's drug-smuggling racket.

McCauley's statements came soon after Mick Corby's cousin, Alan Trembath, claimed on the ABC's *Lateline* program that the Queensland-based Corby patriarch had been involved in the drug trade for at least 30 years. McCauley, who has just spent 15 months in jail for his role in a drug syndicate that transported 100 kilograms of cannabis from South Australia to Queensland, also said the reason Schapelle was arrested was that the supposedly 'foolproof' scheme to bribe Bali customs officials with $US1000 didn't work that day.

According to McCauley, the pay-off to corrupt Indonesian airport officials was a well-oiled routine set up by Mick Corby that had always worked in the past, but that day it all went wrong. Someone had removed the bribe from the side pocket of the boogie-board bag before it reached security at Denpasar, leaving Schapelle with 4.1 kilograms of cannabis and no bribe.

Schapelle's Bali-based sister, Mercedes, publicly admitted to making a frantic dash to Denpasar Airport with cash in hand as the nightmare was unfolding, but by the time she arrived, it was too late. McCauley said the 'excellent South Australian hydroponic' marijuana he sold to Mick Corby was highly sought after in Bali, where it fetched four times as much as Corby paid for it and was distributed among a network of surf and souvenir shops, who sold it to expats and tourists. In a bizarre coincidence, Mercedes Corby's Balinese husband ran a surf shop.

McCauley's involvement with the Corbys was revealed after a police raid on his Adelaide house in November 2005 unearthed photographs of him visiting Schapelle Corby in jail. Footage recorded by the documentary filmmakers shows Mercedes Corby thanking Mr McCauley for attending Schapelle's hearing, and McCauley and Schapelle chatting away like old buddies in a holding cell.

Since this all began in 2005, Schapelle's sister Mercedes has made hundreds of thousands, perhaps millions of dollars, from a successful defamation suit against Channel 7, a bestselling book, a *Ralph* magazine bikini shoot and interviews with other magazines and the media.

Yet, at Christmas 2009, Mercedes flew home to Australia to be with her family, leaving Schapelle alone in her filthy prison cell with the rats and cockroaches.

Perhaps Schapelle might have been in better company.

48 | LONDON'S NOTORIOUS KRAY TWINS

While it could be said that England is notorious for some of the worst murderers in history, it could hardly be recognised as a country famous for its gangsters. Mainland Europe and north and south America are far better known for organised crime, through the Mafia and the drug cartels. Yet it was in London's East End that arguably two of the most recognised gangsters in history created a crime empire they called 'the Firm', which is still operating to this day. It began back in the days when armed robberies, arson, standover, torture, protection and assault with extreme violence were the bread and butter of organised crime, long before drugs became the underworld's currency. It was the time of the Kray twins.

Identical twins Reggie and Ronnie Kray were born in London's working-class East End on 24 October 1933, to a mum who adored them all their lives. They would develop into a formidable yet unusual duo – one a paranoid schizophrenic and the other a violent homosexual. Their brother Charlie Jr, six years older, was named after their rag-and-bone-man father, whom they seldom saw as he was on the run from the army after deserting in 1939. Influenced by their boxing grandfather Jimmy 'Cannonball' Lee, in their early teens the twins took up boxing and became very good at it.

The increasingly violent twins made their first appearance at the Old Bailey in 1950, where a case of assault was dismissed for lack of evidence. And in keeping with the family tradition, when they were drafted into the military service in 1952, they repeatedly deserted and bashed the civilian police officers sent to arrest them. After numerous periods in military custody they were dishonourably discharged and embarked on their real career as gangsters.

Tall with broad shoulders and rugged good looks, and always immaculately groomed in suits and ties, the twins recruited other thugs and began their takeover of the business houses in the East End. Brawls broke out in the pubs and clubs that didn't pay protection money. Worse still, a mysterious fire could burn the place to the ground. Everyone paid.

Their expanding empire of violence became known as the Firm and Ronnie and Reggie became the Lords of the Firm. By 1960 it ran teams of successful armed robbers, hijackers and firebugs for profit, and their thriving protection racket affected the entire neighbourhood. But their livelihood wasn't without its occupational hazards. On 5 November 1956, Ronnie was jailed for three years for assault. While in prison he refused to eat, shaved only one side of his face and suffered wild mood swings, sitting still for hours before erupting into a violent frenzy. He was diagnosed as a criminally insane paranoid schizophrenic and after his release his violence increased. In February 1960, Reggie was imprisoned for 18 months for protection-related threats.

In 1961, slumlord Peter Rachman, who had been paying the Krays exorbitant protection money for his many rundown tenements that were leased out as brothels, decided it was better to get rid of the Krays in one deal instead of paying them forever, so he gave them the Esmeralda's Barn nightclub and gambling casino in Knightsbridge. The Krays paid Lord Effingham, the sixth Earl of Effingham, to greet people at the door and give the club the style that Londoners loved.

It worked and soon the twins found themselves entertaining Diana Dors, Frank Sinatra, Judy Garland, politicians and knights of the realm, which gave the Krays a veneer of respectability. In doing so they became celebrities in their own right, being photographed by David Bailey and interviewed on television.

While Reggie found himself in bed with Barbara Windsor, the famous actress from *Eastenders,* his gay brother Ronnie wound up on the front pages of the *Sunday Mirror* accused of having a sexual relationship with one of the club's regulars, Lord Bob Boothby, a UK Conservative politician, whom he had met through the many gay parties that they both attended.

Although no names were printed, Lord Boothby threatened to sue and the newspaper backed down, sacked its editor, apologised, and paid Boothby £40,000 in an out of court settlement. As a result, other newspapers were less willing to uncover the Krays' connections and criminal activities and they lived a charmed existence as respected club owners. But it wouldn't last.

On 9 March 1966, Ronnie Kray shot and killed George Cornell in the Blind Beggar pub in Whitechapel Road in front of a packed bar. Cornell had made the mistake of calling Ronnie a 'fat poof' in a nightclub months earlier. Police questioned everyone in the bar but such was the reputation of the Krays that no one saw a thing. The killing only enhanced the stranglehold the Kray twins had on crime in London's East End.

In October 1967, Reggie was encouraged by his brother to kill Jack 'the Hat' McVitie, a minor member of the Kray gang who had failed to fulfil a £1500 murder contract paid to him in advance by the Krays. McVitie was lured to a basement flat in Newington and as he entered, Reggie Kray, in front of four witnesses, pointed a handgun at his head and pulled the trigger twice, but the gun failed to discharge. Ronnie Kray then held McVitie while Reggie stabbed him in the face, stomach and neck until McVitie lay on the floor dying. McVitie's body was never recovered.

A year later in May 1968, Reggie, Ronnie and 15 senior aides of the Firm were arrested and charged with a huge variety of offences, including the murders of George Cornell and Jack the Hat. Once the Firm was behind bars, witnesses to both murders came forward and the fate of the Kray twins was sealed. The Krays were convicted of murder and the 14 others were sent to prison on lesser charges. Condemned from the bench of the Old Bailey as 'criminals of the worst possible kind', the twins were sentenced to life imprisonment, with the then record of 30 years in custody before they could apply for parole. Their brother Charlie got 10 years for being an accessory to murder. Their mum, of course, said her boys would never do such things and were at home with her when the offences took place. The only time the twins would ever see the outside of prison again was to go to her funeral in August 1982.

In jail Ronnie was again certified insane and lived the remainder of his life in Broadmoor psychiatric hospital for the criminally insane, with the likes of Peter Sutcliffe, the Yorkshire Ripper. He died on 17 March 1995 of a massive heart attack, aged 61. His funeral on 29 March 1995 was a huge event, with the coffin paraded through the streets of the East End in a glass hearse drawn by six black horses, and thousands of mourners and curious bystanders lining the streets. Getting sicker by the day, Reggie kept himself in the public eye, giving television and radio interviews from jail. He was released from prison on compassionate grounds in August 2000, a few weeks before his death from terminal bladder cancer.

Such is the legend of the Kray twins that over the years they have appeared or been referred to in at least six movies, a dozen books have been written about them, they have numerous mentions in songs and countless mentions in English TV series such as *Eastenders, Walking the Dead* and *Whitechapel 11*.

49 | THE JURY'S STILL OUT ON SIR JOH

There are people in Australia who still believe that arguably the two greatest myths ever perpetrated on the Australian public are true. The first one is that Lindy Chamberlain killed her baby daughter Azaria. The second is that former Queensland premier Sir Joh Bjelke-Petersen was bone honest. The Lindy Chamberlain case has been resolved; the dingo definitely took the baby. Lindy has been pardoned and compensated for her years behind bars, for the greatest miscarriage of justice in our history.

Sir Joh? Now that's a different story. Although it was painfully obvious that there was something terribly wrong in Queensland while he was in power, he was never convicted of anything and it would be fair to say that the jury's still out. And if it's one of Sir Joh's juries, you can bet that any verdict that ever comes out of it will be suspect. Sir Joh was accused of the lot: bribery, corruption, running a crooked government and an even more corrupt police force. And, of course . . . jury tampering.

Almost from the day that Bible-bashing Joh Bjelke-Petersen and his National Party swept to power in Queensland in 1967, the odour of corruption spread like a plague across the Sunshine State, which was like a ripe mango just waiting to be plucked by developers with brown paper bags full of cash. And Joh and his cronies were only too happy to help them out.

The first indication of things to come happened just a few weeks after the Nationals gained office, when the Premier granted oil companies leasing rights on the Great Barrier Reef. This had always been considered a sacrilege and the oil companies' applications to explore the reef had been overwhelmingly rejected. Perhaps it was just a coincidence that Joh had shares in the oil companies.

Then, one at a time, dozens of Brisbane's treasured heritage-listed buildings were reduced to rubble overnight – literally. Citizens were woken in the early hours of the morning by wrecking crews smashing down some of the city's most famous buildings to make way for blocks of apartments or high-rise office buildings. Under the previous state governments such a thing could never happen – the buildings were protected. But under Joh's regime, where a bag full of fifties could solve anything, nothing was safe.

In 1975 Joh saw an opportunity to cause trouble for the incumbent Whitlam federal Labor Government – and he took it. When a Queensland Labor senator died, Joh broke with established political convention and ignored the Labor Party's nominee as a replacement, instead appointing a man known for his hatred of the Whitlam Government, a stooge named Albert Patrick Field, a furniture polisher with little knowledge of politics.

When the government tried to pass the federal budget, the new senator conveniently went on leave, thus giving the Coalition control of the Senate. As a direct result the Supply Bill could not be passed and it was the beginning of the historic sacking of the Whitlam Government.

Joh used electoral boundary redistributions to stay in government and while Joh's Nationals won seat after seat at the elections, there were in fact fewer and fewer Queenslanders voting for him. He won one election with less than 40 per cent of the vote. In another it was said that he won only 20 per cent of the vote in the city but had a clean sweep in the country seats due to the wider electoral boundaries and his big appeal in the bush. After all, he was a peanut farmer by profession.

Joh also had another of his stooges installed as Police Commissioner. In November 1977, Inspector Terry Lewis – who was the boss at Charleville, a bush town in Western Queensland with 35 officers under his command – found himself in the top job. It was Joh Bjelke-Petersen himself who apparently gave the final nod.

It all happened so fast that few had time to protest. What had transpired personally between the new Commissioner and the Premier prior to the appointment can only be subject to speculation. But detractors could read nothing into it other than corruption. And time would prove them 100 per cent correct.

Under Terry Lewis, corruption ran rampant at every level. Crooked politicians, illegal casino bosses and brothel proprietors, drug traffickers and corrupt police did little to hide their activities. But sadly for the now *Sir* Joh, his dimwitted police commissioner was always going to be a liability.

Voted Father of the Year in 1980, Terry Lewis moved into a mansion worth $500,000 – a staggering amount of money back then for a public servant's salary. In 1986, after constant lobbying from his family and supporters, Terry Lewis became Sir Terence – the only police commissioner in Australian history to receive a knighthood.

By July 1987, Queensland's Fitzgerald Inquiry into corruption heard that Sir Terence was collecting around $120,000 a year in kickbacks from organised crime, which ran Queensland's illegal casinos and brothels. After the Commission's findings Sir Terence was sacked, convicted on 14 counts of corruption and jailed for 14 years.

After he banned street marches and failed miserably with his ridiculously naive 'Joh for PM' campaign, Sir Joh was on the slide. When the Fitzgerald Inquiry saw to it that four of his corrupt Cabinet ministers were jailed, Joh resigned as Premier in December 1987 to save face. But that was not to be the end of it . . . not by a long shot.

In 1990, the Fitzgerald Inquiry recommended that Sir Joh be charged with two counts of perjury and one of corruption. It was alleged that in 1986 Sir Joh received $100,000 from Mr Robert Sng so that Sng's company would receive favourable consideration as the developer for the Brisbane Port Office site. It was also alleged that Sir Joh knowingly lied to the Fitzgerald Inquiry about the donation and that he didn't receive the cash personally from Mr Sng.

Sir Joh's trial, during which the defendant constantly 'exercised his right to remain silent' and didn't give any evidence or call witnesses on his own behalf, lasted 16 days. As the jury retired to consider its verdict – it seemed blatantly obvious that Sir Joh was guilty – it was revealed that the jury foreman, 20-year-old Luke Shaw, was an active member of Joh's National Party and a campaigner with the Friends of Joh, a group openly raising funds for Joh's defence. The Crown applied for a retrial but it was dismissed.

The jury was out for 61 hours over five days and in the end could not break a deadlock of 10–2 in favour of a conviction. The judge called for a mistrial and an investigation into the selection of the jury in the first place. It stunk to high heaven of corruption but in 1993 it was found that there was no case of deliberate jury tampering to answer to. Sir Joh was never brought to trial again.

In 2003 at age 92, Sir Joh filed compensation claims on behalf of himself and his family against the Queensland Government for $350 million, for stress and emotional and financial hardship. It was rejected. Sir Joh died on the 23 April 2005 in a Kingaroy Hospital, aged 94. He was given a state funeral.

50 | PROTECTING PAEDOPHILES FROM THE PULPIT: THE NAIVETY OF PETER HOLLINGWORTH

Before we get underway with this story, it's important to note that Peter Hollingworth did not actually commit any crime personally to warrant his appearing in a book of Australian crimes. But it does indeed appear that the former Governor-General of Australia defended – or in the very least did little about – a succession of abhorrent criminal acts that took place under his watch. These crimes destroyed the lives of a number of young Australians, stealing their innocence in the most despicable of ways – paedophilia.

Prime Minister John Howard appointed the recently retired Anglican Archbishop of Brisbane Peter Hollingworth to be the nation's Governor-General on 22 April 2001. It was a controversial decision – it was the first time a clergyman had ever been accepted in such a lofty position, though by that stage Hollingworth already had a long line of credentials to his name, including being appointed an Officer of the Order of the British Empire in 1976, and being named

Victorian Father of the Year in 1987 and Australian of the Year in 1992.

But just six months after Hollingworth was named our 23rd Governor-General, allegations surfaced that Kevin Guy – the Senior Boarding School Master at the Anglican School in Toowoomba, Queensland – had raped or sexually abused as many as 80 young girls between the years of 1987 and 1991.

Making the situation even worse was the fact that the school's headmaster and the Diocese decided to let their lawyers sort things out, rather than going directly to their aggrieved flock. It has also been alleged that the school's business manager contacted the Diocese directly, requesting that the story be kept from the school's council. Shockingly, the majority of the parents of the children who had been molested were not even told of the allegations.

The police were informed about Kevin Guy, though, and they charged him with multiple counts of child abuse. Then, on the day that he was scheduled to appear before the judge, Guy took his own life.

The headmaster of the Toowoomba Anglican School allegedly later sent a letter of condolence to the parents of each of his pupils, telling them of the 'tragic death' of Kevin Guy. The letter went on about how deeply the deceased Senior Boarding School Master would be missed, and spoke of the great amount of effort he had put into the school. There was no mention of the innocent young girls that he had sexually abused.

But one of those victims wanted something done about it all. She wrote directly to the then Anglican Archbishop of Brisbane, Peter Hollingworth, asking for his help. The girl's psychologist and the school nurse also wrote to Hollingworth, but the future Governor-General didn't respond to any of the correspondence.

Much later in the scandal, Hollingworth was asked why he failed to answer their letters. He said that he had stayed out of it all because he had been informed that there was nothing to investigate. To the best of his knowledge, no cases of abuse had

Protecting Paedophiles From the Pulpit

come forward. There was no questioning about why Kevin Guy had committed suicide.

But that wasn't the only time Hollingworth's name would be linked to sexual abuse charges against minors. It came out in 2002 that he had given the go-ahead on the appointment of Canon Ross McAuley to a Church Sexual Abuse Committee, despite the fact that he knew the choirmaster had been accused of the repeated sexual abuse of a teenage boy two decades earlier.

When Hollingworth was called on the matter, he said that he had known McAuley for a long time and that he had previously asked him about the allegations. He also said that he spoke to the teenage boy involved, and that McAuley had assured him that he was innocent of the claims. McAuley gave him an unconditional guarantee of this.

Basically, Hollingworth believed his friend rather than the teenager. To him, McAuley's assurance was enough for Hollingworth to decide not to pass the information on to the committee. But when the other members heard about the accusations against McAuley, they were justifiably horrified.

Anglican priest John Elliott was another paedophile with connections to then Archbishop Peter Hollingworth, who let him continue as the rector of a parish even though he knew that he had been tampering with young boys. One of serial offender Elliott's many victims finally spoke out in 1993. By then a young man, he told his parents about the sexual abuse he had suffered at the hands of Elliott for three years. Elliott had been working as the financial manager of the Anglican Church Grammar School in Brisbane and went on to join the ministry. He eventually became a rector in rural Queensland.

When Elliott heard that one of his victims had spoken out against him, he went to his boss Hollingworth and admitted that he was guilty. Hollingworth organised a meeting between Elliott, the young man and himself. He heard directly from the victim about how he had suffered for three tortuous years. He heard the victim explain that Elliott was a serial paedophile who had abused many other boys while acting as the minister of the Anglican churches in Bundaberg, Dalby and Nanango.

The victim's story was harrowing to say the least, and Hollingworth took action – to a point. Elliott was told to apologise to the young man and his family. He also underwent a damning psychiatric evaluation, and had to go through the indignity of telling his wife what had happened. And that was enough for Hollingworth, who not only decreed that Elliott could remain a priest, but he insisted that he remain at Dalby. After all, it would look suspicious if the local rector left after only having been there for a year. It wasn't Hollingworth's wisest decision.

The law finally caught up with Elliott nine years later, in 2002, when he pleaded guilty to 28 sex charges – including 10 counts of sodomy – and was jailed for seven years and six months. The other 18 charges were for indecent dealing, and dated back to the early 1970s in Wide Bay, Queensland – before he joined the Anglican priesthood. They involved five boys between the ages of 10 and 13. Elliott's sentence was increased in February 2003 when he pleaded guilty to the case that Hollingworth had swept under the rug a decade earlier.

By this time, of course, Hollingworth was acting as Queen Elizabeth II's representative in Australia. Our Governor-General was big enough to admit that he had made a 'serious error of judgement' when he let a known paedophile remain in the position of Rector in the Church of which he was then Archbishop. He apologised personally to the family involved, and agreed that he should have handled the issue differently.

Hollingworth was quite rightly condemned in public for the way he handled at least six separate serious sexual abuse matters while he served as Brisbane's Anglican Archbishop. But there was still trouble in store for him.

Donald Shearman was a married Anglican priest who had an affair with a 14-year-old girl who was in his care in the mid-1950s. Shearman went on to become the most senior bishop in his Church. Hollingworth had been aware of the affair since 1995, but he appeared to find no problem with it. Indeed, he later went on television to defend Shearman, turning the tables and accusing the young girl of soliciting the priest.

Protecting Paedophiles From the Pulpit

It was 18 February 2003 when Hollingworth appeared on the ABC's *Australian Story* program and declared:

The great tragedy about this situation is that the genesis of it was 40 years ago and it occurred between a young priest and a teenage girl who was under the age of consent. I believe she was more than 14. I also understand that many years later in adult life, their relationship resumed and it was partly a pastoral relationship and it was partly something more. My belief is that this was not sex abuse. There was no suggestion of rape or anything like that. Quite the contrary, my information is that it was, rather, the other way around.

But the evidence provided by witnesses, as well as hundreds of letters written by Shearman during his tenure as both a priest and bishop, told a very different story. When these were produced on the episode of *Australian Story*, it became clear to the world that Governor-General Hollingworth didn't have any insight on the matter whatsoever. It was an embarrassment to the Church and the country.

The facts were that Shearman had seduced a 14-year-old girl. He then proceeded to make her life a misery for more than 40 years – even after she miscarried their child. The whole time, Shearman was married and bringing up his own children. Shearman was defrocked in 2004. The people of Australia felt Hollingworth deserved a similar fate.

After it was announced that 76 per cent of Australians – including the majority of local politicians, with the notable exception of Prime Minister John Howard – wanted Peter Hollingworth out of the position of Governor-General, he resigned from the post on 25 May 2003, admitting that he 'got it wrong'. 'In accordance with my oath of office,' he continued, 'I bear no ill will to anyone. The rest I leave to God and the judgement of history.'

It's still too soon to see how history will judge Peter Hollingworth – former Anglican Archbishop of Brisbane and disgraced Governor-General of Australia – and God is yet to issue a statement on the matter.

51 | THE ADVENTURES OF CAPTAIN MOONLITE

The notorious Australian bushranger Captain Moonlite was flamboyant both by name and by nature. But unfortunately for the young men he surrounded himself with, he led most of them to tragic ends.

Born Andrew George Scott to a deeply religious family in Northern Ireland in 1842, the 26-year-old came to Australia in 1868. In Victoria he was appointed lay preacher for the Church of England and sent to Bacchus Marsh to assist the Reverend HW Cooper. The following year he was transferred to his own parish in the gold-mining settlement of Mt Egerton, where he became close friends with the local schoolmaster, James Simpson, and Julius Wilhelm Ludwig Bruun, the manager of the local London Chartered Bank.

One night after dinner, when the bank manager Bruun was returning to the bank where he lived, he was bailed up by a man with a full face mask and a gun. The man held the gun to his head, forced him inside and demanded the contents of the safe.

The Australian Crime File 3

Bruun immediately recognised the voice as that of his friend, the Reverend Scott, who was aware that the bank was holding an unusually large amount of gold at the time.

The robber put the contents of the safe into two bags and then led the now blindfolded manager over to the church, where he told Bruun that he was waiting for his mate. When no one arrived they went on to the schoolhouse, where Bruun was forced to face the wall while the man wrote a short note saying 'Captain Moonlite has stuck me up and robbed the bank', signing it 'Captain Moonlite'. Bruun was then tied up and left in the classroom while the robber made his escape.

The young bank manager freed himself and raised the alarm, accusing the Reverend Andrew Scott of being the man who had committed the crime. Andrew Scott acted dumbfounded and categorically refuted the claims, explaining that he had just arrived from Melbourne, and produced a train ticket to prove his innocence.

The Reverend even went so far as visiting Bruun's father, demanding that he advise his son to apologise. He was so convincing that the police believed he was innocent and therefore diverted their attention to Bruun, who was duly arrested. They also took into custody the schoolmaster, James Simpson, who was accused of being an accomplice and author of the 'Moonlite' letter.

In July 1869, Bruun and Simpson were tried at Ballarat and included among the witnesses for the prosecution was the Reverend Scott, who testified against his former friends. Both men were acquitted due to insufficient evidence. Shortly after the trial, Scott boarded a ship from Melbourne to Fiji, then sailed back to Sydney soon after, owing a large amount of money.

In Sydney, Scott sold an ingot of gold and purchased a yacht with intentions of moving on. But before he could leave, he was arrested for passing bad cheques. On 20 December 1870, he was charged with false pretences and sentenced to 12 months in jail. During this time the former bank manager at Mt Egerton, Julius Bruun, hired a private detective named George Sly to investigate Scott, whom he found in Parramatta Gaol.

The Adventures of Captain Moonlite

Sly also discovered that the ingot of gold Scott sold to the bank in Sydney was of identical weight to one stolen from Mt Egerton. On his release, Scott was arrested and extradited to Victoria to face a re-opening of the Mt Egerton Bank Robbery. Captain Moonlite was charged and found guilty of bank robbery, and sentenced to 10 years.

In jail, Scott formed a relationship with 19-year-old James Nesbitt. Following his release in March 1879, Scott decided to become a bushranger and teamed up with Nesbitt, who would become his constant companion and partner in crime for the rest of their short lives.

A young man named Tom Williams joined them, and when the local Lancefield Bank was robbed the trail led to Scott, Nesbitt and Williams, who were living together in Fitzroy, but there wasn't enough evidence to charge them. Soon after, a convicted horse thief, 22-year-old Thomas Rogan, and Augustus Warneckie, the 19-year-old son of a prominent Melbourne publican, joined the gang.

Having no money and with no prospects of getting any, Scott walked out of Victoria into New South Wales with his gang and newcomer 22-year-old Graham Bennet. Unemployment was high and Scott and his friends tramped from homestead to homestead, looking for work. Finally Scott and his party reached Wantabadgery Station, 38 kilometres east of Wagga Wagga, where they asked for work. They were told to try again the next day. The men returned and once again asked for work, or in the least something to eat. They were told to clear out.

Scott, now as his alter ego Captain Moonlite, and his young gang returned to Wantabadgery Homestead and stole guns and food, and over three days they bailed up 35 hostages. The following day four constables from Wagga Wagga arrived to see why people hadn't returned from the station and, having observed the hostage situation, called on the bushrangers to surrender. Scott and his gang opened fire and the troopers drew back and fled back to town for reinforcements.

With the police now gone, the bushrangers decided it was time to leave, and after commandeering all of the horses and

The Australian Crime File 3

guns, Captain Moonlite and his gang left armed to the teeth. As the district was alerted, armed constables came from every direction. In the ensuing running gun battle, which ended near Gundagai and was the longest in Australian outlaw history, Captain Moonlite shot and wounded Constable Edward Webb-Bowen, saw the 19-year-old Augustus Warneckie shot and killed, and cradled his friend and companion, James Nesbitt, in his arms as he died from gunshot wounds.

Captain Moonlite and what was left of his gang were brought before the Gundagai Court and charged with robbery under arms and wounding with intent to murder Constable Webb-Bowen. But when the Constable died the following day, they were charged with murder; they tried in Sydney and were all found guilty. The judge recommended mercy for Williams and Bennet, whose sentences were commuted to life imprisonment. But Captain Moonlite and Thomas Rogan would be executed.

Just before he was hanged at Darlinghurst Gaol, Captain Moonlite's last wish was that he be buried with his friend James Nesbitt in the Gundagai Cemetery. He pleaded:

> *I want to rest in the grave of my friend, James Nesbitt. Gratify my last wish if you can. The only thing I long for is the certainty that I may share his grave. When he died my heart was crushed . . . my fondest hope is to be with him in Eternity. We were one in heart and soul, he died in my arms and I long to join him, where there shall be no more parting. When I think of my dearest Jim, I am driven nearly mad.*

Wearing a ring made of Jim Nesbitt's hair, Captain Moonlite was hanged alongside Thomas Rogan on 20 January 1880 and buried at Sydney's Rookwood cemetery. One hundred and fifteen years later, in 1995, Captain Moonlite's wish was granted and his remains were dug up and interned at Gundagai Cemetery, just a few metres from his friend James Nesbitt.

Also nearby are the graves of his friend and gang member, Augustus Warneckie, and the murdered constable Edward Webb-Bowen. For these nostalgic reasons alone it's worth a trip to Gundagai.

52 | DEAD WRONG: WHEN THE LAW MAKES A FATAL MISTAKE

When Timothy Evans fell to his death on the gallows at England's Pentonville Prison on 9 March 1950, the 24-year-old lorry driver had no way of knowing that his execution would become the catalyst for the many anti–capital punishment arguments of the future.

Timothy Evans went to the gallows for the murder of his baby daughter, Geraldine. At Evans' trial the main witness for the prosecution was his landlord, John Christie. Three years after Evans' execution, Christie confessed to murdering six women and having sex with their corpses. The women's bodies, including that of Evans' young wife, Beryl, were found in wall cavities, under the floorboards and buried in the backyard of his house. As well as killing Timmy Evans' wife, Christie also confessed to murdering their baby Geraldine.

John Reginald Halliday Christie went to the gallows at Pentonville Prison in July 1953. The unfortunate Evans was eventually granted a posthumous royal pardon in 1966. His body was exhumed from Pentonville Prison and reburied in consecrated ground. The Christie Murders are told in chilling detail in the movie *10 Rillington Place*. (The full story of the Christie murders is in chapter 11 of this book.)

The other most quoted case by the anti–death penalty lobbyists is that of Derek Bentley, whose hanging was the classic misuse of the death penalty and possibly the most shameful act in the long and disgraceful history of alleged British justice.

Although Bentley never pulled the trigger and, for that matter, never even held the gun, he was convicted of the murder of a policeman when his associate, 16-year-old Chris Craig, deliberately shot and killed a constable while caught on a rooftop after attempting to rob a store in London in 1953. Because the underage Craig couldn't pay the ultimate price for the life of the policeman, Bentley, who suffered with epilepsy and had the mental age of an 11-year-old, was rushed to the gallows under mammoth protest from an outraged public.

The sacrificial lamb, Bentley, was heard to say, 'Let him have it,' seconds before Craig opened fire on the policeman. The prosecution maintained that Bentley was calling to his partner, telling him to shoot to kill. The defence argued that Bentley was telling Craig to hand the gun over and surrender.

The jury chose to believe the prosecution, and the luckless Bentley went to his death in what criminologists now claim is the indefensible argument against capital punishment. Chris Craig served 10 years of his life sentence and was released from prison in 1963. He never came to the attention of police again.

While such travesties of justice were allowed to happen in the 1950s, experts believe that it could never happen today with modern technology such as DNA. Yet, where the death penalty is still in existence, there is always the possibility that an innocent person could be the victim of a miscarriage of justice. Where it is abolished, the possibility does not exist.

This in itself is a very strong argument against capital punishment and there seems little doubt that the unfortunate executions of Evans and Bentley played a significant role in the eventual abolition of the death penalty in England.

Dead Wrong

But while the British justice system has always been the yardstick used in the argument against execution, Australia's anti–capital punishment lobby has its own classic case against the reintroduction of capital punishment.

In November 1973, Johann Ernst Siegfried (Ziggy) Pohl was convicted of strangling his wife, Kum Yee 'Joyce' Pohl, at Queanbeyan in southern New South Wales. He was sentenced to life in prison. He appealed against the conviction but the appeal was dismissed in August 1974. Ziggy stayed in goal.

Ziggy Pohl vehemently proclaimed his innocence, saying that his English was very poor and he did not know that the answers he was giving to the police would be misinterpreted to go against him. But the circumstantial case against him was strong. On the surface, Ziggy was the only person likely to kill his wife. Furthermore, he could not account for his actions at the time of the murder. It looked like an open and shut case.

But there was no motive. No one could come up with a logical reason why the outwardly happy and secure Ziggy Pohl would want to kill the woman he so obviously loved and shared his every moment with. But that aside, the kindly German immigrant with the big smile and the sad eyes was bundled off to Long Bay jail to serve out his term with the most vile killers in captivity.

Ziggy Pohl was a model prisoner and was released on parole after serving only 10 years of his life sentence. Having taught himself to read and write English during his prison years, Ziggy Pohl set about trying to prove his innocence. But his efforts were to no avail. No one would listen and no one cared. It appeared that Ziggy would spend the rest of his life with the stigma of being a convicted murderer.

In September 1990, 17 years after Ziggy Pohl's conviction and seven years after his release from prison, the most amazing thing happened. Roger Graham Bawden (aka Roger Graham) walked into the Queanbeyan police station and confessed to the murder of Mrs Pohl. It had been on his conscience for almost two decades and he had to get it off his chest.

While he was interviewed by detectives, Bawden gave information that only the killer could have known. When asked why he had not come forward earlier, Bawden maintained that he had left the district shortly after he strangled Mrs Pohl when she surprised him burgling the house, and that he had no idea her innocent husband had been found guilty of his (Bawden's) crime. Bawden claimed he first heard of Ziggy Pohl's conviction when he returned to his home town only weeks before he confessed to the killing. He claimed that he had gone all of those years thinking that the murder was unsolved.

Ziggy Pohl was unconditionally pardoned in May 1992 and eventually awarded $1 million compensation for his decade behind bars. In a strange irony, Roger Graham Bawden pleaded guilty to murder and was sentenced to only eight years in prison.

But what if capital punishment had been the law at the time of Mrs Pohl's murder? What if the kindly German immigrant Ziggy Pohl had been put to death for strangling his wife? And if capital punishment had still been in force 17 years down the track, would Roger Graham Bawden also have been hung for the same murder?

Admittedly, all of these questions are hypothetical, but it does lay a very solid foundation for the argument against the death penalty. Some of the best legal brains in the country agree that there is no way that Ziggy Pohl would have been put to death if capital punishment had been in force at the time of his wife's murder. The fact that he was released after serving only 10 years of his life sentence is, in itself, an indictment of what the parole board thought of Mr Pohl's conviction. In other words, it would appear that there was always some doubt in a lot of people's minds that Mr Pohl did indeed murder his wife. There was no eyewitness, no confession and no motive.

And if he did commit murder, then it certainly wasn't premeditated. It was more of a crime of passion or a violent act committed in a fit of rage. Even the strongest advocate of capital punishment would find it hard to hang a man under those circumstances.

However, had the death penalty been in force in New Zealand in 1970, there seems little doubt that an innocent man would have gone to the gallows for a double murder he did not commit.

On 17 June 1970, in the small farming town of Pukekawa, south of Auckland, Harvey and Jeannette Crewe were shot and killed in the lounge room of their home and their bodies dumped in the local river, where they were found several months later. One of the bodies had been weighed down with a trailer axle, which led police to the nearby house of Arthur Thomas.

Arthur Thomas had unsuccessfully courted Jeannette 10 years earlier and police claimed that Thomas was still besotted with her, and murdered her and her husband in a jealous rage, even though Thomas' wife swore that her husband was at home in bed with her when the murders took place.

A spent cartridge shell found at the scene of the crime, which was alleged to have been planted by police, loosely linked the murder weapon to Thomas. The rest of the evidence was circumstantial and even though there were no fingerprints, footprints or eyewitnesses, a spirited prosecution case saw to it that Thomas was found guilty of murder and sentenced to life imprisonment.

But Arthur Thomas' friends and family never gave up in their belief in his innocence, and he was eventually granted a retrial in 1973. Amid public outrage and disbelief, Thomas was again found guilty and again sentenced to life imprisonment.

A further appeal was rejected. It wasn't until 1979, soon after the publication of David Yallop's worldwide bestselling book about the case, *Beyond Reasonable Doubt*, which offered evidence beyond any reasonable doubt that Arthur Thomas had been railroaded for a crime he definitely did not commit, that New Zealand's Prime Minister, Mr Muldoon, took the extraordinary step of overruling the entire New Zealand judicial system by personally granting an immediate pardon.

Arthur Thomas was eventually awarded $1 million in compensation for his nine and a half years behind bars. The real murderer was never found.

Arthur Thomas had been convicted twice of the same double murder and with all avenues of appeal exhausted, had the death penalty been the law of the land at the time, the kindly, mild-mannered dairy farmer would most certainly have gone to the gallows.

On the other hand, pro–death penalty advocates will argue that there is a list of criminals who have been released from jail to kill and that if they had been executed in the first place, their further victims would still be alive.

They cite such cases as that of Barry Gordon Hadlow, who was sentenced to life imprisonment for the sexual assault and murder of a five-year-old girl in Townsville in 1962. Hadlow was released in 1985 and in 1990 he sexually assaulted and murdered a nine-year-old girl in almost identical circumstances to that of the first murder.

Rodney Francis Cameron, aka 'the Lonely Hearts Killer', served just 16 years in New South Wales and Victorian prisons after being sentenced 'for the term of his natural life' for the 1974 serial murders of a man and a woman. In 1990, just three months after he had been released on parole, Cameron murdered a 44-year-old woman he had met through a matchmaking show on radio 3AW in Melbourne a month earlier.

Cameron has since confessed to another 1974 murder, two unsolved murders in Victoria in 1990, another in South Australia and another in New South Wales.

Though it is of little consolation to the families of his victims, this time Cameron will stay in prison until he dies.

Then there is the case of Leonard Keith Lawson, the talented portrait artist who was sentenced to death by hanging in Sydney in 1954 for the rape of two young models. After heavy lobbying by the anti–death penalty movement, Lawson's sentence was commuted to 14 years and he was released after seven years; he murdered two schoolgirls within six months of being set free.

This brings us to the age-old debate: should we execute our worst criminals or should we let them rot in jails around the country at the taxpayer's expense?

Dead Wrong

A recent estimate in New South Wales put the cost of keeping the prisoners who are sentenced to 'never to be released' at $65,280 per year. It seems that a lot of people would rather have them strung up and the money put to better use. Shortly after the horrific abduction, rape and murder of nursing sister Anita Cobby by five men in New South Wales in 1986, a Sydney TV station conducted a phone-in survey on capital punishment. Of the thousands of callers, more than 90 per cent agreed with the reintroduction of the death penalty.

In the New South Wales Parliament in May 1994, Tony Windsor, independent MP for Tamworth and an advocate of capital punishment since the murder of Ebony Simpson, the nine-year-old schoolgirl who was sexually assaulted and thrown in a dam to drown at Bargo in New South Wales in 1992, lodged a petition of 400,000 signatures requesting a referendum on the reintroduction of the death penalty 'in extreme cases of murder where there is absolutely no doubt that the offender committed the crime'.

Admittedly, emotions run high when the general public is confronted with atrocities such as the murders of Ebony Simpson and Anita Cobby, but opinions appear to be evenly divided as to whether or not the individual Australian states should reintroduce capital punishment.

Martha Jabour, executive director of the NSW Homicide Victims Support Group, which has counselled hundreds of families who have lost relatives to homicide, said in an interview:

I won't give an opinion on the reintroduction of the death penalty but I believe that it would make the task of a jury all that much harder to convict a person knowing that they would be put to death. For this reason alone I fear that a killer could be set free on the conscience vote of a jury rather than on the evidence if the death penalty was allowed back in.

Carol Barnes, the daughter of George Hodson, the warder that Ronald Ryan, the last man to be hung in Australia, shot dead as he escaped from Pentridge, is opposed to the death penalty. 'I got the life sentence,' says Carol, who was 13 at the time of her father's murder. 'Ronald Ryan got the easy way out. I believe that he didn't pay his dues for killing my father. Hanging was too good for him. A life behind bars would have been a much worse penalty than hanging him.'

Sandy MacGregor, whose three teenaged daughters and their girlfriend were blasted to death by a male acquaintance in their home in 1987 at the Sydney suburb of Pymble, doesn't believe that anyone has the right to take another person's life. MacGregor, whose daughters' killer was found to be insane at the time of the murders, said:

> Obviously the cheapest way out is to kill them. But a swift death in front of a firing squad or by hanging is too good for them. The prison environment is far worse than any death sentence. And as they grow old, say 20 years down the track, they have to live with what they've done and the mental trauma of that is far worse than taking the easy way out and killing them.

Gary Lynch, whose daughter Anita Cobby, 26, was abducted, raped and murdered by five men in Sydney's western suburbs in 1986, wouldn't give an opinion of the death penalty, only to say that if we did execute offenders then it would take us back to primitive times, to a level beyond humanity. 'Let us hope that in time social attitudes will change and the would-be perpetrators of horrific crimes will say to themselves, "This is not good, let's not do it". And some day maybe the world will change its attitude to revenge. Let us hope so.'

Gwen Hanns, whose five-year-old daughter Nicole was stabbed to death in her bed in 1974 in Sydney's western suburbs, says that she didn't believe in the death penalty until her daughter's murder. Now her opinion has changed. 'All child murderers should be hung,' she says. 'If capital punishment was in at the time of Nicole's murder, I would have gladly seen John Lewthwaite [her daughter's killer] hang.'

Mrs Hanns concluded, 'I believe that in conclusive cases like child slaying, violent murders, pack rape and murder and serial killings, where there is absolutely no doubt, they should be put to death.'

Beverley Balding, mother of Janine Balding, a young woman who was abducted, raped and murdered by three men in Sydney's western suburbs in 1988, strongly believes in the death penalty. She says:

I agreed with the death penalty before Janine's murder, and I most definitely agree with it now. I also believe that if there was a referendum held in New South Wales tomorrow that the death penalty would overwhelmingly be voted back in. Even though two of the three men who murdered my daughter were teenagers at the time, I believe that they still should have been put to death. Every case should be judged on its merits. In the case of my daughter, her killers should have been executed.

Christine Simpson, mother of nine-year-old Ebony Simpson, who was sexually assaulted and murdered at Bargo in New South Wales in 1992, and whose portrait depicting Ebony's death and the events surrounding it was hung in NSW Parliament House in January this year, is strongly in favour of the death penalty in cases such as hers, where a child is murdered and the verdict is beyond doubt. Her daughter's killer, Andrew Peter Garforth, 29, confessed to the crime and took police to Ebony's body.

'The death penalty is not a deterrent,' Christine says. 'And so it shouldn't be expected to be. It should be used so that the punishment fits the crime. Garforth should have been made an example of and executed and so should all child killers.'

Many fair-minded Australians would agree with her.

53 | WHO FRAMED THE MICKELBERGS? THE STORY BEHIND WESTERN AUSTRALIA'S BIGGEST GOLD HEIST

In Western Australia the saying goes that the police always get their man – eventually. It may not be the right man, but they always seem to get someone in the long run. And when they do, it seems as though they never let the truth get in the way of a conviction. Their track record is appalling.

Deaf mute Darryl Raymond Beamish served 15 years for a murder he did not commit in 1959, after being verballed by police and forced to sign a fake confession. An innocent John Button served five years for the manslaughter of his girlfriend in 1963 after being bullied into signing a confession. Beamish and Button stayed in jail despite serial killer Eric Edgar Cooke, the real killer, providing verbal evidence that only the real killer could have known and two detailed confessions to the killings and another from the gallows. Both men should have been released immediately. Instead, they served their time and only many years later were exonerated, pardoned and compensated.

263

Andrew Mallard spent 12 years in jail for the 1994 murder of Perth jeweller Pamela Lawrence, after making a false confession under extreme duress from the police. Mallard was eventually released, pardoned and compensated after it was revealed that the palm print of the real murderer, which matched prints found at the scene, had been in police files for 15 years, and a mountain of evidence that could have proved Mallard's innocence was either never pursued by the police or covered up.

While these are the extremes of the many miscarriages of Western Australian justice, there is one case that hit the headlines across Australia. After the alleged culprits were convicted and sent to jail for a very long time, it caused angst for their supporters across Australia, so much so that I can recall graffiti on viaducts and expressway walls all across Sydney in the 1980s asking the question 'Who Framed the Mickelbergs?' The graffitists eventually got their answer, but they had to wait a very long time.

In what became known worldwide as The Perth Mint Swindle, on 22 June 1982, 49 gold ingots for a total weight of 68 kilograms and a value of $650,000 ($1,540,000 in today's money) were stolen from the mint without so much as a person being threatened, a truck stolen or a shot fired. To this day it will go down as one of the coolest heists in history, relying almost entirely on the incompetence of the security at the mint.

Earlier, a man had rung the mint and ordered the gold, saying that he would pay for it with three building society cheques (remember, this was 30 years ago) when he picked it up. Instead, the gold was picked up and paid for by a well-known security company, which delivered it to an unattended office in Perth and was then instructed by phone to deliver it to suburban Jandakot General Aviation Airport, about 18 kilometres south of Perth, and leave it on the tarmac. From there, it disappeared. The couriers had not had any connection with any person during the whole process.

Then the cheques bounced. Two of the cheques carried the number of an account operated under a false name by a Ray Mickelberg. Investigation showed that Mickelberg had

Who Framed the Mickelbergs?

substantial dealings in gold, and that his brother flew regularly from Jandakot Airport. According to police, the three Mickelberg brothers, Ray, Peter and Brian, stole cheques from a Perth building society and then fooled the mint into accepting those cheques in exchange for the gold, which was then picked up by a courier. Based on fabricated evidence, the Mickelberg brothers were charged with stealing the gold.

At their trial, police presented unsigned records of interview, or verbals as they are now known, with each of the Mickelberg brothers, in which they allegedly volunteered information that incriminated themselves and each other. The most damaging admissions were supposedly made by Peter, whose interrogation took place at an unoccupied suburban police station where he alleged he was stripped naked and bashed by detectives for four hours.

A highly suspicious fingerprint of Ray Mickelberg was found on one of the cheques used in the swindle. Police evidence was that the fingerprint was found on 24 June, but not identified until after Mickelberg's arrest on 15 July. However, there was no written or photographic evidence of the existence of the fingerprint before 15 July — the same day that police seized bronze and latex casts of Mickelberg's right hand and right index finger (the products of a modelling hobby) from Mickelberg's house.

In 1983, Raymond, Peter and Brian Mickelberg were convicted of swindling the Perth Mint of $650,000 of gold bullion. Based on what can only be described as highly shonky evidence, Raymond, a former SAS soldier, was sentenced to 20 years and Peter to 14 years. After serving nine months in jail and having his conviction overturned on appeal, Brian was released from jail but died in a light airplane air crash in 1986.

Ray and Peter's appeals in 1987 were unsuccessful. Peter's further appeal was dismissed in 1989. While in prison, Ray and Peter embarked on a series of seven appeals against their convictions, essentially on the grounds that their confessions had been fabricated. Ray was released from jail in 1991 after serving eight years of a 20-year sentence. Peter served six years of a 14-year sentence.

The Australian Crime File 3

In a bizarre twist, in 1989, 55 kilograms of gold pellets, presumed to have been from the swindle, were found outside the gates of Channel Seven in Perth with a note addressed to one of the station's reporters, protesting the Mickelbergs' innocence and claiming that a prominent Perth businessman was behind the swindle.

In 2002, midway through a State Royal Commission into police corruption, a retired police officer, Tony Lewandowski, who had been at the centre of the case and who was present at the interviews with the Mickelbergs, made a confession of his involvement in fabricating evidence that was used to help frame the Mickelberg brothers. Mr Lewandowski admitted that he and Detective Sergeant Don Hancock, who later went on to become head of the State CIB, had fabricated confessions from the brothers and had lied at the trial and the appeals.

Mr Lewandowski also admitted that Peter Mickelberg had been stripped naked and beaten by interviewing officers during the investigation. Mr Lewandowski said he had not come forward earlier because he had not wanted to cross Mr Hancock, who had since died in a car bombing in what police believe was a payback killing by Gypsy Joker bikie gang members after the murder of a gang member in 2000. Lewandowski was subsequently charged with attempting to pervert the course of justice, making false statements, fabricating evidence and perjury. In May 2004, just before facing trial, Tony Lewandowski committed suicide.

In July 2004 the Western Australian Court of Criminal Appeal quashed the Mickelberg convictions. The brothers subsequently sued the WA Government for libel, and as part of the settlement, the WA police issued a public apology. In January 2008 the State Attorney-General offered $500,000 in ex gratia payments to each brother for the 'injustice done to them'. The payment followed $658,672 paid to cover legal costs of their appeals. To this day the case remains unsolved, and the remaining 13 kilograms of the stolen gold has never come to light.

54 | THE DEVIL MADE ME DO IT: THE VIOLENT WORLD OF DARREN OSBORNE

The coach captain checked the speedo on his 18-wheeler road liner. No, he wasn't speeding. And he was certain that he hadn't gone over the limit at any time since he had left Perth. Then why would the police want to have a chat with him? He was puzzled as to why they would radio ahead on the two-way radio and tell him to call in to Eucla for an unscheduled stop. And it was annoying. He was 15 hours into his journey to Adelaide and was dead on schedule. Still, it would give his passengers a chance to see how remarkable the tiny township is. Eucla is in the middle of the Nullarbor and sits on the top of the huge white cliffs that look across the Great Australian Bight. It is like a strange oasis.

As the coach captain pulled into the roadhouse parking area he was met by two plain-clothed policemen, who quietly boarded his bus.

'Morning, Captain,' said Sergeant George Johansen. 'Sorry to interrupt your trip. Do you mind if we take a look around?'

'Not at all,' he replied, relieved that they appeared to be looking for someone. This was no traffic pinch.

The passengers looked up at Johansen as he slowly moved down the aisle. He hardly spared a glance at the young honeymooners cuddled up at the front, but threw a quick smile at the two pretty American tourists. They smiled back at the man who looked so out of place in a suit in the middle of the Nullarbor Plain. Then Sergeant Johansen had a close look at the hands of the clean-shaven young man who was asleep with his head resting against the window. No. That wasn't him.

Finally his eyes rested on a young man. Short, bearded and pudgy, he was sitting at the back of the coach. The man was stooped over with his head in his lap, as if to hide his face. Johansen stood over the man for a few seconds, but did not speak. Although they had never met, Sergeant Johansen knew the man.

'Show me your hands,' Johansen demanded. The man complied. On the back of his hands were tattooed crosses. And on his forearm was a tattoo of a stickman.

'Are you Darren Osborne?'

'Yes.'

'Grab your gear and come with me.'

Osborne offered no resistance but fearing otherwise, Johansen had his hand inside his jacket and around the butt of his police-issue .38 Smith and Wesson. The madman could come at him with a knife. If he did, then he was ready. But it seemed unlikely. The coward Osborne specialised only in attacking defenceless women. Besides, by now other police had arrived and surrounded the bus. Osborne's opportunities to escape were nil. Chances are that the passengers on the bus on that day in May 1987 never found out that they were sharing their journey with one of Australia's most wanted criminals.

Such was the ferocity of the sexual assault and murder of Susan Frost at Albany in southern Western Australia three days earlier that police had prepared themselves for the worst. This was an extremely dangerous homicidal maniac and their instructions were to approach with extreme caution.

The Devil Made Me Do It

Police also believed that Osborne could help interstate detectives with their inquiries into a series of extremely violent sexual assaults in Queensland and Victoria. There was also the recent assault of a 16-year-old girl at East Perth, in which the suspect answered Osborne's description. In one of the attacks in Queensland, the victim had been left for dead with her throat cut from ear to ear.

When apprehended, Osborne confessed to all of the crimes.

Darren Osborne's career as a violent rapist began in Queensland when he was just 18. He assaulted three girls at knifepoint and was sentenced to nine years' jail. Released on parole in 1986 after serving just four and a half years, within a week of his release he launched one of the most savage knife attacks in Queensland's criminal history.

Brisbane beautician Shari Davies was kidnapped at knifepoint from a car park on 5 November 1986. Her attacker told her to drive her car into remote bushland on the city's outskirts. There she was viciously bashed and then stabbed 12 times in the neck and body before her throat was cut and she was left for dead. Semiconscious, she managed to crawl 50 metres to the side of the road where she lay for 10 hours before she was found the next morning. Shari hovered between life and death for a week, but she eventually recovered and was able to describe her attacker and the tattoos on the back of his hands. A massive manhunt was launched but her attacker had fled.

From her hospital bed, Shari Davies made a prophetic plea to police all around Australia. 'Please find my evil attacker before an innocent girl is murdered,' she begged. 'He'll kill next time. He's got nothing to lose.'

Osborne next struck on 27 November 1986, when he assaulted a 33-year-old mother of two at knifepoint in the toilets of a McDonald's in the heart of Melbourne. She described her attacker as having tattoos of crosses on the back of his hands. Police knew Osborne was on the run, violating women as he went, but where would he turn up next?

When a man with the now familiar tattoos violently assaulted a 16-year-old girl at knifepoint in Perth on 24 April 1987, police circulated a description of the man and his tattoos to the press. On 5 May, in Albany, in southern Western Australia, Osborne stole a knife and on Mother's Day, 10 May, he abducted 23-year-old barmaid Susan Frost and assaulted her at knifepoint in a nearby car park, before stabbing her to death with 22 blows from a butcher's knife. Her body was found the following morning.

Soon after committing the murder, Osborne buried the knife, washed off the blood, arrived at the home of a lady he had befriended and borrowed enough money for a coach ticket to Queensland. Osborne had told the lady of the murderous assault he had committed upon Shari Davies in Queensland and explained that he wanted to go back and confess.

The following morning when Miss Frost's dead body turned up, the poor woman realised that the man the police were looking for was Osborne; she gave them details of Osborne's bus trip and he was arrested. But instead of acting like the knife-wielding monster police were pursuing, on the long trip back to Perth their suspect broke down in tears, confessed his crimes and begged forgiveness because 'the Devil made him do it'.

Upon hearing of Osborne's arrest, Ian Davies, the father of Shari, the young lady lucky to escape with her life in Brisbane, was extremely critical of Osborne's release after having served only half of his sentence for raping the three girls.

Darren Osborne was described in court as being one of the most evil killers in our history, and was sent to prison without ever the possibility of parole. The judge added, 'You should never be released until senility overtakes you.'

In 1988, Shari Davies sued for damages and was awarded a record $40,000 compensation from the Queensland Government. In June 2001, the story of Shari's bravery and survival was the subject of an episode of the ABC's *Australian Story*.

Darren Osborne committed suicide in Perth's Casuarina Prison in 1997.

55 | THE JAPANESE TOURIST MURDER MYSTERY: THE CRIMES OF ROBERT RAYMOND DAY

The trial and sentencing of Robert Day for attempted murder is one of the most unusual in Australia's history. In all major trials, juries are protected as well as can be from any knowledge of a defendant's previous record, as it is deemed that it may sway their vote and the defendant may not get a fair trial. Also deemed to be prejudicial against the defendant is the introduction to the court by the prosecution of what is known as 'similar fact' evidence, which is evidence of an identical nature from a previous trial in which the defendant may have been convicted of a crime.

One case that comes immediately to mind is that of Barrie Gordon Hadlow. After he had been convicted of murdering a nine-year-old girl in Roma in rural Queensland in 1990, the jury was informed that Hadlow had committed an identical crime upon a five-year-old girl in Townsville 28 years earlier. Hadlow had been released five years earlier, after serving 23 years of a life sentence. One of the ladies in the jury fainted to think that they could have found the double child murderer not guilty.

In the case of Robert Day, none of that ultimately mattered to the judge, who had just sat through a previous trial in which Day was charged with murder but was eventually found innocent. To the judge's mind, Day was obviously as guilty as sin. The judge used what he had seen and heard in the previous murder trial in the sentencing of Day in the new attempted murder case in which Day was found guilty. As it turned out, the judge's controversial decision proved to be an excellent one when the murder victim's body turned up a few years later.

In 1990, Brisbane labourer Robert Raymond Day, 37, was sentenced to life imprisonment with no parole for the attempted murder of Danish tourist Hendrik Enevoldsen in December 1988. Explaining why he recommended that Day never be released, Justice Shepherdson said that a psychiatric report described Day as being capable of extremely violent behaviour.

Day was described as a 'dangerous man', and Justice Shepherdson believed there was an extremely high risk that he would reoffend in the same manner. The judge went on to order that gaol authorities be informed of his remarks 'for the protection of fellow prisoners'. Two years earlier, on 23 December 1988, Day had appeared in the Cleveland Magistrates Court charged with the attempted murder of 21-year-old Enevoldsen. Seven days later, on 30 December 1988, Day was also charged in the Brisbane Magistrates Court with the murder of 22-year-old Japanese tourist Noriyuki Oda, who had last been seen buying bus tickets to Alice Springs on 4 December. From there Mr Oda had vanished.

Day entered no plea to charges of the bodyless murder of Oda, attempted murder of Enevoldsen and assaulting a police officer, and was remanded in custody. It was alleged in court that detectives found Japanese-brand items – including shampoo, conditioner, tissues and a pen – in a flat used by Day. A friend of Mr Oda's was flown in from Japan and identified the pen as similar to one she had given Mr Oda when they worked together in Japan. The witness also identified an unusual brand of tissues

The Japanese Tourist Murder Mystery

found at Day's apartment as the same ones she had sold Mr Oda before he left for Australia. On top of this evidence, authorities found an Oriental amulet, alleged to have been Mr Oda's, in a rubbish bin at Day's flat. They also found a pair of handcuffs.

During the case, Hendrik Enevoldsen, the Danish tourist Day was charged with attempting to murder, told the court he had travelled with Day to Redland Bay, and that Day had attacked him there from behind with a piece of timber. Enevoldsen was taking pictures of a hollow tree near a bushland swamp at the time. He said Day then tried to drown him in the swamp, but he managed to escape and flag down a passing motorist.

At his trial for the murder of Mr Oda, it was alleged that Day had confessed the Japanese tourist's murder to two Brisbane Gaol inmates. And there was more: it was said that he had asked one of the men who was about to be released if the man could murder another Japanese person to give the impression that there was a serial killer on the loose, which would help Day's defence case.

In his alleged confession to the two prisoners, Day is said to have told them he had handcuffed Mr Oda to a tree before pouring petrol at his feet and taunting him, saying, 'You burn, you burn.' As Mr Oda was set ablaze, Day said he pleaded and cried out in Japanese. Day was alleged to have buried the dead body in a 44-gallon drum full of chemicals.

During the trial, Mr Justice Shepherdson ruled that a Japanese handwriting expert could only give evidence according to a particular basis of comparison with Japanese characters on documents accepted as Mr Oda's, and characters written on a cassette case found in Day's flat. But the expert went further in his evidence. Acting for Day, Bill Cuthbert then submitted that his case had been prejudiced because he could not cross-examine on evidence that the jury had heard, but the judge had then ruled inadmissible.

The trial was aborted after 20 days of legal argument. It had heard from 20 witnesses, including 13 flown in from Japan. In discharging the jury, Justice Shepherdson said that regardless of the hundreds of thousands of dollars in costs incurred, if he allowed the case to continue he would be left with a strong sense of unfairness to Day.

Day was finally retried for Mr Oda's murder in June 1990 and he was acquitted. But he remained in custody facing the charge of the attempted murder of Hendrik Enevoldsen. On 1 November 1990, Day was found guilty on that charge. This time, Justice Shepherdson said that he was concerned about similarities in the evidence about the death of Mr Oda and the attempted murder of Hendrik Enevoldsen. 'I heard sworn testimony in the Oda death trial that certainly suggested this man killed the Japanese man Mr Oda,' Justice Shepherdson said. 'I realise that Day has been acquitted of that charge but what concerns me is that this offence involving Mr Enevoldsen occurred two to three weeks after Mr Oda disappeared when it was said, in Mr Oda's case, the accused had killed him.'

On 7 December 1990, Day was sent to prison with the recommendation that he never be released. In the psychiatric report that played such an important role in the judge's sentence, it was revealed that at the age of 18, in 1971, Day had entered a block of flats one afternoon and confronted a 55-year-old crippled woman with a knife. The report stated that Day had attacked and sexually assaulted the woman as she was crawling across the floor to change the television channel. Day was released in 1982 after serving 11 years for the crime.

On 8 April 1993, the remains of Noriyuki Oda were found in a bush grave in the Beerburrum State Forest, on Queensland's Sunshine Coast. He had died from severe head injuries administered by an 'instrument of some kind'. To this day, Robert Day maintains his innocence in relation to the crimes.

56 | AMERICA'S WORST SERIAL KILLER EVER: POGO THE KILLER CLOWN

Recent DNA tests Chicago, Illinois revealed that bones found more than 30 years ago are those of 19-year-old Chicago construction worker William George Bundy, one of the eight unnamed victims of America's worst-ever serial killer. Their killer, John Wayne Gacy, described as generous, charming and civic-minded, will forever be infamous as Pogo the Clown, a character he dressed up as to entertain local children.

Born in Chicago on 17 March 1942, Gacy was a boy scout who at 16 was found to have a heart condition that caused him to put on weight. Gacy dropped out of school and became involved in community groups, where he met Marlynn Myers. They married in 1964 and had a son and daughter.

But Gacy was always in the company of young boys and in May 1968 he was found guilty of tying up and sexually assaulting a teenager; he was sentenced to 10 years and paroled after serving 18 months. His wife and children left him. Released in June 1970, Gacy worked as a chef and bought a house at 8213

West Summerdale Avenue in suburban Norwood Park. It would become one of the most notorious addresses in the world. In November, Gacy was charged with disorderly conduct after he picked up a boy at a bus station and forced himself upon him. The charges were dropped when the boy didn't show up for court.

But Gacy played his double role as a deviant and an upstanding citizen well. When he wasn't participating in fundraising events for local charities, he was at the hospital or kids' functions as Pogo, a big jolly clown with a huge painted smile and a rainbow-coloured clown suit. Pogo was such a hit with the locals that he became a regular feature at every function where kids were involved.

In June 1972, Gacy married Carole Huff, a newly divorced mother of two. Carole and her daughters moved into Gacy's house and would often comment on the strange smells that permeated through the floorboards, like an animal had died under the house.

Gacy started a construction business in 1974, employing mostly teenage boys. His marriage broke up when his wife found pornography featuring naked males in the house.

One of the boys working for Gacy, 16 year-old Tony Antonucci, told friends that Gacy had made advances towards him, but had retreated when Antonucci threatened to hit him with a chair. Weeks later, at his house, Gacy tricked the boy into a pair of handcuffs, but he managed to get out of them. But 17-year-old co-worker Johnny Butkovich wouldn't be so lucky. After driving two friends home from Gacy's house, he vanished. Michael Bonnin, 17, was next to disappear, followed by 16-year-old Billy Carroll, 17-year-old Gregory Godzik and 19-year-old John Szyc (Zick), who was last seen driving in his 1971 Plymouth Satellite on 20 January 1977.

Not long after Szyc went missing, the police picked up another teenage boy driving the same car. The youth told them it belonged to John Gacy, who told them he had bought the car from John Szyc. But if the authorities had run a simple title check, they would have noted that the papers were signed over to Gacy 18 days *after* John Szyc went missing.

The next boy to disappear was 18-year-old Robert Gilroy, who was last seen on 15 September 1977 on his way to catch a bus to meet friends. An investigation was launched but nothing would come of it until a year later, when 15-year-old Robert Piest also disappeared. Piest had disappeared after telling his mum he was meeting a man answering Gacy's description about a contracting job. It was the beginning of the end for Gacy. An investigation was launched and Gacy became a prime suspect when police checked his record, to find that he had served time for sexual assault on a teenage boy.

Alarm bells rang and a search of Gacy's home revealed marijuana and amyl nitrate, nylon rope, gay and child pornography, handcuffs, two driver's licences, several items of clothing that were obviously too small for Gacy and a collection of rings, including one with the initials JAS engraved in it.

With no other options, the police booked Gacy with possession of marijuana while they waited for their experts to come back with the results on the items seized in the search of Gacy's house. Bingo. The engraved ring belonged to the missing teen John Szyc and hair found in the boot of Gacy's car was Robert Piest's.

Then they discovered that three former employees of Gacy's had also disappeared. Then Gacy admitted that he had indeed killed someone and buried the body under his garage. Investigators marked out the garage but instead they began with the crawlspace below the house, where they uncovered the first decomposing corpse. Gacy confessed to multiple murders, but in their wildest dreams investigators didn't imagine how many young men he had killed until the bodies just kept coming, and coming and coming out of the house. In all there were 29. Two bodies were also found set in concrete under Gacy's patio. The remains of another four were found in the Des Plains River.

Gacy confessed that he had committed his first murder in January 1972 and buried it under his house. His second killing was two years later, while he was married to Carole Huff and living there with her and her young daughters. His modus operandi was to trick his victims into being handcuffed, before stuffing their underwear into their mouths and assaulting them while holding a rope or board to their throats until they stopped breathing.

Often he did it in his Pogo outfit. He kept the corpses under his bed for days, often interfering with them, before they were buried under the house.

With Pogo safely behind bars, by the spring of 1979 his house at 8213 West Summerdale, the killing field and graveyard for so many young men, had been reduced to ruin by the locals. They had thrown bricks at it, smashed the windows and even set fire to it. When the remains of the house were finally bulldozed down, a conspicuous vacant block of mud and slush was left that was a constant reminder of the bodies that had been buried there.

And still the onlookers came by the busload, to be reminded of Chicago's most terrible resident since Al Capone. Grass was planted there as a silent memorial but, despite there being no logical explanation for it, neither grass nor trees would grow. A few weeds, but nothing peaceful would take hold in that horrible place. The lot remained vacant for a few years before it was bought and a new house was built on the spot.

Gacy's murder trial began on 6 February 1980, with the prosecution painting a chilling picture of a monster that preyed on young men. Gacy's only defence was that he was insane at the time of the murders, but the jury didn't buy it and took just two hours to find him guilty of murdering 33 young men and violating them both alive and dead. To this day, it is the most convictions for any murderer in America's history.

Gacy was sentenced to death and after years of frivolous appeals, on 9 May 1994 he was executed by lethal injection. That certainly took the smile off Pogo the Killer Clown's face.

57 | THE CASE OF THE PERSISTENT POISONER

In Australia's bleak homicidal past, cases of murder by poisoning are commonplace. And the one thing that most of them had in common was that women were behind the dastardly crimes. One of the better-known cases was Melbourne's Martha Needle who, from the mid-1880s to 1894, murdered her entire family and her boyfriend with an arsenic-based rat poison named Rough on Rats. Three other similar cases immediately spring to mind: in the early 1900s Martha Rendell murdered her three stepchildren and, in the 1940s and 1950s, great-grandmothers Caroline Grills and Gladys Fletcher saw seven people off between them with the help of a thallium based rat poison.

In the mix with all of these larcenous ladies was a bloke – and the only male administer of potent potions of note I can find – who could arguably be titled 'the world's worst poisoner'. This blunderer allegedly made six blatant attempts to murder his wife for no apparent reason and was eventually sentenced to death by the most notorious hanging judge of the time. But

279

that wasn't to be the end of it, not by a long stretch, if you'll pardon the pun.

George Dean was the least likely murderer imaginable. The tall, handsome Sydney Harbour ferryboat captain, with an easy smile and a pleasant nature, was highly regarded for his bravery when he dived from his ferry to save two women who had slipped and disappeared into murky Circular Quay. George and his wife Mary lived happily with their newborn baby in a cottage in Miller Street, North Sydney. If there was a problem it was that George didn't always see eye-to-eye with his mother-in-law, Mrs Seymour, who had stayed with them following the birth of the baby. However, after she had left, it seemed to be a joyous household.

But it seemed that from mid-January 1895, George tried to kill his wife on six occasions by putting a mysterious white powder in the beverages and meals he served her. And there was no mistaking that something was going on as, according to Mary, he was so careless about it. The food and drinks he prepared for her had a strange bitter taste and there was a white powder residue around the bowl or cup. Each time Mary had managed to swallow the food or drink she was violently ill.

When George allegedly mixed some white powder into a lemon syrup drink in front of her, and she drank it and was violently ill, against Mary's wishes George insisted on calling the doctor. In front of her husband Mary asked the doctor if the powder was part of her medicine. The doctor said no and her husband denied mixing it in. Mary gave a sample of the drink to her mother who couldn't get it to the police quickly enough. Sure enough, it contained traces of both arsenic and strychnine. On 9 March 1895 George Dean was arrested and charged with the attempted murder of his wife.

But although according to his wife and his mother-in-law George Dean was as guilty as sin, he had one huge factor in his favour – the lack of a motive. He was an absolute cleanskin with no girlfriends and had never missed a day's work in order to provide fulsomely for his little family, whom he adored. Why on earth would he try and murder his wife? It was up to Richard

The Case of the Persistent Poisoner

Meagher, who was Sydney's most promising defence lawyer, to prove that George had no case to answer and that there was a lot more in play than met the eye.

At the committal hearing Richard Meagher had some curly questions to ask. Why would the happily married family man attempt to kill his wife? And if he did, why so openly? And why would Mary continue to eat and drink substances from her husband when she allegedly suspected him of tampering with them? And when Mary did not want to call the doctor it was George who insisted. His concern for her health was hardly the behaviour of a scheming poisoner.

When George Dean's mother-in-law, the purse-lipped Mrs Seymour, took the stand she found herself the subject of a vicious personal attack. Was it true that she had once boarded known criminals in her home? Was she a part-time madam in a brothel? Had she been in jail for a conviction of petty theft 30 years earlier? To each accusation she hissed that she had not. But Mr Meagher's attempts to cast aspersion upon the characters of the mother and her daughter and conjure up a theory of conspiracy to frame George Dean were fruitless and he was committed for trial.

At his trial George Dean contradicted every word his wife and mother-in-law said. He stood stoically in the box denying everything. His lawyer's pompous three hours' of summing up didn't help matters and Judge Windeyer, better known as the 'hanging judge' who had sentenced nine youths to death in the infamous Mount Rennie Rape Case, was not impressed. In his brief summing up, the judge said that he did not believe that Mary Dean had tried to poison herself – six times over!

When the jury wasn't back in eight hours, His Honour called them back and told them that if they hadn't reached a guilty decision by midnight he would lock them up until the court resumed on Monday morning. They were back in 10 minutes with a sympathetic guilty verdict with a strong recommendation for mercy.

Judge Windeyer's version of mercy was to send George Dean to the gallows. This brought public outrage. Most people believed that Dean was innocent because there was no proof that he had purchased the arsenic – all chemists were bound by law to keep a register of poisons sold to the public and all such registers had been checked by police.

A Dean Defence Committee was formed and thousands of citizens protested across the colony. It worked. George Dean's sentence was commuted to life in prison. Then a Royal Commission inquired into Judge Windeyer's performance and the flimsy evidence on which Dean was convicted. Richard Meagher convinced the commissioners that, urged on by her mother, Mary Dean – although she risked certain death on six occasions – poisoned herself in order to bring charges against her husband for no particular reason. George Dean was pardoned and set free. He returned to his ferry and became Sydney's biggest tourist attraction.

Then, for reasons known only to himself, Richard Meagher, George Dean's lawyer, told the colony's most distinguished barrister, Sir Julian Salomons, that Dean *was* guilty of the poisonings; that he had confessed to him that he had purchased the poison from a chemist named Smith who hadn't entered it in his ledger. Smith was hauled in and admitted his guilt. George Dean was sent to trial again but the best they could get him on was 'for falsely swearing he had not bought the poison'. He went back to prison for 14 years. Upon his release in 1907 he disappeared into oblivion.

Richard Meagher, George Dean's lawyer who knew all along that his client was guilty, went on to a successful career in politics and became President of the Labor Party, Speaker of the House and the first Labor Lord Mayor of Sydney.

58 | SHOULD THE BULLI RAPIST BE FREE TO WALK AMONG US?

There are some criminals who should be behind bars for the rest of their lives: the serial killers, child killers and those who rape and murder in packs. And so, too, the serial rapists should be locked away forever. The Bulli Rapist is a serial rapist of the worst imaginable kind. His crimes are incalculable in terms of human suffering and their administration was beyond appalling. But he is now a free man.

So why then are we now living our lives with one of the most – if not *the* most – terrifying rapist Australia has ever known walking the streets among us? It is because this man, Terry John Williamson, better known as the Bulli Rapist, was released on 16 February 2012, albeit under strict bail conditions, after serving only 22 years of his 24-year sentence. Not only is Williamson a free man in the prime of his life – when he should have been put away forever – but he has also been released two years early, no doubt for good behaviour.

The truth of the matter is that he shouldn't have had the option of ever being released in the first place. He should have been put away forever, never to be released. Let's not lose sight of the fact that the Bulli Rapist acted alone, time after time, after time. He had no mates to urge him on, which could be deemed as an excuse in similar crimes. This was all his own work.

And let's forget about giving him leniency for his age. He was 21 at the time, which may have played a part in the judge handing down such a light sentence. But younger men have been put away forever without the possibility of parole. Bronson Blessington was just 14 and Matthew Elliott 16 when they were sentenced to never be released for the rape and murder of bank teller Janine Balding in Sydney in 1988.

Two 18-year-olds, John Travers and Michael Murdoch, were sent to jail forever for their part, along with three older men, in the abduction, rape and murder of nursing sister Anita Cobby in Sydney in 1986. All of these teenage offenders will die in jail. So age has nothing to do with leniency.

When they tried leniency on 20-year-old Queensland child-killer, Barry Gordon Hadlow, who was released after serving 23 years of a life sentence, he murdered another little girl in identical circumstances to the first. Hadlow has since died in prison. And good riddance, I hear you say.

In preparation for his release, the Bulli Rapist was allowed out of jail under supervision twice a month to adjust back into a society which doesn't want to have anything to do with him. The last time he was released without supervision was on bail in 1990 and he raped a 20-year-old woman.

In what must be the understatement of the century, NSW State Parole Authority spokesman Robert Cosman told the Sydney *Sunday Telegraph* in January 2011: 'Many victims would never want the offender released from jail. I understand that. But the reality is that these people have been sentenced by a court to only a certain length of time in jail.' And therein lies the problem.

The logic behind allowing the Bulli Rapist out on day release was that if the Parole Authority stalled his release until the very

Should The Bulli Rapist Be Free To Walk Among Us?

end of his sentence in 2014, it would place the community at high risk of him re-offending without the restrictions of parole that ends when his sentence ends. 'It is much safer to release a person on supervision,' Robert Cosman also said. 'The statistics show that they are less likely to re-offend with supervision in the community than without it.' And, in all fairness, the Parole Authority can only play the hand it has been dealt.

So now that the Bulli Rapist is free, it has dawned upon us that his sentence was far too lenient in the first place. For his crimes the Bulli Rapist was sentenced to 24 years in prison with a non-parole period of just 14 years. Have a look at his list of crimes and judge for yourself.

The Bulli Rapist began his nine-month reign of terror on 5 August 1989, when a 13-year-old schoolgirl was raped at knife point in broad daylight at Bulli High School near Wollongong, by a man in a balaclava.

On 18 September, a 15-year-old girl was dragged at knife point from her family home in Bulli and raped by a masked man. Both victims were told they would be killed if they made a sound.

On 6 November, an 11-year-old boy was abducted from his bed at his family home in Bulli by a masked man with a knife. The terrified boy was bound and gagged and placed in the boot of a stolen car and driven to nearby Mount Kembla where he was raped and abandoned.

On 5 February 1990, a 24-year-old Bulli woman was raped at knifepoint in her bed by a man in a balaclava. Soon after, over 750 people attended a public meeting called by police to calm community fears.

On 16 February, although all Bulli residents were warned to lock their windows and doors, he broke into a house in Tarrawanna, near Bulli, and threatened to rape a young mother at knifepoint. Realising that the woman was seven months pregnant, he instead turned on her five-year-old daughter and raped her in front of her mother.

On 15 April, three women were attacked by a masked man with a knife in two separate incidents in North Wollongong. On both occasions they foiled the attacker's rape attempts.

On 4 May, a 16-year-old girl fought off a would-be kidnapper with distinctive red hair at nearby Balgownie and her description of the attacker led police to the arrest of 21-year-old local truck driver, Terry John Williamson, the following day.

On 7 May, Williamson appeared in court charged with attempted kidnap and assault charges and was granted $25,000 bail. A week later he raped a 20-year-old Wollongong woman and was arrested soon after and eventually pleaded guilty to 19 of 67 charges, was convicted on five and jailed for 24 years with a minimum of 14.

Six rapes on young girls and young boys, attempted rapes, kidnappings, threatening with a deadly weapon. You name it, this bloke's done it. And he gets 14 years minimum when many fair-minded people believe that he should have got life with no parole? At least when he came up for parole after serving the 14 years, each year he applied to be released it was rejected.

The smartest bloke in the world on these matters is Corrective Services Commissioner Ron Woodham, who opposed Williamson's release. Ron believes the Bulli Rapist of boys and girls and teenagers should serve his full term. He believes that's the least society should make him do under the appalling circumstances.

But so, as of Thursday, 16 February 2012, the beast has been walking among us again. 'Will he rape again?' That's not the issue. He should never have been freed in the first place for us to worry about it. I believe that his crimes were so terrible that he has forfeited his right to ever be free again.

But it's all too late now.

INDEX

A
Abagnale Jr, Frank 165, 169
Abbandando, Frank 'the Dasher' 147
Adams, Michael 129
Adams, Rod 188
Adelaide 11, 12, 15, 220, 232, 267
Adler, Rodney 61, 62, 63, 64–5
Adonis, Joe 23
Afghanistan 13, 14
al Qaeda 11, 13, 14
Albania 12
Albany 268, 270
Alcatraz 74
Alexander Maconochie Centre 129
Ali, Muhammad 210
Ali, Veronica 210
Alice Springs 272
America *see* United States
Anastasia, 'Mad' Albert 23, 146, 147–8
Anderson, Paddles 131
Anderson, Rosemary 89
Anglican Church Grammar School 243
Antonucci, Tony 276
Assyrian community 97–8, 100
Auckland 257
Australian Capital Territory 129
Supreme Court 135
see also Canberra
Australian Electoral Commission 156

Australian Federal Police 13, 35, 121, 123, 129, 132, 170, 230
Australian Labor Party 48, 58, 96, 150, 155–6, 158, 238, 282
Australian Parliament 40, 152, 156, 226
Australian Prudential Regulation Authority (APRA) 63
Australian rugby league team 101
Australian Quarantine and Inspection Service 35
Australian Securities and Investments Commission (ASIC) 98–9, 100
Australian Story 245, 270
Australian of the Year 224, 242

B
Bailey, David 235
Bali 229, 230, 231, 232
Baker, Allan 141
Balding, Beverley 261
Balding, Janine 141, 284
Balmain 38
rugby club 101, 102, 104
Barbaro, Tony 152
Barnes, Carole 259–60
Barnes, Robert 125, 126, 127, 128
Bates, Norman 91, 94

Bawden, Roger Graham 255–6
Bazley, James Frederick 152
Beach, Michael 137
Beamish, Barbara 90
Beamish, Darryl Raymond 87–90, 263
Beattie, Peter 158, 226
Beaumont, Arnna 220
Beaumont, Grant 220
Beaumont, Jane 220
Bennet, Graham 249, 250
Bentley, Derek 254
Berkman, Pnena 88, 89
Berkowitz, David 218
Betts, Raechel 194
Beyond Reasonable Doubt 257
bin Laden, Osama 13
Birchgrove 38
Bjelke–Petersen, Sir Joh 237–9
Black Hand gangs 22
Blackburn, Estelle 90
Blackburn, Harry 'the Hat' 75–8
Blair, Cherie 211
Blair, Tony 211
Blanch, Reg 3, 4
Blessington, Bronson 284
Bloch, Robert 94
Bob 'the Basher' 132–4
Boggo Road prison 166
Bonanno crime family 24
Bondi 41, 199–203
Bonnin, Michael 276
Boothby, Lord Bob 235
Boston Strangler 215

287

Boyce, William 144
Bratanoff–Firgoff, Jean–Pierre 201–2
Brennan, Teresa 136, 137–8
Breslin, Jimmy 217
Brewer, Jillian 87–9, 90
Britain *see* United Kingdom
British Home Office 52
Brisbane 150, 155, 166, 187, 231, 238, 239, 243, 269, 270, 272
  airport 229, 230
  Anglican Archbishop 241–5
  Gaol 273
  Magistrates Court 227, 272
  Police Headquarters 168
  Port Office 240
  Supreme Court 227
Brixton Prison 52
Broadmoor psychiatric hospital 236
Brook, Simon 19
Brown, Arthur Stanley 219–22
Brown, Charlotte 220
Brown, Hester 220
BTK serial killer 113–20
Buchalter, Louis 'Lepke' 146, 148
Bundaberg Base Hospital 224–6
Burgess, Ray 93
Burrell, Bruce 1, 2, 27–31
Bruun, Julius Wilhelm Ludwig 247–8
Budd, Gracie 84
Buffalo Bill 79, 80, 94
Bulletin 160
Bulli Rapist 283–6
Bundy, William George 275
Burrell, Bruce Allan 27–31
Bush, George W 14, 96
Butkovich, Johnny 276

Butterly, Archie 68–9, 70
Button, John 90, 263

C
Cabramatta 57–9
Cameron, Rodney Francis 192
Camperdown 38
Canberra 17, 18, 19, 121–9, 149, 152, 156
Canberra Cop Killer 121–9
Caplin, Carole 211
Capo De Tuti Capi 24, 145
Capone, Al 'Scarface' 71–4, 278
Captain Moonlite 247–51
Carni, Sophie 2, 3
Carr, Bob 48
Carr, Sam 218
Carroll, Billy 276
Carruthers, Justice Kenneth 129
Castellammarese War 22
Casuarina Prison 270
Catch Me If You Can 165
Celebrity Apprentice 155, 159
Chamberlain, Azaria 1, 237
Chamberlain, Lindy 1, 231, 237
Chan, Angel 152
Chicago 71–4, 275–8
Chikatilo, Andrei 82
Christie, Ethel 49, 50, 51, 52
Christie, John Reginald Halliday 49–52, 253, 254
Church Sexual Abuse Committee 243
Ciliberto, Francesco 192
Clark, James 73
Clarke, 'Ratty' Jack 206
Claxton, Marcella 196
Cleveland Magistrates Court 272

Clinton, Bill 96
Coalition, the 238
Cobby, Anita 141, 259, 284
Cochrane, Johnny 183
Colombo crime family 24
Commission, the (Mafia organisation) 24, 146–8
Coningham, Alice 7, 8–9, 10
Coningham, Arthur 7–10
Coningham, Vincent Francis 9
Coningham Conspiracy 7–10
Cooke, Eric Edgar 89–90, 263
Coombes, John Leslie 191–4
Coombes, Sandra 193, 194
Cooper, Bradley David 61, 63, 65
Cooper, Reverend HW 247
Corby, James 229, 230
Corby, Mercedes 229, 230, 232
Corby, Mick 229, 231–2
Corby, Ros 229
Corby, Schapelle 229–32
Cornell, George 235, 236
Cosa Nostra 25, 145
see also Mafia, the
Cosman, Robert 284–5
Coulston, Ashley Mervyn 78
Court TV 116
Cowdrey, Nicholas 40
Cox, Thomas 81
Craig, Chris 254
Crewe, Harvey 257
Crewe, Jeannette 257
Crick, WP 20
Crime File 191
Cronulla 18
Crowley, Peter 122
Crump, Kevin 141

Index

Curtain 18
Cuthbert, Bill 273

D

Dahmer, Jeffrey 83
Daily Telegraph (Sydney) 28, 111, 112, 137
Dancing with the Stars 155
Dangar Place 162–3
Dannemora Prison 25
Darlinghurst Gaol 144, 250
Darwin 187
Davies, Ian 270
Davies, Shari 269, 270
Davis, Dorothy 1, 29, 31
Day, Robert Raymond 271–4
Dean Defence Committee 282
Dean, George 279–82
Dean, Mary 280, 281, 282
de Salvo, Albert 215
Deer Park Prison 70
Denton, Andrew 212
Denzel, Dorothy 109–11
Department of Defense (US) 13
Dewey, Thomas E 25
Diel, John 216
DiLorenzo, Anthony 201, 202
Directors of Public Prosecutions (DPPs) 3, 4, 5, 30, 40, 77, 202
Domican, 'Tough' Tom 47–8, 48
Donnellan, Mick 144
Dors, Diana 235
dot-com boom 95
Downing Centre Court 136
Dr Death 223–7
Duffy, George 144
Dunlop, William (Billy) 171, 172–4
Dupas, Peter Norris 183–6

E

Eastenders 235, 236
Eastman, David Harold 122–4, 126–8
Effingham, Lord 234–5
Einfeld, Justice Marcus Richard 135–9
Einfeld, Syd 135
Elliott, John 243–4
Elliott, Matthew 284
Enevoldsen, Hendrik 271, 272, 273
England *see* United Kingdom
Enough Rope 212
Ermenegildo Zegna 176
Esau, Alexander 217
Ettridge, David 158, 159
Eucla 267
Evans, Beryl 50, 51, 52, 253
Evans, Geraldine 50, 51, 52, 253
Evans, Timothy 50, 52, 253

F

FAI Insurance 62, 63
Falconio, Peter 1, 2, 187–90
FBI 25, 170, 175
Federal Court of Australia 135
Fergie 210
Field, Albert Patrick 238
Fife-Yeomans, Janet 5
Fiji 187, 209, 212, 248
Firm, the 234–6
Fish, Albert 83–5
Fitzgerald Inquiry 239–40
Flannery, Christopher Dale 47
Fletcher, Yvonne 101, 279
Foster, Peter 209–13
Fox, Samantha 210
Fraser, Andrew 183–4, 185–6
Frazer, Graham 163–4
Freeman, George 131

Freund, Christine 216
Friends of Joh 240
Froggy Group 95, 96, 97–9
Frost, Susan 268, 270

G

Gacy, John Wayne 275–8
Garland, Judy 235
Garden Island 19
Garforth, Andrew Peter 261
Gambino crime family 24
Gein, Ed 79–80, 91–4
Genovese crime family 24
Genovese, Vito 23
Georges Hall rapist 75, 76, 77
Gibb, Peter 67–70
Gilroy, Robert 277
Giuliani, Rudy 21
Glover, John Wayne 216
Godzik, Gregory 276
Goeliner, Maria 193
Gold Coast 78, 209–10, 229
Gold Coast Balaclava Rapist 78
Goldner, Viva 137
Goldsmith, Lord 172
Gonzales, Clodine 33, 34
Gonzales, Mary Loiva 33
Gonzales, Sef 33–6
Gonzales, Teddy 33, 34
Gordon, Kirste 220
Goulburn 29, 30
Goulburn Jail 60
Graham, Joseph 108
Granny Killer 216
Grans, Hans 81
Grassby, Albert 'Al' Jaime 149–53
Grassby, Ellnor 152
Green, Dan 10
Greenburg, Les 101
Greenhill, Robert 81
Griffith 150–1

289

Grills, Caroline 101, 279
Guantanamo Bay 11, 12, 14
Guider, Michael Anthony 42–4
Guider, Tim 44
Gun Alley: Murder, Lies and Failure of Justice 108
Gundagai 250–1
Gurino, Vito 'Chicken Head' 147
Gusenberg, Frank 73, 74
Gusenberg, Pete 73
Guy, Kevin 242
Gypsy Joker bikie gang 266

H
Haarmann, Fritz 81
Hadlow, Barry Gordon 191, 258, 271–2, 284–
Halvagis, Christina 186
Halvagis, Mersina 183–6
Hancock, Don 266
Hand, Derek 4
Hanns, Gwen 260–1
Hanns, Nicole 260
Harding, John 106, 163–4
Harris, Jodie 165–70
Harris, Thomas 79, 80, 94
Hartley, Evelyn 93
Heidnik, Gary 80
Herald Sun 152
Heyer, Adam 73
Hicks, David 11–15
Hicks, Mary Jane 142
HIH 61–6
Hitchcock, Alfred 91, 94
HMAS *Cerberus* 19
HMAS *Sydney* 19
Hobart 81
Hodson, George 259–60
Hofman, Toni 224
Hogan, Mary 93, 94
Hogg, Julie 171, 172, 173, 174

Hollingworth, Peter 241–5
'Honored Society', the 152
Hoover, J Edgar 25–6
Hornby, Raymond 46
Howard, Bill 65–6
Howard, John 61, 158, 159, 242, 245
Huff, Carole 276, 277
Hunt for BTK, The 120
'Hydraulics' 175–6

I
Immigration Control Association 151
Indonesia 229–32
internet service providers (ISPs) 97
Ipswich 155–6
Ireland 211
Italy 25, 150

J
Jabour, Martha 259
Jack the Ripper 215
Jackson, Emily 196
Jackson, Florence Edith 192, 193
James, Justice Bruce 139
Japan 12, 272, 273
Johansen, George 267–8
Junee Prison 100

K
Kandahar 13
'Kangaroo Gang' 177–9
Karl Suleman Enterprises (KSE) 96, 97, 98, 99, 100
Katoomba 193
Kay, Adrian 131–4
Kells, Henry Desmond 193
Kelly, Ned 105
Khancoban 18
Kid Tycoon 210
Killing Jodie 5
Klarenbeek, Louis 128
Knight, Samantha 41–4
Knight, Tess 41
Kosovo 12

Kray, Charlie Jr 233–4, 236
Kray, Reggie 233–6
Kray, Ronnie 233–6
Kroll, Joachim 81–2

L
Labor party *see* Australian Labor Party
Lancefield Bank 249
Lanfranchi, Warren 161–4
Lansky, Myer 24, 26, 146
Larcombe, Jodie Maree 1–5
Las Vegas 146
Lashkar-e-Tayyiba group 12
Lateline 231
Lauria, Donna 216
Lawrence, Pamela 90, 263–4
Lawson, Leonard Keith 258
Lectr, Hannibal 79
Lee, Jimmy 'Cannonball' 234
Lees, Joanne 187–90
Levi, Roni 199–203
Lewandowski, Tony 266
Lewis, Sir Terence (Terry) 239
Lewthwaite, John 260
Liata, Angela 138
Liberal Party of Australia 151, 155–6
Lithgow jail 42
LJ Hooker 36
London 49, 50, 176–7, 233–6, 247, 254
'Lonely Hearts Killer', the 193, 258
Long Bay Gaol 112, 161, 255
Loombes, JJ 208
Luciano, Charles 'Charlie Lucky' 21–5, 145
Lucchese crime family 24
Lulham, Bobby 101–4

Index

Lulham, Judith Anne 103, 104
Lynch, Gary 260

M
MacDonald, Jayne 196, 198
Macdonald, William 'the Mutilator' 215–16
MacGregor, Sandy 260
Mackay, Barbara 149, 152
Mackay, Donald Bruce 149, 151, 152
Mackay, Judith 219, 221, 222
Mackay, Susan 219, 221, 222
Mafia, the
  Australia 126, 152, 205
  United States 21–6, 71–2, 145–52, 233
Magna Carta 171
Magoon, 'Blue Jaw' 147
Maher, Michael 152
Maione, 'Happy' 147
Mallard, Andrew 90, 263–4
Many, Frederick Glen 45–8
Maranzano, Salvatore 22, 23
Martin, Joseph 144
Marysville 50
Masseria, Giuseppe 'Joe the Boss' 22
Matthews, Ivy 106
May, Johnny 73
McAuley, Canon Ross 243
McCann, Wilma 196
McCauley, Malcolm 231–2
McComb, Ally 229
McGrath, Anthony 62–3
McGurn, Jack 'Machine Gun' 72, 74
McIntosh, Bob 'the Blender' 133
McPherson, Lennie 131, 205–6, 207, 208

McVitie, Jack 'the Hat' 235, 236
Meagher, Richard 280–1, 282
Mekong Club 58, 60, 61
Melbourne 2, 17, 19, 53–6, 67–9, 105–7, 125, 168, 179, 183–5, 186, 193, 194, 248, 249, 269, 279
  Cup 96, 175
  press 53, 106, 152, 231, 258
  radio 192
  Remand Centre 67
  Supreme Court 183
Mickelburg, Brian 265–6
Mickelburg, Peter 265–6
Mickelburg, Ray 264–6
Millar, Vince 188
Mills, Alan 121
Milosevic, Slobodan 12
Ming, Ann 171, 172, 173
Ming, Charlie 172, 173
Minkley, Phil 76, 77, 78
Mitting, Judge John 195, 196
Monty, Alfred 104
Monty, Judith Anne *see* Lulham, Judith Anne
Monty, Veronica 102–4
Moonlite, Captain 247–51
Moore, Rod 163–4
Moran, Cardinal 8
Moran, George 'Bugs' 72, 73, 74
Morgan, Kevin 107–8
Morse, Virginia 141
Moskowitz, Stacy 217
Mount Rennie Rape Case 141–4, 281
Moxley, William Cyril 109–12
Mr Big 208
Mr Froggy 95–100
Mt Egerton Bank Robbery 247–8, 249
Muldoon, Robert 257
Mundine, Anthony 'the Man' 210

Mundine, Tony 210
Murder Inc. 145–8
Murdoch, Bradley John 1, 189–90
Murdoch, Michael 284
Murphy, Chris 4
Murphy, George 108
Murray, Kevin 195–8
Myers, Marlynn 275

N
National Bank of the Federated States of Micronesia 212
National Crime Authority (NCA) 47, 150, 152
National Party of Australia 151, 226, 238–9, 240
Needle, Martha 279
Nelson, Ricky 206
Nesbitt, James 249, 250
Nettle, Justice Jeffrey 194
New South Wales 2, 5, 17, 18, 27–9, 48, 58, 60, 136, 141, 152, 169, 192, 193, 249, 255–6, 258, 258–9, 259, 261
  Bureau of Crime Statistics 177, 179
  Central Coast 46
  Department of Public Prosecutions 3
  Director of Public Prosecutions 3, 30, 40, 77, 202
  Government 42, 78
  Homicide Victims Support Group 259
  Law Society 38
  Legislative Assembly 150, 152
  Parliament 259
  Parliament House 261
  police 47, 76, 192, 201, 258
  Postmaster General 20
  prisons 192
  Rugby League 102

291

State Parole
    Authority 284–5
Supreme Court 30–1,
    37, 39, 40, 135
Upper House 159
New York 21–4, 83–4,
    145–8, 216–17
Police
    Department 217
New York Times 217
New Zealand 10, 187,
    256–7
Newman, John Paul 57–
    60
Ngo, Phuong 58–60
North Ryde 33–4, 36
North Shore 43, 136,
    169
Northern Alliance 13
Northern Ireland 247
Northern Territory 12,
    187–90
Notting Hill 49–52
Nullabor Plain 267–8

O
O'Connor, Ducky 208
Oda, Noriyuki 272–3,
    274
Ognall, Justice 173
O'Haran, Dr Denis
    Francis 8–10
Oklahoma City
    bombing 155
Old Bailey 51, 171, 234,
    236
Old Melbourne
    Gaol 108
Oldfield, David 158
Oldfield, George 197
O'Meagher, Peter 43
Omerta, code of 25
One Nation 158–9
O'Reilly, Judge 42
Osborne, Darren 267–
    70
Otero, Charlie 113, 114
Otero, Julie 113, 114,
    117, 118, 119, 120
Otero, Joseph 113, 114,
    116, 117, 118, 119,
    120

Otero, Joseph Jr 113,
    117, 118, 119
Otero, Josephine 113,
    117, 118, 119
Owen, Justice Neville
    John 61
Oxley 155–6, 159

P
Packer, Kerry 65
Pakistan 12, 13
Parker, Heather
    Dianne 67–70
Parramatta 28, 30
Parramatta Gaol 248
Patel, Dr Jayant 223–7
Pauline Hanson Support
    Movement 159
Paull, Kevin 76
Payne, Michael 63
Pearce, Alexander
    80–1
Penthouse 210
Pentonville Prison 253,
    254
Pentridge Prison 2, 3,
    67, 259
Percy, Derek 17–20
Percy, Ernie 17, 18
Perkins, Charles 157
Perth 87–90, 264–6,
    267, 269, 270
Perth Mint Swindle,
    the 264
Phillip Island 194
Piest, Robert 277
Piggott, Lester 210
Podesta, Rodney 201,
    202–3
Pogo the Clown 275–8
Pohl, Johann Ernst
    Siegfried (Ziggy)
    255–6
Pohl, Kum Yee
    'Joyce' 255–6
Police Integrity
    Commission 40, 202
Pooncarie 2
Ponzi schemes 95–100
Port Philip Prison 184
Price, Charles 107
Psycho 91, 94

Puerto Rico 114
Pukekawa 257

Q
Queen Victoria Nursing
    Home 192
Queensland 155–6,
    158–9, 165, 192, 219–
    22, 224–7, 229, 231,
    232, 242, 243, 244,
    269, 270, 271–4, 284
Fitzgerald
    Inquiry 239–40
Government 238–40,
    270
Health 225
District Court 159
police force 169, 227,
    230, 237, 239
premiers 226, 237–40
Public Health
    Commission 226–7
Public Hospitals
    Commission of
    Inquiry 226
Senate 159
see also Brisbane; Gold
    Coast
Queensland Times 156

R
Rachman, Peter 234
Rader, Dennis L 113–20
Ralph 232
Ratcliffe, Joanne 220
Read, Robert 144
Redston, Allen
    Geoffrey 18
Reles, Abe 'Kid
    Twist' 147, 148
Rendell, Martha 279
Richards, Katrina 229
Richardson, Irene 196
Rogan, Thomas 249,
    250
Rogerson, Roger 161–4
Roma 271
Ross, Colin
    Campbell 105–8
royal commissions 61,
    63, 78, 151, 266, 282
Russia 13, 82

Index

Russo, Andrew 123
Ryan, Barney 206
Ryan, Ronald 259–60

S
Sale prison 185
Salomons, Sir Julian 282
Saporito, Bill 21
Saudi Arabia 13
Schapelle Corby: The Hidden Truth 231
Scarlett, Paul 185
Schley, Arthur 92
Schmidt, Marianne 18
Schwimmer, Reinhardt H 73
Scott, Reverend Andrew George 247–51
Serbian forces 12
Sergi, Tony 152
September 11 attacks 13
Seychelles Islands 134
Seymour, Mrs 280, 281, 282
Sharrock, Mary 18
Shaw, Justice Jeffrey William 37–40
Shaw, Luke 240
Shearman, Donald 244
Shepherdson, Justice 272, 273–4
Shooters Party 159
Siegel, Benjamin 'Bugsy' 23, 146
Sievers, Robert Theo 191
Silence of the Lambs, The 79, 80, 94
Simpson, Christine 261
Simpson, Ebony 259, 261
Simpson, James 247, 248
Simpson, OJ 155, 183–4
Sinatra, Frank 235
Sing Sing 145
Singular, Stephen 120
Ski Beach 19
Sly, George 248–9
Smith (chemist) 282
Smith, Neddy 131, 161–3

Smith, Stan 'the Man' 131, 206–7
Sng, Robert 240
Snowy Mountains 18
'Society Murders', the 53–6
Son of Sam 215–18
South Africa 210
South Australia 189–90, 231, 232, 258
police 190
prisons 190
Sparrow, Jodie 12
Speirani, Michael 193–4
Spiller, Shane 19
St Kilda 3, 4
St Mary's Cathedral 8, 10
Stilwell, Linda 19, 20
St Valentine's Day Massacre 71–4
Stanley, Bill 142–3
Stockton-on-Tees 174
Strauss, 'Pittsburgh Phil' 147
Stump, Peter 80
Suckling, Daryl Francis 2, 3, 4–5
Suleman, Karl 95–100
Sunday Age 231
Sunday Mirror 235
Sunday Telegraph 284
Sunshine Coast 274
Supermax prison 60
Surfer's Paradise 209
Suriani, Valentina 217
Sutcliffe, Peter 195–8, 215, 236
Sutcliffe, Sonia 198
Sutherland shire rapist 76, 77
Sutton, Candace 28
Sweetman, Charles 142, 143
Sydney 8–10, 13, 17, 18, 19, 27, 28, 29, 33, 41–4, 57–9, 75–8, 96–100, 101–4, 109–12, 131–4, 135, 136, 141–4, 150, 152, 159, 161–4, 177, 179, 180, 181, 187, 193, 199–

203, 205–8, 215–16, 231, 248, 249, 250, 258, 260, 261, 264, 280–2, 284
Central Criminal Court 103
Central Local Court 169
Downing Centre Court 136
Drug Squad 151
Hospital 143
journalists 5
Latin Quarter 208
North Shore 43, 136, 169
solicitors 4
press 28
TV station 259
Syyc, John 276

T
Tactical Intelligence Unit (TIU) 76
Taliban 13, 14
Tamworth 259
Tasmania 80–1
Taylor, Robert 72
10 Rillington Place 49, 51, 52
10 Rillington Place 52, 254
Teesside Crown Court 172
Thailand 161
Theo Notaras Multicultural Centre 149, 152
Thomas, Arthur 257–8
Thornthwaite, Jim 76
Time magazine 21
Tingle, John 159
Tirtschke, Alma 105–8
Tirtschke, Viola 108
Tizzoni, Gianfranco 152
Tolson, Clyde 26
Toowoomba Anglican School 242
Townsville 219–22, 258, 271
Travis, Victor 93
Treasury 122, 123

293

Trembath, Alan 231–2
Trimbole, Robert 152
Tuohy, Yvonne 19, 20
Turner, Eric Thomas 191
Travers, John 284
Twining, Andrew 169

U
Unholy Messenger 120
Unione Siciliane 24–6, 146
   see also Mafia, the
United Kingdom 8, 49–52, 101, 171–4, 195–8, 210, 211, 233–6, 253, 254
United States 11, 13, 14, 15, 21–6, 28, 68, 71–4, 80, 83, 91–4, 96, 113–20, 136, 145–8, 187, 210–11, 211, 227, 275–8
   Department of Defense 13
   government 25
   Supreme Court 14

V
Valachi, Joe 25, 145
Valenti, Jody 216
Vanuatu 212
Victoria 17, 19, 56, 78, 105–8, 167, 169, 179, 183, 184, 192, 247, 249, 258, 269
   Attorney-General 108
   Father of the Year 241–2
   Government 107
   Institute of Forensic Medicine 108
   police force 168, 169, 184
   prisons 258

Supreme Court 186
Violante, Robert 217
Voskerichian, Virginia 216

W
Wagga Wagga 249
Wales-King, Margaret 53–6
Wales-King, Maritza 54, 56
Wales-King, Matthew 54
Wales-King, Paul 53–6
Walker, Ray 162
Walker, Robert 'Pretty Boy' 206
Walking the Dead 236
Wanda Beach 17, 18, 19
Wanda Beach Killer 17–20
Wang, Lucy 58, 59
Want, Jack 9
Wantabadgery Station 249
War on Terror 14
War Reserve Police 50
Warneckie, Augustus 249, 250, 251
Warneet 19
Webb-Bowen, Constable Edward 250, 251
Weckler, Georgia 93
Weinshank, Al 73
Wentworth 4
Wentworth Falls 192
'Werewolf of Hannover' 81
West Yorkshire 196, 197
Western Australia 87–90, 263–6, 267–8, 269–70
   Court of Criminal Appeal 266

Government 266
   police force 266
   Supreme Court 135
Whelan, Bernard 27–8
Whelan, Kerry 1, 27–9, 30, 31
Whitechapel 11 236
Whitlam, Gough 150
Whitlam Government 150, 238
Wilkinson, Frank 109–11
Williams, Peter 197
Williams, Ray 61–2, 63, 64, 65
Williams, Tom 249
Williamson, Terry John 283–6
Winchester, Colin 121–9
Winchester, Gwen 124, 125
Windeyer, Justice 143–4, 281, 282
Windsor, Barbara 235
Windsor, Tony 259
Wisconsin 91–4
Wollongong 285–6
Woodham, Ron 286
Woodward, Justice Philip 151
Worden, Frank 92
Worden, Bernice 92, 93, 94
World War I 49, 81
World War II 50
Wran, Neville 151
Wyrama Station 4

Y
Yatala Prison 15
Yallop, David 257
Yorkshire Ripper 195–8, 215, 236